3step
vegetable
gardening

First Published in North America in 2009 by
CREATIVE HOMEOWNER®
Upper Saddle River, NJ 07458

CREATIVE
HOMEOWNER®

Creative Homeowner® is a registered trademark
of Federal Marketing Corporation.

Copyright © 2009 Toucan Books

Toucan Books

Design: Leah Germann
Editor: Theresa Bebbington
Managing Editor: Ellen Dupont
Editorial Assistant: Hannah Bowen
Picture Research: Paul Matthews
Picture Manager: Christine Vincent
Indexer: Jackie Brind
Proofreader: Constance Novis

Creative Homeowner

VP/Publisher: Timothy O. Bakke
Art Director: David Geer
Managing Editor: Fran J. Donegan
Junior Editor: Jennifer Calvert
Editorial Assistant: Sara Markowitz
Design Intern: Mary Dolan
Digital Imaging Specialist: Frank Dyer

Current Printing (last digit)
10 9 8 7 6 5 4 3 2 1

3-Step Vegetable Gardening, First Edition
Library of Congress Control Number: 2007938378
ISBN 10: 1-58011-407-5
ISBN 13: 978-1-58011-407-3

CREATIVE HOMEOWNER®
A Division of Federal Marketing Corp.
24 Park Way
Upper Saddle River, NJ 07458
www.creativehomeowner.com

Planet Friendly Publishing
✔ Made in the United States
✔ Printed on Recycled Paper
Learn more at www.greenedition.org

GREEN EDITION

At Creative Homeowner we're committed to producing books in an earth-friendly manner and to helping our customers make greener choices.

Manufacturing books in the United States ensures compliance with strict environmental laws and eliminates the need for international freight shipping, a major contributor to global air pollution.

And printing on recycled paper helps minimize our consumption of trees, water, and fossil fuels. *3-Step Vegetable Gardening* was printed on paper made with 10% post-consumer waste. According to Environmental Defense's Paper Calculator, by using this innovative paper instead of conventional papers, we achieved the following environmental benefits:

Trees Saved: 11

Water Saved: 4,039 gallons

Solid Waste Eliminated: 668 pounds

Air Emissions Eliminated: 1,232 pounds

For more information on our environmental practices, please visit us online at www.creativehomeowner.com/green

Contents

1

Getting Ready

THIS BOOK HAS "3 STEPS" IN ITS TITLE, but as in all endeavors, spend some time doing a little planning before you embark on the first step. Even experienced gardeners use the winter to do as much preparation as they can and to formulate a plan. The first decision you'll need to make is where to grow your vegetables. You might think the only place to grow them is in a dedicated vegetable plot. However, there are three easy ways to incorporate vegetables (and herbs and fruits) into any backyard, no matter how small: make space in your ornamental borders for vegetables that have decorative leaves, flowers, or fruit; build a raised bed—you'll be surprised how much a 4 × 10-foot (1.2 × 3m) bed can produce; and grow vegetables in containers. If you opt for a vegetable plot, a good starting point is to learn about your soil, the medium in which your vegetables will flourish. One surefire way to improve any soil and produce better vegetables is to add organic material, and your own compost pile is the most convenient source of organic matter.

The next step is deciding what to grow. Think about what to grow where, grouping crops together, and when to sow and plant. Vegetable growing can be unpredictable, and you will have to adapt and improvise. However, being organized at the beginning will reduce the work later.

Vegetables in the Border

making room for your vegetables

IF YOU DON'T HAVE SPACE in your backyard to dedicate a plot for vegetables, you can still grow them by planting them in a flower bed. Many vegetables have attractive foliage, flowers, and fruit. (However, avoid planting invasive types, such as mint and Jerusalem artichoke, which can quickly spread.) As with flowers and shrubs that you choose for a flower border, when choosing vegetables, consider how they will look when planted next to neighboring plants. Don't forget to consider the plant's height as well as its appearance.

Most vegetables are annuals, and you can use the less tender types to fill gaps early in spring. For example, lettuce makes a neat edging that can be eaten in early summer and replaced by annual flowers. Chard, such as the multicolored 'Bright Lights', is worth a place in any flower border for its ornamental value alone, and you can always spare a few stems for the kitchen. As the year progresses, any of the fruit-bearing vegetables—peppers, beans, eggplant, and tomatoes—will add color

Leeks (right) blend into this ornamental garden.

and interest to a summer flower border. Consider corn as an alternative to the purely ornamental grasses. Make sure the vegetables have enough space to reach their full potential, and be prepared to feed and water them; otherwise, their yields can be disappointing.

You can use the winter-hardy vegetables to fill gaps left by tender flowers in milder areas. Leeks, kale, chicory, and some of the Asian greens should provide greenery through the winter.

Architectural and climbing plants

There aren't many perennial vegetables, but they make attractive permanent additions to an ornamental garden. They are all large and will need plenty of space. However, the bold leaves and flower heads of globe artichoke and the large leaves of rhubarb are striking. And the feathery fronds of asparagus make a good foil for flowers.

Climbing vegetables are good candidates for training on fences, trellises, or freestanding tepees. Choose pole bean varieties with colorful flowers or beans, and pick them frequently to prolong flowering.

Fruit and herbs in the border

Currants and brambles, such as blackberries and raspberries, make good subjects for ornamental borders, too; position raspberries and blackberries next to a fence to make training them easier. Blueberries are ornamental in their own right—with flowers, berries, and fall foliage—but they need an acidic soil, and protecting the fruit from birds may be tricky in a flower border.

All herbs can be grown in an ornamental border and, if you don't want a permanent herb bed, this is a good place for woody perennial herbs, such as bay and rosemary, and the sages that have colorful leaves. Annual

Zucchini and lettuce form a small island bed.

herbs bought as plants can be treated as annual bedding. The bright green foliage of parsley makes a great foil and chives and basil have attractive flowers.

The practicalities

Don't expect huge crops. The vegetables will be competing for food, water, and light with vigorous, established perennial flowers, so be prepared to give them a helping hand. Whether you sow seeds directly into the border or plant started plants—young plants purchased from a garden center or mail-order company—first fork over the area, remove any weeds, and add some compost. A handful of general-purpose plant food won't do any harm either.

The usual rule of planting in rows doesn't apply to borders, except as edging. Sow seeds in irregular patterns by making short rows or swirls into which to sow; this will help you to tell the seedlings apart from any weeds. Plant transplants in groups or drifts as you would ornamentals. Water the seedlings or transplants well until they are established, and give them preferential treatment in dry weather, too. Once the vegetables are well established, water with a liquid plant food every couple of weeks to keep them growing strongly. Pests will still find vegetables in a flower border. Check regularly, and take action if necessary. Don't forget to have replacements ready, either flowers or more vegetables, when you start to harvest your vegetables.

Ornamental Vegetables

Here is a list of attractive vegetables suitable to grow among ornamental plants:

ANNUAL VEGETABLES

Bean, bush (yellow or purple podded varieties)
Beet ('Bull's Blood' is colorful)
Cabbage (red or savoy types)
Carrot (ferny foliage)
Chicory (especially radicchio)
Eggplant (look for varieties with purple foliage)
Fennel (feathery foliage)
Kale (especially Tuscan or red types)
Kohlrabi (purple varieties)
Leek (blue-green foliage in winter)
Lettuce (especially red and loose-leaf types)
Okra (types bearing purple pods)
Asian greens (good winter fillers)
Pepper (types bearing colorful peppers)
Summer squash
Swiss chard (types with colorful leaves or stems)
Tomato (may need support)

CLIMBING VEGETABLES

Bean, pole (with purple flowers or colorful beans)
Cucumber
Pea (tall varieties tied to supports)
Scarlet runner bean (types with red flowers)
Tomato (trained up trellis)
Winter squash (varieties with small squash)

Tomatoes and marigolds create a bright color combination.

Raised Beds

a dedicated bed for your vegetables

A RAISED BED IS A SIMPLE SOLUTION

if you don't have suitable soil for growing vegetables. A raised bed is basically an area of soil built up above the normal soil level. You can make a single raised bed, or if you have a larger garden, you can create a system of several beds. Simply raising the soil surface just a few inches has several benefits:

- Normally wet or waterlogged soil will drain more quickly.

- Cold wet soil will warm up more quickly in spring, so you can start sowing seeds earlier.

- The soil structure will remain more open, so roots will be able to get established faster.

- You will be able to improve any soil by adding organic matter and, in particular, you can increase the depth on poor, thin soil.

Once the bed is made, dig the soil and add plenty of compost.

- You won't need to walk on the soil. This means the beds won't become compacted, so there won't be a need to dig every year. In fact, raised beds are ideal for a no-dig system (See "No-Dig System," page 19.)

- Organic matter, food, and water will be concentrated on the growing area, not wasted on walkways.

- You will feel you are making progress by working one bed at a time—whereas raking or weeding a large area of garden can seem daunting.

- As the soil level settles, it will be obvious when a raised bed needs extra organic matter, especially if it has edges.

Low beds

To gain the benefits of a raised bed, a low bed needs to be only 6 inches (15cm) high. Ideally, the bed should be no more than 4 feet (1.2m) wide—any wider and you won't be able to reach the center without treading on it. No longer than about 10 or 12 feet (3 or 4m) is best, otherwise you'll find it frustrating getting from one side to the other. Walkways between beds should be 12 inches (30cm) wide to allow for foot access and 18–24 inches (45–60cm) wide for a wheelbarrow. Mulching the walkways with permeable plastic, gravel, or chipped bark will help to keep weeds down.

In its simplest form, you can mark out a bed and walkways by digging the bed and incorporating organic matter. It will be raised above the level of the walkways. However, enclosing a bed in a permanent edging, such as lumber or recycled plastic "wood," creates a neater finish, and you will be able to raise the bed surface even higher. If you don't have poor soil, raising it 6 inches (15cm) is fine, but if you have poor soil, raise the bed to 12 inches (30cm) and you'll be able to ignore the underlying soil, however poor, and treat the bed as a large container—but with less need for watering.

High Beds

Some situations call for a high raised bed, perhaps for landscape reasons—to add height in a garden—or because the gardener wants to avoid bending over or relies on a wheelchair. To create a high raised bed, you'll need a firm, level base, such as concrete. You can use wood, metal, or other materials to make the sides. The bed should be 24–30 inches (60–75cm) high for a wheelchair user or 3 feet (90cm) high for a standing gardener; in either case, make it no more than 4 feet (1.2m) wide. The plants need only 12 inches (30cm) of soil, so fill the bottom of the bed with building debris.

Raised beds are attractive planted with ornamental vegetables.

Making a basic raised bed

To make a raised bed, start by marking out the area on the ground, making sure it is square. Cut lengths of 1×6 (2.5×15cm) boards into two 4-foot (1.2m) sections for the ends and two longer sections for the sides. Nail them to 3×3 (7.5×7.5cm) posts 12 inches (30cm) long; these should be flush with the top of the boards—the rest will be buried to hold the bed in place. For long beds, nail a post to the center of each side, too. Dig a hole for each post. Level the top of the boards, excavating soil from beneath them if necessary. Pack soil into the holes until the boards are firmly in place. Dig the soil inside the bed as deeply as you can to loosen it; add a generous amount of compost or well-rotted manure to fill the bed. You can dig this in or leave it as a mulch.

Maintaining and using raised beds

Simply add a generous layer of compost or other organic matter every other year. This will act as a mulch to retain soil moisture and suppress weeds. Soil critters, such as worms, will eventually incorporate it into the soil. Raised beds will not need digging each year, but after several years the soil may settle and need a little breaking up with a garden fork when you add extra organic matter. Raised beds lend themselves to intensive production. Because the soil is improved, vegetables can be spaced

Mini Vegetables

Baby vegetables often command a high price in the supermarket, but they are easy to grow and a good choice in raised beds. Many vegetables can be picked small and tender, such as summer squash and bush beans—but the plants can take a lot of room. Leafy or root vegetables can be grown at closer spacing than normal to produce small roots or heads. Look for small varieties.

Beet	Carrot	Lettuce
Broccoli	Cucumber	Snow pea
Cauliflower	Kohlrabi	Squash, patty pan

Vegetables in Containers

growing vegetables in limited space

IF YOU DON'T HAVE a vegetable plot, you can still grow a huge range of vegetables (and fruit and herbs) by planting them in containers. And even if you do have a vegetable plot, there are a few advantages to growing some in containers, too: for that special first pick; for crops that don't do well in your soil; or for herbs and salad greens that are handy to have close to the kitchen door.

Which container?

Plastic containers are light and inexpensive, come in any style or shape you want, and are ideal for growing vegetables and fruit. Avoid clay or terra-cotta pots. They may look rustic, but, unless you line them with plastic, they lose moisture rapidly. If you don't plan on making them permanent fixtures, make sure you can move the pots when they are full of soil, which can be surprisingly heavy. If you grow larger vegetables and

Make sure you choose a deep container if you want to grow carrots.

want to move them, invest in a caddy or other device on wheels specifically designed for moving large containers.

Window boxes are ideal for growing herbs and leafy lettuce crops. Another alternative is to use hanging baskets for colorful herbs, small bush tomatoes—especially trailing varieties—or strawberries.

For practical reasons, the bigger the container the better. A pot that is 8 inches (20cm) in diameter will take proportionally more watering than a 12-inch (30cm) one. As a rough guide, a container about the size of a bucket—about a 2-gallon (7.5L) capacity and 12 inches (30cm) in diameter will suit most vegetables, and it will be easy to move around and maintain. However, larger plants, such as cucumbers, squash, and melons, will need a container about twice this size.

The depth of the container is important, too. Choose containers that are at least 12 inches (30cm) deep to allow a good root run and a reservoir of moisture. Shallow pots will dry out quickly; deeper ones will retain water but will need more potting mix. Whichever container you choose, make sure it has plenty of drainage holes.

What potting mix?

For the novice, the best bet is to buy packaged potting mix from a garden center or store. It will be weed free and free draining, and it will retain moisture and contain sufficient nutrients to give the plants a good start. If you have an ample supply of garden compost, you can use it to fill containers, provided it is fully decomposed and looks like rich soil. However, if you want to avoid introducing weeds or diseases, fill only the bottom half of the container with compost and the top half with store-bought potting mix.

Chili peppers have attractive fruit and foliage.

At the end of the season, don't waste the contents of your containers. You can recycle it by adding it to the vegetable patch as a mulch, adding it to the compost pile, or reusing it for next year's containers by fluffing it up and using it to fill the containers halfway, then filling up with fresh mix.

If you are tempted to use really large containers, remember that these can require a huge quantity of potting mix to fill them up. However, most vegetables will grow well in 12 inches (30cm) or so of soil, so you can fill the bottom of the pot with an inert material, such as gravel. This will help excess moisture drain away, too, and make tall pots more stable.

Because blueberries and currants are in their pots for longer, a soil-based potting mix is better than soilless mixes. Blueberries are easier to grow in containers than in the garden because you can fill a container with the acidic soil they need. For long-term plants, start them in a small container and then move them into a larger one when the roots fill the smaller one.

Sowing and planting

Provided the container is in a warm, sheltered spot and the soil is kept moist, you can sow all vegetables directly into the containers. For closely spaced crops, such as onions, lettuce, or greens, scatter the seeds as thinly as you can, allowing a few spares. Cover with potting mix and keep the surface moist. Thin the seedlings in stages until you have an even distribution of plants.

Larger plants, such as cucumbers, eggplant, peppers, and tomatoes, are best planted individually. Provide them with a large container with at least a 2-gallon (7.5L) volume or 12-inch (30cm) diameter.

Urban Living

Apartment residents who have a roof terrace or balcony can use these limited spaces to grow vegetables in containers. However, large soil-filled containers can be heavy enough to put a strain on the building's structure. A building professional can advise you whether your space can support the weight of heavy containers and what steps to take, if necessary, to make it safe.

Even if you use only window boxes and hanging plants, you'll still need to think of safety. These containers should be completely secured so that they cannot be knocked or blown to the ground below. Even a drop of only one story can do damage or injure someone.

For the earliest harvest, move the container into a greenhouse, well-lit room, or garage with grow lamps until it is warm enough outside. If late frosts are predicted, cover the pot with a row cover or another frost protector. (See "Extending the Season," page 39.) The nutrients in the potting mix should last about four weeks. Afterward, vigorous vegetables need a regular feed. Choose a general-purpose or balanced fertilizer for leafy and root crops and a high-potassium one for fruit-bearing vegetables, such as eggplant, peppers, and tomatoes.

Watering

This is the biggest chore when growing vegetables or other edible crops in containers. Get into a routine with a watering can or hose, and water edible and ornamental containers at the same time. You may have to water twice a day for thirsty plants in the hottest part of the year. Mid-morning and late afternoon are best because less water is lost to evaporation. Try to avoid splashing water on the leaves, because this can encourage disease.

Moving containers into shade or partial shade is one way to help reduce water loss in the hottest weather. Mulching the surface with organic matter or gravel can reduce water loss, too. However, the best solution is to rig up an automatic watering system. This is comprised of a hose supplying fine tubes fitted with drippers or emitters to each container. Larger containers need more drippers, and it may take a couple of days to make sure each container is getting sufficient water. Afterward, all you need to do is turn the faucet on for a set time twice daily.

Attractive eggplant will add color to a patio.

Container Candidates

Here are some suggestions for vegetables and fruit that will do well and look attractive grown in containers:

VEGETABLES

Asian greens	Potato
Bean, bush	Radish
Beet	Scallion
Carrot	Spinach and all greens
Cucumber *	Summer squash *
Lettuce	Sweet potato
Okra	Swiss chard
Onions	Tomato *
Pepper	Turnip

* Choose small bush varieties

FRUIT

Blueberry	Strawberry
Currant	

An arrangement of herbs in containers makes an attractive display.

One labor-saving device is an automatic water timer that will turn the faucet on and off for you. These are available at garden centers and from mail-order suppliers. After you get it running, check weekly that each container is sufficiently moist, and adjust the timing or individual drippers as needed.

Planting combinations

Fruit-bearing vegetables, such as peppers, eggplant, and tomatoes, are ideal choices for ornamental containers; peppers and eggplant are attractive plants in their own right. Before you start planning interesting vegetable combinations, consider the consequences. If you mostly want vegetables to eat, stick to one type per container, especially if you'll want to harvest some vegetables all at once or over a short period. Some vegetables—for example, potatoes—are not the most attractive plants and do not combine well with other vegetables.

When growing several kinds of vegetables in one container, try to match their requirements and vigor or one will swamp the rest. For example, avoid mixing hungry crops, such as chard, with slower-growing ones, such as kale. Try quick-growing salad greens with longer-term crops, such as tomatoes, to make full use of the container. Annual flowers or herbs can also be used to underplant tomatoes. Combinations of leafy greens work well in larger containers, provided you pick individual leaves as required instead of whole plants, or the effect will look messy.

Growing herbs in containers

Herbs are a natural choice for containers, even if you have a vegetable garden.

- Invasive kinds, such as mint, can be kept from spreading.

- Some, such as thyme and rosemary, like poor, free-draining soil.

- Tender types, such as bay, can be kept in a warm sheltered spot over winter; you can move some, such as parsley or basil, indoors in winter to improve leaf quality.

- It is sometimes useful to be able to pick a sprig of a fresh herb without going right out into the garden.

The same rules apply as with vegetables. For practical reasons, grow each herb on its own in a medium-size pot—one that is 12 inches (30cm) in diameter is fine—so you can give it the conditions it prefers. Sow annual herbs in a succession of small containers so that when one is harvested, the next one is reaching its peak.

If, for aesthetic reasons, you want to grow several perennial herbs in a larger container, choose ones with variegated or colorful leaves for the best display. Try to match herbs that like the same growing conditions. Because you will need to pick only a few shoots at a time, the container should look good all year. If necessary, divide or take cuttings from vigorous plants; replace tired ones; and replant the container each year. Remove about one-fifth of the potting mix and replace with a fresh mix.

Finding Out about Your Soil

which soil is best for your garden?

BEFORE YOU START GROWING vegetables you'll need to assess your soil. For example, is it free-draining soil or prone to waterlogging? Is its texture light and sandy or heavy clay? Is it acidic or alkaline? Some soils are naturally better for growing vegetables, and most others can be improved to make them suitable. There are ways of coping with even the most difficult soil.

Drainage

The best way to find out whether you have free-draining soil is to dig a hole 18 inches (45cm) deep in early spring, when the soil is not frozen. Fill the hole with water, and monitor how long it takes to empty. If it drains away within an hour, you have free-draining soil; if it is still full the next day, it is waterlogged.

Sandy soil has large particles, making it free draining.

Vegetable plants prefer a free-draining soil. If your soil is waterlogged in winter, it may be slow to warm up in spring. You should be able to grow summer crops, but for early spring sowings, consider using raised beds. (See "Raised Beds," pages 10–11.)

Texture

Dig a couple of holes around the garden and examine the soil that comes out. If it is wet and sticky or clings together into clumps, it has a high proportion of clay. If it separates easily into grains, it has a high proportion of sand. Look for a change of color—this could indicate that the soil is waterlogged in winter or there is a hard layer below the surface impeding drainage. Try the following tests to identify your type of soil:

- Grab a handful of soil from 4–6 inches (10–15cm) deep and squeeze it. If it springs back, it is high in organic matter.

- Rub it between your thumb and index finger. If it feels gritty, it contains sand particles; if it feels smooth and silky, it contains mostly clay.

- Try rolling it into a ball. If it falls apart easily, it is mostly sand; if it sticks together reasonably well, it is loam; and if it can be molded into any shape, it is mostly clay.

Most soil falls between the two extremes of clay and sand; loamy soil contains a mixture of larger sand particles and minute clay particles. The soil's texture will determine whether you need to add organic matter:

- Clay can be hard to work into a fine soil for seeds, remains wet in winter, and is slow to warm up in the spring. It is fertile but benefits from plenty of bulky organic matter to open up the soil texture.

- Sandy soil drains easily and warms up rapidly in the spring. It is easy to work but may be lacking in nutrients and may dry out in warm weather. Adding organic matter will increase its water-holding capacity and add nutrients.

Loam soil has a crumbly texture made up of sand, clay, and silt.

Clay soil has tiny particles that trap water, leading to waterlogged soil.

- Loamy soil with roughly equal proportions of sand and clay particles is ideal for growing vegetables. It is free draining in winter yet retains moisture in the summer. It is easy to work and reasonably fertile, but it still benefits from the addition of moderate amounts of organic matter.

Acidic or alkaline?

Most vegetables prefer a soil that is near neutral, neither too acidic nor too alkaline. Most garden soil is suitable for growing vegetables, but if you are not sure about your soil, buy a pH test kit from a garden center or send a sample of your soil to your local Cooperative Extension Service or a private laboratory. A report from a private laboratory will give a more accurate reading but will cost more than one linked with the Cooperative Extension Service. A pH test kit will give you only a rough guide. Test several samples across the area or from each bed before you add fertilizer or soil ammendments.

To take a soil sample, use a clean trowel to dig down about 6 inches (15cm). Remove stones, roots, and other debris, and mix the sample thoroughly. Add a little soil to the tube from the kit, and follow the instructions to obtain a reading, usually by comparing the color of the resulting solution to a chart that indicates the pH. Or mix five or six samples from different parts of the vegetable garden together to send to a soil laboratory.

A pH of 7.0 is neutral (neither acidic nor alkaline); higher readings are alkaline and lower readings acidic. You can increase the soil pH (to make it less acidic) over several years by adding lime. Around 3 pounds per 100 square feet (1.36kg per 9.3m²) should raise the pH from 6.0 to 7.0 on sandy soil, about twice this for loam soil, and even more for clay. Decreasing the pH of an alkaline soil is more difficult, but you can use acidic organic matter, such as pine bark or sulfur chips. Test the pH each year to take corrective action if necessary.

Ideal pH for Vegetables

Below are the ideal pH levels for different vegetables:

- **5.5–7.0** Chicory, eggplant, endive, pepper, rhubarb, squash, turnip

- **6.0–7.0** Brussels sprouts, carrot, celery, corn, cucumber, garlic, kale, melon, parsnip, pea, radish, Swiss chard, tomato

- **6.5–7.5** Asparagus, bean, beet, broccoli, cabbage, cauliflower, leek, lettuce, onions, spinach

Soil Preparation

IF YOU ARE STARTING with a fresh site, especially one that has not been cultivated or is under grass, the soil may be firm and compacted. In order to grow well, vegetables need an open soil structure so that rain will drain through quickly and air can reach the roots. This will mean digging up the area.

Cultivating

Digging with a fork or spade is difficult work, although some people find it therapeutic and it is good exercise in moderation. Opening up a new vegetable garden can be daunting, but if you dig a portion of the garden each year in fall, it will not be too much of a chore. Cultivating the soil achieves three things:

Use your foot to help push the fork deeply into the soil.

- It breaks up compacted soil into smaller lumps—leave these over the winter, and let the frost and rain work on them. By spring, the soil should have settled so that it has a nice open texture. If you leave footprints when you walk across the bed, that is a sign of a good soil. However, try to keep off the areas you are intending to plant to avoid compacting the soil.

- It allows organic matter to be incorporated deep into the soil. Spread a good inch (2.5cm) of compost or well-rotted manure on the surface before you dig or till, and aim to mix it in thoroughly. This will help improve the texture of the soil and provide nutrients for the plants.

- It allows you to remove any perennial weeds with underground runners or deep taproots. It is worth spending time getting these out at this early stage because tackling them later on will be much more of a challenge. Annual weeds can be buried below the surface, where they should not cause a problem.

Fall is the best time to dig—especially in cold regions where the ground freezes—because it allows the weather to help break down any lumps over the winter. If you have heavier soil, especially clay, you might prefer to use a fork instead of a spade or shovel for digging. To avoid back strain, do some gentle stretching exercises before you begin to dig. Hold the tool with one hand near the blade when lifting, and don't overload it with too much soil. If you have stony soil, it may be worthwhile to remove any larger stones; however, you'll find that trying to completely destone the soil is a futile exercise.

At the end of the growing season, dig sections at a time in fall when space becomes available after a harvest. Remember that you won't need to break up any clods because of the effects of the weather.

If you don't like the thought of all the work involved in digging, you can rent a powered rotary tiller—or better still, hire someone with a rotary tiller—and get

A rotary tiller takes the labor out of digging up a plot.

the whole vegetable plot done at once. Don't till the soil when it is very wet or very dry, and don't over-till; one pass should be sufficient.

Problem soils

Most soil types can be improved simply by adding bulky organic material. (See "Organic Matter," pages 20–21.) And you can avoid some underlying problems by building raised beds. (See "Raised Beds," pages 10–11.) However, if the soil is waterlogged in winter and slow to warm up in spring, this could be due to a hard layer below the surface. If soil has been cultivated to the depth of a typical garden spade or fork or a powered tiller for years, a layer of compacted subsoil can result

that impedes drainage and roots. In this case, the only solution is to dig a trench and break up the bottom using a fork. This is known as "double digging," and it involves digging a series of trenches and backfilling the previous one with the soil. Unless you are a masochist, this is not recommended. However, digging a single trench each fall will help to gradually improve part of the garden at a time. Break up the bottom; fill it with bulky plant remains—for example, cabbage stalks, corn stems, and woody prunings—refill in the spring with soil; and grow a crop that likes plenty of moisture in the summer, such as cauliflower or pole beans.

No-Dig System

While there is a certain logic to digging, a no-dig system involves a lot less labor. This system assumes that your soil has an open (not compacted) structure to start with. If not, you'll still need to cultivate it first. If your soil structure is good, add a layer of organic mulch to the soil surface and simply leave it to disappear instead of digging the soil each fall or spring. The combination of plant roots and earthworms dragging the mulch into the soil will gradually improve the soil. The only cultivation you'll need to do is planting your vegetables and pulling out weeds. Any buried weed seeds will stay buried because you won't be bringing them to the surface as you dig, so you should find weeding will become less of a chore.

If you don't walk on the soil, it should not become compacted—and because compacted soil needs digging, this is something to avoid. The best way to achieve this is to adopt a bed system to separate growing areas from walkways. (See "Raised Beds," pages 10–11.)

Improving Your Soil

adding organic matter and composting

IF YOU HAVE A VEGETABLE GARDEN, you cannot have too much organic matter, and if you garden organically, without relying on chemcials, this will be even more the case. Organic matter, when dug into the soil, provides several benefits:

- It improves any soil, opening up heavy clay soils and binding free-draining sandy soils.

- Organic matter provides food for soil organisms, which in turn increases the fertility of the soil.

- It holds moisture in the soil, making it available to plants.

- As it breaks down gradually, it will release nutrients that can be used by the plants, and it will moderate the pH by acting as a buffer.

Most types of soil can be improved by adding some organic matter.

Used as a mulch, organic matter has several advantages:

- It prevents weed seeds in the soil from germinating and competing with crops.

- It will prevent moisture from evaporating from the soil.

- A mulch acts as an insulator, maintaining an even soil temperature when the air temperature is too hot or cold or fluctuates wildly between day and night.

Sources of organic matter

There are several different sources of organic matter. Leaf mold is useful for adding bulk to the soil, although it has little in the way of nutrients. Rake up fallen leaves in the fall, and stack them in a pile; you can use a circular enclosure made from wire or plastic mesh and a couple of stakes to keep them in place. Leave them and after a year they should have broken down into a rich crumbly leaf mold.

Animal manure, if you can get it in bulk, is especially useful because it contains significant quantities of plant nutrients. Stable manure often contains bedding, too, and if this is mostly straw, it will break down into great compost. Avoid manure with a lot of sawdust because it takes a while to decompose. Well-rotted manure is best, but if you can get hold of only fresh manure, stack it in a corner; cover it with a tarpaulin; and give it a year to decompose before spreading it on the garden. Poultry manure is too strong to use as a soil additive, but it makes a good organic fertilizer when well-rotted for several months. (See "Feeding," pages 47–49.)

You may see soil conditioners for sale in large bags at garden centers. They may be based on peat, recycled organic materials, bark, or composted manure. They'll work well, but to buy enough to make a significant difference to a vegetable garden can be expensive.

Keep compost in a hidden area but near the house for convenience.

Homemade garden compost

You can make your own compost with anything of plant origin from your garden or house. (See "Composting Ingredients," right.) Simply pile it in a heap, use a plastic compost container, or build your own enclosure.

You can build an enclosure out of lumber using old or recycled boards or rough-cut lumber. Make it at least 3-feet (90cm) on every side because this lets the material heat up during decomposition. Heat will help kill weed seeds and plant diseases. Use four fence posts to form the corners and nail boards to the sides and back. Place two vertical boards inside the cube behind the front posts, creating grooves so that you can slide loose boards down to make a removable front. (This will be helpful when it's time to empty the enclosure.)

A well-made compost pile will rot down into a fresh-smelling, soil-like material in six months to a year. Try to add material containing a mixture of one part moist green material to three parts dry woody material. The classic approach is to layer the materials, but mixing them up works, too. To speed up the process, shred or chop the materials before adding them to the pile, and occasionally mix up the pile to aerate it.

If the compost pile is wet and smelly or dry and undecomposed, the most likely causes are letting it get too wet or too dry or getting the mix wrong. The composting material should be moist but not wet. Cover the pile to prevent rain from making it waterlogged over winter, but water it, if necessary, in hot weather. If you are adding a lot of fresh green material, try adding torn-up newspaper or cardboard to bulk it up.

If you have enough material to fill them, build two enclosures side by side. Fill the extra one while the full enclosure is "maturing." When you empty the finished compost, refill it with half-composted material from the other. This mixing and aerating will kickstart the process all over again, and the pile will mature more quickly.

Composting Ingredients

Below is a list of items you can add to your compost pile, and those you should avoid:

WHAT TO COMPOST

Lawn clippings (but not if treated with chemicals)

Dead garden plants

Remains of vegetable plants after harvest

Shrub and hedge clippings (best shredded first)

Vegetable trimmings, including peels, from the kitchen

Coffee grounds and other uncooked plant-based waste

Cardboard (tear up or shred first, then add in small quantities)

Fallen leaves (if not using to make into leaf mold)

Waste from certain pets, such as rabbits and guinea pigs (but not cats)

Weeds (except mentioned below)

WHAT NOT TO COMPOST

Perennial weeds with their roots

Annual weeds that have flowered or set seed

Cooked food, bread, or meat, or food with oil-based dressings

Cat litter

Garden plants with obvious pests or disease

Crop Rotation

moving crops to help prevent pests and diseases

A USEFUL JOB during winter is planning your vegetable plot for the following year and ordering seeds and started plants.

Crop rotation is one of those traditional techniques that made perfect sense in the days before modern fertilizers and pesticides. Its aim was to prevent pests and diseases from spreading and to avoid problems that could not be cured easily. Now that many vegetable gardeners want to grow plants without man-made chemicals, it is as relevant today as it ever was.

Separate beds will help make crop rotation easier to follow.

The theory is that you should group annual vegetables that require similar conditions to thrive or that are susceptible to attack from the same soil pests or diseases together; grow these vegetables in the same part of the vegetable garden. Move these groups around in a set order each year so that they occupy the same part of the garden only every three or four years. This plan has several major benefits:

- Growing the same crop year after year can deplete the soil of the nutrients they use the most of. However, because each vegetable roots at different levels and uses different quantities of nutrients from the soil, moving them around will be less draining on the soil.

- Some crops, such as carrots and peas, need few nutrients, whereas others, such as cabbages and beets, need a lot. You can, therefore, concentrate organic matter and fertilizer where it will do the most good if you grow these crops together.

- Soil diseases and pests, such as cabbage root maggot, tend to attack specific groups of crops. By growing the same crop year after year in the same place, you allow pests to build up to damaging levels. However, if you rotate crops and grow unrelated vegetables in the same space for two years, the pests from the first year won't be able to live on their natural hosts in the second year, so their numbers will decline.

- Insect pests are more mobile than soil pests. However, some will overwinter beneath the crops they attack. For example, flea beetles overwinter beneath the previous cabbage family crops and cucumber beetles beneath squash. Moving crops around can prevent them from getting established among these crops.

Remember that crop rotation will not prevent most diseases that are airborne or spread by insects, nor flying pests or slugs. However, in the war against pests and disease every little bit will help. You may need to take other measures to get rid of pests and diseases, but following this system should cut down on your work.

Creating a rotation plan

Start with the list of what you intend to grow. Put each vegetable into its family group and assign each family to one of four areas. (See "Crop Families," right.) You'll have to combine some of the families. Possible combinations include potatoes and roots; pea and carrot families; pea and spinach or lettuce crops. Fit unrelated crops where there is most room, trying to match groups with similar needs. (See "Feeding Vegetables," pages 47–49.) One simplified method is a thee-year rotation plan with three groups: roots, cabbage family members, and all others.

Next year rotate all the groups to the next space, with light feeders following heavy feeders. Peas and beans are light feeders that fix atmospheric nitrogen in nodules on their roots, so they make a good break after heavy feeders, such as cabbage family members or squash. Don't worry about following a rotation plan too closely. You'll need to adapt it as your plot evolves and if you want to try new crops. If all else fails, just try to keep the crops with the most severe soil problems—potatoes, onions, and members of the cabbage family—moving on a three- or four-year cycle and do your best with the rest.

Beans from the pea family

Cabbage from the cabbage family

Potatoes from the potato family

Carrots from the carrot family

Crop Families

Family ties in the plant kingdom are not necessarily obvious—for example, the turnip ia a cabbage relative, and the potato is related to the tomato. Although you might decide to keep all the roots together, here are some family groupings that can be grown together:

- **CABBAGE FAMILY**

  Bok choy, broccoli, broccoli raab, Brussels sprouts, cabbage, cauliflower, Chinese cabbage and other Asian greens, collard, kale, kohlrabi, mustard, rutabaga, and turnip; also arugula and radish

- **ONION FAMILY**

  Garlic, leek, onions, scallion, shallot

- **POTATO FAMILY**

  Eggplant, pepper, potato, tomatillo, tomato

- **CARROT FAMILY**

  Carrot, celery, celeriac, fennel, parsley, parsnip

- **PEA FAMILY**

  Bush, fava, pole, runner, and soy beans, peas; also many cover crops, such as alfalfa and clover

- **CUCUMBER FAMILY**

  Cucumber, melon, pumpkin, summer and winter squash

- **UNRELATED CROPS**

  These are not related to any of the above and can be fitted in wherever there is room. Try to put heavy and light feeders together. (See "Feeding," pages 47–49.)

  Beet, chicory, lettuce, okra, spinach, sweet corn, sweet potato, Swiss chard

◄ Once you have divided the vegetables into groups, rotate them each year so that they do not grow in the same space more than once every three or four years.

Hardiness & Heat Zones

choosing the right vegetables for your climate

FOR SUCCESS IN GROWING CROPS, it is important to choose the vegetables and their varieties that will thrive in your climate. As well as knowing where to expect sunlight in your garden, you'll need to know how cold and hot it can get and when to expect the first and last frost dates in your area. Your local Cooperative Extension Service can help you learn about your local climate, especially the frost dates, and these maps can be used as guidance, too.

United States Hardiness Zone Map

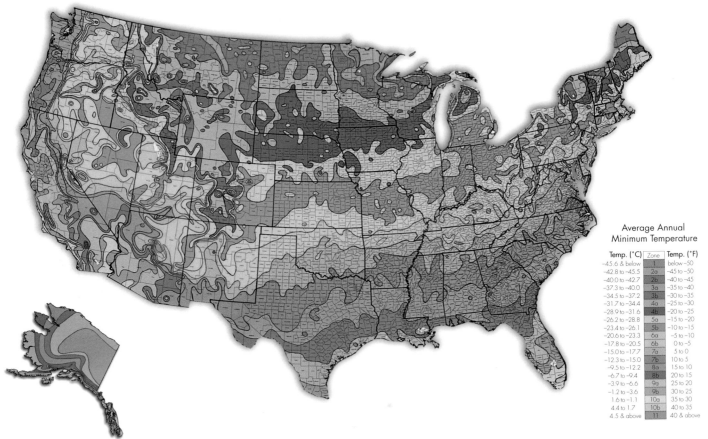

Average Annual Minimum Temperature

Temp. (°C)	Zone	Temp. (°F)
−45.6 & below	1	below −50
−42.8 to −45.5	2a	−45 to −50
−40.0 to −42.7	2b	−40 to −45
−37.3 to −40.0	3a	−35 to −40
−34.5 to −37.2	3b	−30 to −35
−31.7 to −34.4	4a	−25 to −30
−28.9 to −31.6	4b	−20 to −25
−26.2 to −28.8	5a	−15 to −20
−23.4 to −26.1	5b	−10 to −15
−20.6 to −23.3	6a	−5 to −10
−17.8 to −20.5	6b	0 to −5
−15.0 to −17.7	7a	5 to 0
−12.3 to −15.0	7b	10 to 5
−9.5 to −12.2	8a	15 to 10
−6.7 to −9.4	8b	20 to 15
−3.9 to −6.6	9a	25 to 20
−1.2 to −3.6	9b	30 to 25
1.6 to −1.1	10a	35 to 30
4.4 to 1.7	10b	40 to 35
4.5 & above	11	40 & above

The United States Department of Agriculture (USDA) has developed a Hardiness Zone Map. In the map, various regions throughout the United States have been divided into zones based on records of the average minumum temperatures in those areas. Zone 1 has the coldest temperatures, while Zone 11 has the warmest.

If you live in Zone 5, you can include plants that will thrive in Zones 1–4, too. When you buy seeds or transplants, the labels often include the hardiness zones in which the plants will survive. Within these zones, there are smaller microclimates, so you should use this information only as a guide and try experimenting.

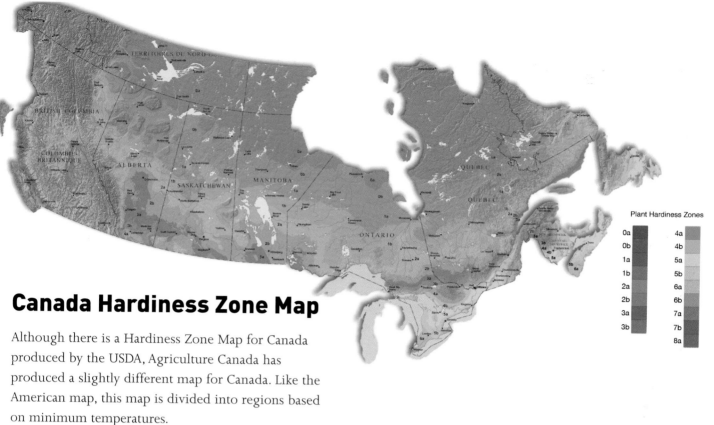

Canada Hardiness Zone Map

Although there is a Hardiness Zone Map for Canada produced by the USDA, Agriculture Canada has produced a slightly different map for Canada. Like the American map, this map is divided into regions based on minimum temperatures.

Plant Hardiness Zones

0a	4a
0b	4b
1a	5a
1b	5b
2a	6a
2b	6b
3a	7a
3b	7b
	8a

United States Heat-Zone Map

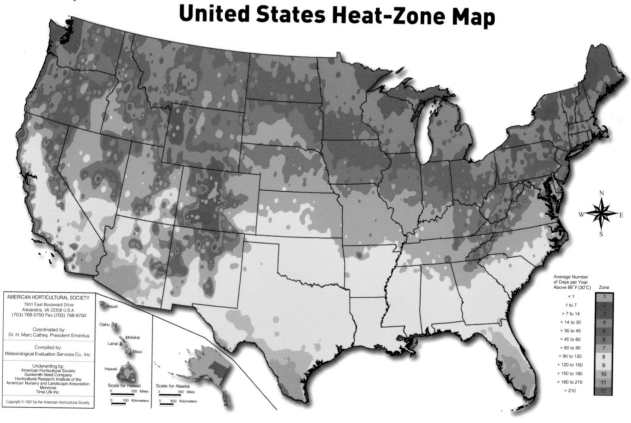

AMERICAN HORTICULTURAL SOCIETY
7931 East Boulevard Drive
Alexandria, VA 22308 U.S.A.
(703) 768-5700 Fax (703) 768-8700

Coordinated by:
Dr. H. Marc Cathey, President Emeritus

Compiled by:
Meteorological Evaluation Services Co., Inc.

Underwriting by:
American Horticultural Society
Goldsmith Seed Company
Horticultural Research Institute of the
American Nursery and Landscape Association
Monrovia
Time Life Inc.

Copyright © 1997 by the American Horticultural Society

Average Number of Days per Year Above 86°F (30°C)	Zone
< 1	1
1 to 7	2
> 7 to 14	3
> 14 to 30	4
> 30 to 45	5
> 45 to 60	6
> 60 to 90	7
> 90 to 120	8
> 120 to 150	9
> 150 to 180	10
> 180 to 210	11
> 210	12

The American Horticultural Society introduced their Heat Zone Map in 1998. It divides the United States into 12 zones, each one based on the average number of days over 86°F (30°C) for the region—these are known as "heat days." If you live in Zone 1, don't expect any days above 86°F (30°C), while Zone 12 will have 210 heat days in a year. Many plant breeders are now including this information in their labeling.

2

Sow

SEEDS USED TO BE THE STARTING POINT FOR GROWING NEARLY ALL VEGETABLES, and planting seeds is an easy way to grow most of them. For the best chance of success, start with good-quality seeds and give them all the conditions that they need. As long as you follow the instructions on the seed packet carefully, you should produce a bountiful harvest.

Today, many people prefer to buy started plants from a mail-order supplier, garden center, or a local nursery, which is a great way to save time. You will cut out all the germinating and handling of tiny seedlings and go straight to the outdoor planting stage. The choice of vegetables available is increasing all the time. Unless you want a particular variety that is not available or a lot of plants, it may be more convenient to buy started plants than to grow vegetables from seeds.

For the beginner, just filling the plot with vegetables will be an achievement in itself. The downside—if this is one—is that just when you can stand back and admire your handiwork, the first crops will be ready to harvest. As you harvest, you will open up space in the garden. However, you can keep sowing and planting throughout most of the growing season to fill any gaps.

Starting from Seeds

buying and storing seeds

A SEED IS A LIVING THING, and within its casing there is an embryonic plant, plus some stored energy. When warmth and moisture reach the dormant plant, they trigger it to start to grow. As long as you take care of your seeds—and follow the packet instructions—you should be able to grow them successfully. However, if you store seeds incorrectly, they will have a short life expectancy.

Buying seeds

Start off by purchasing fresh seeds each year. If you buy from a mail-order supplier, the seeds should be fresh and should have been stored in ideal conditions. However, if you buy seeds from a store or garden

Large seeds are easy to handle.

center, they may be last year's seeds or they may have been kept in less than ideal conditions. If you can, buy early in spring when there is a fresh stock of seeds.

Check the date on the packet. This will tell you when the seeds were packed and by what date you should use them. As long as the seeds have been enclosed in a sealed foil packet, they should keep for a few years. However, if the seeds were packed in a paper packet, use them in the year you buy them.

Saving seeds

Seeds will start to deteriorate as soon as they are ripe, and the process will speed up the warmer and more humid the atmosphere. Therefore, you should keep the seeds cool and dry until you are ready to sow them. When you open the packet, the seeds will deteriorate even faster. Reseal a foil packet by rolling it over tightly and return it to a cool dry place as soon as possible. The seeds should be fine for the remainder of the year if you are making several sowings. In particular, make sure you use seeds from lettuce, carrots, parsnips, and onions during the year because the quality will not be as good the next year.

Long-term storage

For some vegetables, you won't need to sow a whole packet of seeds, and you can store the unused seeds for the next year. For example, you can store the seeds of cabbages and their relatives, tomatoes, peppers, and eggplant, and all members of the cucumber family long term. This is particularly worthwhile if the seeds are the more expensive hybrid types. As soon as you've sown what you need, reseal the packet and put it in a sealed container (a plastic box container is ideal). Put a bag of silica gel in the container to absorb any moisture

Seed Terms Explained

You'll find several terms on a seed packet whose meanings might not be understood by a gardening novice. Knowing what they mean can help you to select your seeds.

F1 HYBRID: This is a term applied to seeds produced by crossing distinct parent plants. You don't need to know how the seeds were produced, but you do need to know what you are getting. The plants produced from F1 hybrid seeds will be almost identical to each other in terms of size, appearance, and maturity. This is a distinct advantage for farmers but not necessarily for home gardeners. However, F1 hybrid plants are more vigorous and heavier cropping than other varieties, and many have some resistance to pests or diseases bred into them. These seeds are more expensive than the alternative, the open-pollinated varieties (see below).

OPEN-POLLINATED VARIETIES: These are seeds collected from plants that have been pollinated naturally, so they contain a mixture of parents. The offspring can exhibit a lot of variation and may be harvested over a longer period.

HEIRLOOM VARIETIES: These are varieties that have been around for a long time, sometimes kept going by gardening enthusiasts. Many are just good, reliable varieties that have stood the test of time and hold up well against modern hybrids. Whether they taste better than modern hybrids is a matter of opinion.

ALL-AMERICAN SELECTION WINNERS: Each year new varieties are trialed all over the country, and the winners are those judged to be distinct improvements over existing varieties and are the ones likely to succeed in all geographic areas. Recent winners should be a safe bet, but winners from years back may have been improved upon.

DAYS TO MATURITY: Some varieties are faster to mature than others. Seed suppliers quote a number of days from when the seeds are sown to when the crops are ready to be harvested or the days from transplanting to harvest for transplanted crops. Use this as only a rough guide to compare varieties. The actual time will depend on where you live and on the weather each year. Days to maturity have been given in the varieties listed in this book where appropriate.

and keep it in a cool place, such as a cool cabinet or even in the salad compartment of the refrigerator.

Checking old seeds

If you have some old seeds but aren't sure if they are still viable—whether they will germinate—and if you have enough, you can test them to see if they will grow. Fold up a piece of paper towel; put it into a bowl and moisten it. Place about a dozen seeds on the towel; then seal them with the bowl in a plastic bag

and store in a dark place at room temperature. Check occasionally to make sure the towel is still moist for the next ten days.

On the tenth day, check to see how many seeds have germinated. If fewer than half of them have, dispose of the seeds. If between one-half and two-thirds of the seeds have sprouted, you can use the seeds but you'll need to sow them more thickly. If even more have germinated, they are safe for sowing.

Sowing Methods

SOWING SEEDS STRAIGHT into the ground is easy, provided you get the basics right. There are several requirements before you can begin to sow: the soil should be moist (but not too wet) and warm enough, with an open structure to let the seedlings push through to the surface. However, if the soil is too warm—above 86°F (30°C) in most cases—the seeds will struggle to germinate. When the soil is ready, instead of rushing out and sowing all your seeds at once, plan how to spread out the harvest as much as possible. (See "Using Space Efficiently," pages 40–41.)

Minimum Sowing Temperatures

It should be emphasized that these are the minimum temperature at which vegetables will germinate. All will germinate much more quickly as the soil temperature rises. The exception to this is lettuce, which germinates poorly at soil temperatures above 70°F (21°C).

- **40°F (5°C)**
  All leafy cabbage family crops, including Asian greens, fava bean, lettuce, pea, radish, rutabaga, turnip

- **45°F (7°C)**
  beet, carrot, leek, onions, parsnip, Swiss chard

- **50°F (10°C)**
  Celeriac, celery

- **55°F (13°C)**
  Bush bean, pole bean, runner bean, cucumber, squash, sweet corn, tomato

- **65°F (18°C)**
  Eggplant, pepper, okra (in cool areas, these are best started indoors).

When to sow

Although the calendar is a good guide to when you can start sowing, the soil temperature is a more accurate indicator. You can invest in a soil thermometer, which has a probe that you push into the soil roughly to the same depth as you will sow the seeds. For an accurate reading, measure the temperature in early morning, before it has time to warm up in the sun. When the soil reaches the minimum germination temperature needed by the seeds for several days running, it should be safe to sow them. If the soil is a little cooler than the preferred minimum temperature, the seeds may still germinate, but it can take an extra week or longer.

Preparing a seedbed

Seedlings will struggle through soil even if it is lumpy. However, if they are struggling above the surface, the roots underground will be having a hard time, too. If you haven't dug or tilled the soil the previous fall, use a garden fork to loosen it, breaking up large lumps with the back of the fork. Then, even if you did break up the soil in fall, using a rake, work back and forth to break

Use a rake to help prepare a fine tilth in a seedbed.

the surface down into a fine texture, known as tilth. At the same time, rake off any stones or debris. When the soil surface is smooth and level, it is ready to sow.

Seed rows and furrows

Most vegetables are sown in rows and there are good reasons for this:

- Because the vegetable seedlings appear in straight lines, they are easy to tell apart from any weed seedlings.

- It is easier to hoe between straight rows.

- It is easier to space plants evenly apart to give them an equal chance.

- Vegetable seeds need to be buried, and it is easier to gauge the correct depth by making a seed furrow.

A seed furrow is simply a shallow V-shape or flat-bottom trench in the soil made with a trowel or the corner of a hoe. An alternative is to use the edge of a piece of lumber pressed into the seedbed to the correct depth. (See "Seed Sowing Depths," right.)

For long rows, use a piece of string held taut between two pegs to mark the line and run the furrow along it. Space rows evenly and the ideal distance apart for the particular vegetables you plan to grow in them, and check that the furrows are the right depth. If the soil is dry, dribble water into the bottom of the furrow and let it soak in before sowing the seeds.

Seed Sowing Depths

Vegetables prefer different soil depths for germination. Some are shallow so that the seeds receive light for germination, but other seeds prefer deeper soil.

- **¼ INCH (6MM):** Arugula, chicory, fennel, lettuce, celery

- **½ INCH (12MM):** Carrot, all members of the cabbage family, eggplant, leek, melon, onions, parsnip, pepper, radish, spinach, tomato

- **1 INCH (2.5CM):** Beet and chard, bush and pole beans, cucumber, okra, pea, pumpkin, squash, soy bean

- **1½ INCHES (3.75CM):** Fava bean, sweet corn

- **1¾ INCHES (4.5CM):** Runner bean

For smaller seeds, such as carrot and lettuce, tip some seeds into the palm of your hand and, taking a pinch between your other index finger and thumb, scatter them thinly along a section of the furrow. Keep in mind the final plant spacing recommended on the packet, but sow plenty of extra seeds to allow for some failures. The extra seedlings can be pulled out later. Cover the seeds by hoeing dry soil over the furrow. Don't forget to label the row with the variety and sowing date.

Use a hoe held on an angle to create a seed furrow.

Let water soak into dry soil before sowing seeds.

A trench is made for double sowing (plank prevents soil compaction).

Larger seeds, such as squash and bean, are easy to place the correct distance apart. Some gardeners like to sow two or three seeds together, then remove the weaker seedlings. Alternatively, you can sow the seeds at half the final spacing recommended on the packet, then remove any extra seedlings, which can be used for filling any gaps where there are failures.

Double sowing

Peas and bush bean seeds are often sown in double or triple rows about an inch or two apart, with wider paths for picking. This is also a useful technique for vegetables that are grown close together, such as radishes, scallions, and baby leaf salad greens. Use a hoe with a blade 4 to 6 inches (10 to 15cm) wide and make a wide, shallow furrow. Keep the depth even or the seeds may emerge erratically. Water the furrow if the soil is dry, and scatter the seeds as thinly and evenly as you can across its width. Cover the furrow and lightly firm the surface with the back of a rake. The drawback to double sowing is that if your soil contains weed seeds—and most soil does— you'll have to pull out weeds until the crop is established.

Raised beds

Instead of sowing seeds in long furrows, the best approach to sowing seeds in raised beds is to sow them in short rows across the bed. Alternatively, you can sow the seeds in double rows, spacing them more closely together, to make blocks of each vegetable. Because you will be able reach all the vegetables from the edges, you don't need to allow for access between rows.

Hill sowing

Large heat-loving crops, such as cucumber, melon, and squash, will benefit from a method known as hilling, where the seeds are planted in a small hill, or mound, of soil. This hill protects the neck of these plants, which are susceptible to rotting. Depending on the spacing between plants within the row, it may be easier to create individual hills or to make a hilled row. Dig either a hole or a trench; then add a bucketful of compost per planting position. Mix it into the soil, and water if necessary. Hoe the soil you excavated and loose soil from between the hills or rows to create a mound up to 12 inches (30cm) high and the same across. Plant two or three seeds per position. The top of the hill will warm up more quickly than the surrounding soil, so your crops will get started faster. The hill will also help shed rain so seeds will be less likely to rot. Make sure the surrounding soil is well watered in dry weather, but avoid watering the hill itself to encourage the roots to spread out.

Vegetables are sown across the width of a raised bed.

Raising Transplants

MOST VEGETABLES CAN BE SOWN directly into the garden, but there are circumstances where it is better to start them off in pots indoors and transplant them into the garden later on. However, if you only want a few plants of any type of vegetable, consider buying started plants instead. (See "Buying Vegetable Plants," pages 36–37.)

Why transplants?

One advantage of raising your own transplants is that you can enjoy watching plants develop from seeds close up. Note how a squash seedling has to push the huge seed out of the potting mix and then split it so the two seed leaves can open. These two cotyledons, or seed leaves, are actually the major part of the seed (although on some plants there is only one seed leaf). The leaves that appear after the seed leaves are known as "true" leaves.

Practical reasons for growing transplants include:

- Vegetables that are attacked by soil pests or diseases will get off to a better start in a pot. It is easier to protect tender young plants from slugs and snails, rodents, or birds if grown indoors instead of in the open garden.

An emerging squash shows its seed leaves.

- Large vegetables that are slow to start are best transplanted when bigger and they need their allocated space. Meanwhile, you can use the space for a quick filler crop. (See "Using Space Efficiently," pages 40–41.)

- Tender vegetables that need high temperatures to bear fruit can be started earlier, providing a longer season. This is especially true in northern regions with a cold spring. However, even in the warmer South, you can extend the season by four weeks or more by starting plants indoors before conditions are ideal outdoors.

- If you want a lot of plants of a particular variety, store-bought started plants can be expensive. Or if you want to try unusual varieties not available as started plants, raising your own is often the only option.

Sowing mixes and containers

Instead of digging up soil from your garden to fill up plant containers, you should buy a good-quality seed-starting mix because it will be free of disease and weed seeds. This can be either a soil-based or soil-free medium, but no matter the type it should be sterile with the loose, free-draining texture seeds need. Unlike a potting mix, it should contain only small amounts of plant nutrients—a seed contains everything a plant needs to grow to a reasonable size. Afterward, you'll need to move it into a larger container or into the garden, where it can continue to grow larger.

You can use any clean container for starting seeds, provided it has drainage holes in the bottom. Keep the pots small to produce compact root systems and stocky seedlings. Vegetables that grow fast or remain in their pots for more than four weeks will do well in a pot 3 inches (7.5cm) in diameter. For most other plants, 1½–2 inches (4–5cm) across is best. If you want to raise a lot of seedlings, invest in plastic seed-starting trays that are divided into individual cells or compartments. Each seedling will have its own space to grow and the root balls will be kept separate, making the seedlings easier to transplant. Being part of a tray, you'll find it easier to care for the seedlings together. You'll need to make sure they have enough light; water them each day; and feed them a half-strength mixture of fish emulsion once a week.

Starting tender plants

Tender plants are those that germinate and grow best when the temperature is a steady 70°F (21°C) at the minimum. (See "Tender or Hardy?," opposite.) Cucumbers, squash, and melons have big seeds, so sow each seed into an individual 3-inch (7.5cm) pot. Push large squash seeds sideways into the seed-starting mix—the seedling will find it easier to germinate.

Plants with smaller seeds, such as eggplant and peppers, take longer to emerge from the seed-starting mix and grow slowly at first. Scatter the seeds thinly over the surface of a seed-starting tray and cover lightly with more mix. When the seedlings are large enough to handle and the first true leaves appear, move them to individual 4-inch (10cm) pots to continue growing. Handle the seedlings carefully, holding a leaf or seed leaf, never the stem or roots. Make a hole with a pencil or your finger, and drop the roots in so the seedling is the same level as before, then push the mix into the hole until the seedling is firm.

Because these are tender vegetables, you'll need to keep them warm. On a table by a well-lit windowsill in a heated room will be fine, but avoid direct sunlight or the seedlings may be scorched. One alternative is in a greenhouse; you'll need to provide a heating mat to provide constant bottom heat—one with a thermostat won't overheat them on sunny days. Another option is a basement or garage if you also provide flourescent lights suspended about 3 inches (7.5cm) above the plants.

Bigger seeds can often be planted into individual pots.

Scatter smaller seeds over a divided seed-starting tray.

Tomatoes are tender plants that can be started indoors.

Tender or Hardy?

There are several vegetables that will be more successful if you start them off as transplants. For the more tender types, it is important that you carefully harden them off before transplanting them outdoors.

TENDER VEGETABLES

Cucumber	Pepper
Eggplant	Squash
Melon	Tomato
Okra	Tomatillo

HARDY VEGETABLES

Broccoli	Kale
Brussels sprouts	Leek
Cabbage	Lettuce
Cauliflower	Onions
Celery	

Starting hardy plants

All you need for hardy plants is somewhere with good light that is frost-free or, preferably, higher than the minimum germination temperature. (See "Minimum Sowing Temperatures," page 30, and "Tender or Hardy?," above right.) A porch is suitable, as is an old-fashioned cold frame. This is basically a square frame positioned over the soil with a window on top. Because these plants grow rapidly and can be planted outdoors after as few as four weeks, seed-starting trays are ideal. Sow a couple of seeds per cell and if more than one emerges, use nail scissors to clip all but the strongest later on.

Hardening off

A simple technique for acclimatizing young plants to life outdoors after they have been raised under controlled conditions indoors is known as hardening off. Without it, the shock of moving tender seedlings straight from a warm sheltered place to cold soil will interrupt, or slow down, their growth and can even kill them.

When the plants have a couple of pairs of true leaves and have more or less filled their pots with roots, it's time to start getting them used to outdoor conditions. Choose a settled period when frosts are no longer predicted in your area. Put the plants in their pots outdoors during the day and bring them back in at night. Leave them outside for longer each day until they can stay outdoors all night. After about a week or so, your transplants should be ready for planting in the ground outside. Another option is to put them in a cold frame where you can prop the window open for longer and longer periods each day until you can leave it fully open, even at night.

Buying Vegetable Plants

transplants ready for planting

STARTED VEGETABLE PLANTS are now sold by mail-order suppliers and garden centers. Although the varieties available are limited in comparison to those sold as seeds, you might prefer to buy these instead of raising your own transplants, especially if you have a small vegetable garden. Started plants are a great way to try out a wide range of different vegetables and varieties. For example, if you only have room for a half-dozen tomato plants, you can try a cherry, a plum, a beefsteak, a slicing variety, one with yellow fruit, and an unusual heirloom—without wasting most of six packets of seeds.

If you live in an area prone to late frosts, don't be tempted to buy plants too early. Wait until they can go straight outdoors, otherwise you'll have to keep them protected from frost and watered regularly.

Leaves on started plants should be healthy, not yellow or dried out.

What to look for

If you choose plants from a garden center, you'll have the advantage of being able to examine the plants before making your selection. Consider the following:

- Avoid any plants if there has been a frost in the area. Ask staff when they expect the next delivery.

- Look for fresh stock. Look for stocky plants with bright green leaves, and avoid plants that look as if they have been allowed to dry out or have been kept poorly. Reject any that are pale or thin and look unhealthy.

- Check that the pots are full of healthy roots but not crowded or "pot-bound." Roots emerging from the drainage holes are a sign that the plant has been in the pot too long.

- Make sure you aren't bringing any pests with your started plant into your garden. Look for aphids, mites, or other insects on the plant, and avoid those with mottled or nibbled leaves.

Caring for started plants

When you get your started plants home, check the local weather forecast. A calm spell of mild weather is ideal for planting hardy plants; wait for an average

Best Started Plants

Some vegetables require a lot of effort to get started. If you lack time or experience, consider buying the following as started vegetables:

Cabbage	Melon
Cauliflower	Onion
Cucumber	Pepper
Eggplant	Squash
Leek	Tomato

Onion sets are small, dry bulbs that are ready to grow to maturity.

temperature of at least 60°F (16°C) before planting tender vegetables. If conditions are not ideal, keep the plants somewhere sheltered and well lit. Water regularly to keep the mix moist but not wet. If you can't plant outdoors for a few weeks, give the plants a little diluted plant food, and make sure you harden off the plants before planting outside. (See "Hardening Off," page 35.)

Other ways to buy vegetables

Some vegetables are sold as dry bulbs or tubers. Potatoes are sold as "seed" tubers in garden centers or as budded eyes (pieces of tubers with a single eye or sprout) by mail-order catalogs. Although it may be tempting to plant potato tubers from a supermarket, seed tubers have been produced under controlled conditions and are guaranteed free of major diseases. When buying seed potatoes, check that they are free from rot or damage, that the tubers are an even size, and that they have several healthy sprouts starting to form. Depending on the cultivar, or variety, you may need to cut them up. Sweet potatoes are sold as "slips," which are rooted shoots produced from a tuber. Put them in a jar of water or into a pot or soil immediately to prevent them from drying out before you are ready to plant them.

Onions can be raised from seeds or bought as bundles of started plants. However, you may also come across

Perennial Vegetables

Globe artichoke, which can be grown as a perennial in mild areas, is mostly sold as plants. Asparagus is usually sold as one- or two-year-old "crowns," which are semidry roots without soil. You may also find them sold as potted plants. Jerusalem artichoke is sold as tubers but can be invasive. Rhubarb is available as small potted plants divided from a mother plant.

Globe artichoke is normally available as a potted plant.

"sets," small dry onion bulbs raised from seeds under controlled conditions. They are ready to grow to full size when planted in the spring. Garlic never produces seeds so is available only as bulbs. Shallots are also sold as dry bulbs. Check the packages and reject any with soft, shriveled, or rotten bulbs. Onion sets should be even in size. Keep garlic bulbs intact until you are ready to plant; only then separate them into individual cloves.

Planting Transplants

moving plants from pots into the ground

WITH THE PROPER CARE, whether from you or the nursery staff, your young vegetable plants grown in containers will be ready to be planted outdoors. You'll find this less work then starting plants from seeds, and they need just a little attention to get started.

Planting outdoors

The main advantage of planting vegetable transplants or starts that began life indoors, as opposed to sowing directly in the ground, is that you don't need a perfect seedbed. Simply hoe off any weeds, scrape back any mulch left from the previous year, and plant. Use a string line or plank of wood if you want to plant in straight rows, and dig a small hole with a trowel or large dibble at the required spacing.

Tap the bottom of the pot gently to release the plant with its root ball intact. Some vegetables, such as cucumbers, resent any disturbance to their roots and must be handled

A plank of wood can be used as a guide when transplanting.

carefully when planted outdoors. To release the root balls from divided trays, push a pencil through the drainage hole. Avoid pulling on the plant itself.

Plant most young plants at the same level they were in the pot. You should plant members of the cabbage family deeper, so the first pair of leaves are resting on the soil. Plant tomato plants deeply, too, and any buried stem will sprout additional roots. However, plant members of the cucumber family so the top of the root ball is level or slightly above the soil surface. This will help prevent moisture from collecting around the base of the stem, causing rot. You can also plant them into hills. (See "Hill Sowing," page 32.)

A good start

Make sure the soil is moist when you plant the vegetables, so the roots are encouraged to grow into the soil and search for water and nutrients. Transplants should be watered frequently in dry weather, until they are well established and growing vigorously. Try to water the soil surrounding the plant instead of the original root ball. It is better to keep the plant itself dry and the surrounding soil moist to deter diseases. Drip irrigation works well for widely spaced transplanted crops. (See "Watering Vegetables," pages 44–46.)

Keeping transplants free of weeds is a lot easier than with directly sown crops. You can mulch with straw or organic matter, which will help control weeds and retain moisture in the soil. (See "Mulching & Weed Control," pages 50–51.) You can also plant widely spaced transplants through a plastic sheet, which is even more effective at suppressing weeds, warming the soil, and preventing moisture loss. Finally, keep floating row covers handy in case of a sudden cold snap. They should keep new transplants warm even in a late frost.

Extending the Season

IN COLD AREAS, gardeners have learned to cheat the weather and stretch the season just long enough to coax a crop out of most vegetables. In other areas, you can use these techniques to extend the growing season to have the most time possible for growing and harvesting your crops. The key is getting plants started a couple of weeks before the conditions outdoors are ideal and to a lesser extent, allowing long-season crops to finish cropping before the weather gets cold again.

Protecting individual plants

A clear, dome-shaped hot cap, sometimes called a cloche, is designed to protect a plant from wet and cold weather and to keep the plant warm. Instead of a store-bought hot cap, you can use a recycled, large, plastic milk container. Simply cut off the bottom and put it over a plant, pushing the edges into the soil to anchor it in place. Keep the lid on at night to retain warmth,

A spun plastic floating row cover will protect the vegetables.

but remove it in the daytime to allow ventilation. You can use hot caps to warm the soil if set in position for a week before you plant a transplant or sow seeds.

Protecting a row

To protect a row of crops, use a row cover made from a sheet of clear plastic and metal hoops. These are inexpensive to buy and use. The advantage is that in addition to the headroom they can provide your plants, the sides can be hitched up to allow ventilation during the daytime and for watering. The temperature inside will be warmer and water evaporation will be greater than outside, so regular watering is essential.

Floating row covers made from perforated plastic sheet or spun polyester fibers are the easiest way to protect young seedlings or recently sown rows. The material is light enough to let the growing plants push it up without it crushing them. It lets light, air, and rain through but keeps the temperature inside a few degrees higher than outside. As a bonus, the spun fiber covers prevent even tiny pests from getting to your young crops. In hot weather, the plants can get too hot and scorch. To protect plants from frost on the coldest nights, double up the cover or add extra layers to trap air. Anchor the edges, either by burying them or with bricks, heavy lumber, or another material, but leave the material slack to give plants room to grow.

Fall protection

There's nothing more frustrating than a crop of tomatoes, melons, or bush beans growing well when the first frost is in the weather forecast. Get those hot caps and row covers out again and you should be able to gain a few precious weeks before harvesting. If necessary, untie staked tomatoes and lay them on a bed of straw before covering with a row cover.

Using Space Efficiently

IT MAKES SENSE TO USE every bit of vegetable garden area as efficiently as possible to get the best harvest. So once you've decided on your main cropping plan for the season, think about how you can fit a little bit extra in. Look for any patch of bare soil throughout the season, and you'll find an opportunity for a quick crop. Here are some successful techniques.

Double cropping

If you can match an early crop (or an overwintered one) and a late crop together, you can grow two crops in the same space. For example, follow an early pea or fava bean crop with a later sowing of sweet corn or bush beans. Or clear a crop of radishes or spinach and plant the area with lettuce or late cabbage family members. With some quick crops, you can count on getting several complete crops from the same area, for example, lettuce or other greens.

Early starters

In early spring, while you wait for the soil to warm up for tender crops, such as squash, tomatoes, and sweet corn, use this space to sneak in an early crop (See "Fillers and Intercrops," opposite.) Sow the seeds in rows, but leave space between them to plant the main crop. In cold areas, cover the early starters until after the last frosts are expected. (See "Extending the Season," page 39.) If the early crop hasn't produced a decent harvest when you plant the main crop, remove enough of it, if necessary, to plant the main crop. Clear the early crop before the next one needs the space.

Intercropping

Many large vegetables are spaced widely apart and do not use their allocated space for weeks or months. You can use the space between them for a quick crop that will be out of the way before the later crop needs the space. The larger members of the cabbage family—kale, sprouting broccoli, and Brussels sprouts—are prime candidates. Choose a related crop, such as kohlrabi, turnip, or radish, if you are following a crop-rotation plan. (See "Crop Rotation," pages 22–23.)

Leeks are another slow-growing winter crop, so you can grow scallions while they are growing. Parsnips are slow enough to allow a crop of baby carrots. The area around the bottom of trained pole bean plants will accommodate a quick crop of lettuce and other greens.

Fast-growing lettuce grow among slow-growing leeks.

Sweet corn is a good choice for intercropping because even when fully grown, the plants don't shade the soil beneath. Native Americans grew corn and pole beans on mounds and planted squash beneath them. A modern version is to underplant corn with pumpkins or winter squash, or to sow bush beans between rows of corn.

Follow-up crops

There's another opportunity for adding to your harvest toward the end of summer, as the summer vegetables are cleared, by planting vegetables for overwintering, such as leeks and garlic. Choose quick-growing crops or ones that can be picked young and that are hardy enough to cope with the first fall frosts. In frost-free areas, keep sowing right through winter.

Successional sowing

Some vegetables produce a crop over a long period, but many come all at once, leading to a glut, followed by nothing. Even vegetables that can be picked over a long period, such as summer squash and pole beans, run out of steam before the season ends. The answer is to make several sowings to extend the harvest period.

Lettuce and other greens and as well as quick-growing plants, such as radishes and scallions, can be sown little and often. Sow a short row or patch each time, enough to harvest over a few weeks. Then sow another batch every couple of weeks so there's always something just reaching the optimum size for harvesting. Later sowings will catch up with earlier ones, but all these plants can be picked smaller or larger to adjust the timing. Instead of occupying a prime spot in the garden, grow these as fillers anywhere you can find space during the season.

Root vegetables that can be eaten young, such as early carrots, baby beets, kohlrabi, and baby turnips, are best sown more than once during the season. For hardier roots, make an early sowing in spring (using row covers to warm the soil), an early summer sowing, and a late summer one to harvest before the fall frosts.

Bush beans and peas can be difficult to keep up with once they start producing pods. Sow shorter rows several times through the summer, the last one timed to finish before the first frosts.

Broccoli and cauliflower are notorious for producing a crop over a short period. Sow a few seeds at a time to spread the harvest, or buy a few plants at a time. Or buy a mixture of varieties that produce a crop after different periods. This technique works well in raised beds. If you sow about two short rows across the bed, you'll never have more than you can eat at any time.

Vegetables that produce a crop over a long period, such as pole and runner beans and summer squash, can start to tire by late summer. Make a second sowing in midsummer to harvest from late summer into fall.

Fillers and Intercrops

Keep a handful of seed packets handy during the season to fill any gaps that appear as you harvest or before you plant new crops. Choose from the quick growers below:

VEGETABLE	SOW TO HARVEST TIME
Arugula	6 weeks (as baby leaf)
Bean, bush	10 weeks (not hardy)
Beet	8 weeks (for baby beet)
Bok choy	6–8 weeks
Carrot	10 weeks (early varieties)
Chinese cabbage	10 weeks
Kohlrabi	10 weeks
Lettuce	10 weeks (less for baby leaf)
Mustard green	6 weeks (as baby leaf)
Pea	10 weeks
Radish	6 weeks
Scallion	8 weeks
Spinach	6 weeks
Turnip	6–8 weeks

3

Grow

YOU'VE SOWN YOUR VEGETABLE SEEDS OR PLANTED YOUR TRANSPLANTS OUTDOORS.
The next stage is to care for them as they grow so that you can reap a bumper harvest. All a plant requires is air, light, moisture, and nutrients. Air, light, and moisture in the form of rain are provided free. Unfortunately, rain doesn't always fall when plants need it, so watering vegetables is important when rain is scarce. In theory, vegetables should get all the nutrition they need from the soil. However, the more plants you grow in the soil, the more the nutrients are depleted, so you will have to put something back in the form of fertilizers. Many modern gardeners choose organic methods for the vegetable garden. The aim is to feed the soil with organic matter, natural nutrient supplements, and cover crops; then the soil can feed the plants.

By providing the ideal conditions for your plants, you will also provide ideal conditions for weeds, so you'll need to take steps to deal with them. Watch out, too, for the pests and diseases determined to steal your harvest. Most pests and diseases can be prevented from damaging your crops or kept at bay long enough to ensure you get a harvest.

Watering Vegetables

keeping your vegetables hydrated

UNLESS IT RAINS EVERY WEEK through the summer, you'll need to provide supplementary water so that your plants can thrive and provide a bountiful harvest. If your plants don't get sufficient water regularly, there will be an interruption to their growth. This can, for example, cause blossoms to form too early, reduce the sugar content in the plant's fruit, and make the plant susceptible to diseases and insects.

In early spring, the soil in most parts of the country will have enough moisture after the winter rain or snow. However, as soon as warm weather begins to evaporate the water, this reservoir will start to disappear. Every time it rains, the soil will be replenished and, as a rule of thumb, an inch (2.5cm) of rain a week will keep plants thriving. As the temperature rises, the water deficit will increase. Wind—which whips moisture away from plants—and humidity are also factors to consider. If it doesn't rain, you'll have to make up the difference. This can mean adding water at a rate of just over half a gallon per square foot (1.9L per 30cm²) a week, but more at higher temperatures.

Watering dos and don'ts

Even if you live in an area with abundant water supplies, you should use water sensibly:

- Provided the soil is moist deep down, most vegetables will be able to exploit it. So even if the surface is dust dry, your vegetables may still be fine. To check, dig a hole a few inches deep to the depth of the plant's roots, and if the soil is still moist at the bottom, the vegetables should not need watering.

- Too much water can be as bad as too little. Permanently wet soil can lead to root rot and other soil diseases and can flush away valuable nutrients. Too much water can cause lettuce heads to split.

- Watering little and often can do more harm than good. It is tempting to sprinkle the surface whenever it dries out, but water doesn't necessarily soak into the soil and become available to the plants. Keeping the surface constantly moist will encourage plants to root close to the surface, and if you stop, they won't have the deep roots they need to see them through dry periods, so water deeply once a week instead of giving a daily sprinkle. The exception to this is with short-term leafy lettuce and other greens.

- Always water newly transplanted vegetables and water seedbeds as the seedlings are emerging unless it has rained. Once they are established and starting to grow vigorously, water only when the weather is dry.

- Concentrate on watering vegetables that are almost ready to be harvested or on those that need to grow fast to produce tender leaves or stems, such as lettuce.

Use a fine spray to water young plants.

A garden hose is a popular choice for watering plants.

- Too much water at the wrong time may just produce a lot of leaves on fruit-bearing crops. Irregular watering can also cause problems—for example, blossom-end rot on tomatoes or bolting of cauliflower. Periods of drought followed by heavy rain can cause root crops to split.

Conserving water

If you live in an arid area or one that has droughts, water conservation is particularly important. Consider any way you can save rainwater during the winter for use on the vegetable garden in the summer. Fit rainwater barrels to collect runoff from the roofs of the house and garage.

- Improve your soil structure by adding organic matter. (See "Improving Your Soil, pages 20–21.) Soil with an open structure holds more water than compacted soil.

- Use mulches to keep the soil cool, prevent competition from weeds, and prevent evaporation from the soil surface. (See "Mulching & Weed Control," pages 50–51.)

- Target water on the vegetables that benefit most and at the stage in their life cycle that will produce the biggest crop. (See "What to Water and When," page 46.)

- Water the soil, not the plants. This ensures that most of the water soaks into the soil instead of evaporating from leaves; wet foliage also encourages plant diseases. Apply a week's water once a week so it soaks in to a good depth. Water when it is cool in early morning or late afternoon to minimize losses from evaporation.

- Get water directly to the roots. Using plastic soda bottles or milk containers, punch a small hole in the lid and cut the bottom off. Bury these halfway in the soil next to widely spaced crops and fill with water. You can also deliver soluble plant food this way.

- You can use gray water—leftover water from the kitchen or bathroom—on the ornamental borders, but it is not recommended for use in the vegetable garden.

Garden hoses

In a small garden, you can use a 2-gallon (7.5L) watering can, but you can waste a lot of time and effort carrying watering cans in a large garden. In this case, invest in a good-quality garden hose, along with an attachment to break up the water into small droplets. Adjustable types are available, and wandlike attachments can help guide water directly to the soil—away from the leaves—and are ideal for hanging baskets.

Irrigation systems

A sprinkler system may be an efficient use of your time—leave it for an hour or two and the whole vegetable garden is watered—but it is wasteful. The most efficient way to deliver water to the plants that need it is to use a drip irrigation system. There are two main kinds:

- Soaker hoses are hoses with small holes at regular intervals. Some are made from porous rubber that leaks water slowly along their length. Run these along rows of crops. Link several lengths together with T-joints and nonporous hose and connect them to your outside faucet.

Watering Vegetables

- Dripper systems use a number of fine tubes that connect to a hose running around the vegetable garden. Each tube ends in a water emitter, or dripper, which can be adjusted to suit the needs of different plants. It may take a little tinkering to get each emitter adjusted properly; you can check their output by running them into a bucket for a length of time.

Once either of these systems is set up, you can water the whole vegetable garden or sections of it by turning on the faucet for a set period of time. You can also use an automatic water timer or water computer to turn the water on and off for you. Some sophisticated systems can override the computer if it rains.

Dripper systems can cater to the needs of individual plants.

What to Water and When

The weekly water volume is given below for typical crops. If it rains, deduct the amount of rainfall from the amount of water you give the plants (you can leave a watering can outside to catch rain to determine this). Do not water vegetables outside the key period unless it is exceptionally dry.

LEAFY CROPS

Broccoli and cauliflower: Water transplants and also when the heads start to form—½ to 1 gallon (1.9–3.8L) per plant.

Cabbage: Water transplants and when the heads start to form; do not water when heads are fully formed—½ gallon (1.9L) per plant.

Lettuce, Asian greens, and other greens: Water throughout their life—1 gallon per 1 foot (3.8L/30cm) of row.

ROOT CROPS

Quick-growing baby crops of beet, carrot, radish, and turnip: Water continuously—¾ gallon per foot (2.8L/30cm) of row.

Leek: Water seedlings or transplants and until cooler fall weather—1 gallon per foot (3.8L/30cm) of row.

Onions: Water when the bulbs start to form; stop when they start to ripen—1 gallon per foot (3.8L/30cm) of row.

Pea and bean: Water when flowers appear and while pods are forming—1 gallon per foot (3.8L/30cm) of row.

Potato: Water early crops throughout growth, main crops when in flower (tubers are forming)—1 to 2 gallons per foot (3.8–7.6L/30cm) of row.

FRUIT-BEARING VEGETABLES

Cucumber, melon, summer and winter squash: Water when the first fruit forms until harvest—1½ gallons (5.7L) per plant.

Eggplant, pepper, and tomato: Water regularly when the fruit starts to form until harvest—1½ gallons (5.7L) per plant up to 2½ gallons (9.5L) for full-grown tomatoes.

Feeding Vegetables

providing the right nutrients

PLANTS GET THEIR NUTRIENTS from the soil. It is a safe bet that most soils contain enough of the major plant nutrients to sustain the vegetation. Whether it's grassland or a forest, natural systems are self-sustaining and the nutrients are constantly used and recycled. However, when you decide to turn a patch of ground into a vegetable garden it can become unbalanced. Some vegetables are more demanding of nutrients, and when you harvest the crop, you are removing a significant amount from the pool. Unless you replace these nutrients regularly and provide extra for greedy crops, your vegetables will not flourish.

Soil analysis

When starting a new vegetable garden, your vegetables should do fine if the site supports good plant growth. If not or you are uncertain, test your soil using a kit

available from a garden center, or take a soil sample and send it to your local Cooperative Extension Service for analysis—this should include pH, organic matter, and major nutrients. (See "Finding Out About Your Soil," pages 16–17.) The report should tell you what you will need to add to your soil to grow vegetables; if you state you intend to grow organically, this should be taken into account. You can choose to make up any deficit with organic or man-made fertilizers.

Major plant nutrients

There are several major plant nutrients that your vegetables will need to flourish. These are:

- Nitrogen, which is particularly important for leafy crops. Lack of nitrogen shows up in plants as yellowing leaves and lack of vigor. Good sources of nitrogen include dried blood, fish meal, and animal manures—poultry manure is a concentrated form of it. Nitrates are soluble, so they are washed out of the soil if they haven't been used by the plants. Organic matter releases it slowly as it breaks down, and cover crops will help prevent it from being lost over winter. (See "Nitrogen Requirements" and "Cover Crops," page 49.)

- Potassium, or potash, which is particularly important for flower and fruit production. It regulates a lot of vital processes inside plant cells. Lack of potassium will show up as pale older leaves, often with brown margins. It is less soluble and is naturally present in some rocks. Wood ash, greensand, or granite dust are good sources of potassium—add this sparingly to the soil or mix it into the compost pile.

- Phosphorous is important for building strong root systems. A deficiency will cause poor, weak growth and the characteristic purple color of leaves and stems. As phosphate, it is present in some rocks, but although it is slow to leach out, many soil types do not have enough. Phosphorous can be added in the form of rock phosphate or bonemeal. Only a small proportion of the phosphate is soluble, and the rest will be released gradually for years.

A well-used plot may benefit from an application of fertilizer.

Minor nutrients

Plants also need other nutrients in smaller quantities; magnesium and manganese are two that are likely to show deficiency symptoms—mottling or yellowing of leaf tissue between the veins. Most of the others can be supplied by regular additions of compost or manure, or by using a tonic, such as a kelp meal or fish emulsion.

Organic fertilizers

These are products of plant, animal, or mineral origin that have high levels of nutrients that are beneficial to plants. Examples include bonemeal, fish emulsion, and rock phosphate. When compost or manure are added to the soil, they improve the soil structure while also adding nutrients to it. Organic fertilizers applied in other forms, such as granules, supply the same nutrients more quickly. They are useful if you cannot provide enough bulky organic matter or to help boost greedier crops. Check the label for the nutrient analysis. Organic fertilizers are often preferred by vegetable gardeners.

Compost tea

You can make an organic concoction known as compost tea by leaving a bucketful of well-made compost or well-rotted manure in a barrel of water. After four days,

When applying granules, keep them off the leaves to avoid scorching.

you can drain off the liquid, which should be the color of tea, and use it to water the plants. Sprayed on the leaves, it acts as a foliar feed. Regular applications help prevent leaf diseases.

Artificial fertilizers

These are man-made products containing known amounts of the three major nutrients. The label will state the amount of each as a percentage, so N:P:K 5:5:5 means there is 5 percent each of nitrogen (N), phosphate (P), and potassium (K). This is known as a balanced fertilizer and is good for most plants. You will also come across fertilizers higher in nitrogen, which are good for leafy crops, or that have more potassium, which is best for fruit-bearing plants.

Applying fertilizers

Fertilizers come in several forms, which will affect how you apply them to vegetables:

- Powder types are available to the plants immediately. However, if they are not used right away, the nitrogen will be rapidly washed through the soil by rain.

- Granules are worked into the soil at planting time or scattered along the rows to boost growth halfway through the growing season—this is known as side-dressing.

- Slow-release fertilizers leach out over a period of time; the speed depends on the soil temperature.

- Liquid fertilizers are diluted and watered onto plants regularly and are particularly useful for vegetables in containers. Follow the instructions for use—applying too much will not benefit the plant and may cause pollution.

How much fertilizer?

Crops differ in the quantity of nutrients they need in a year. Once you've dealt with any initial deficit, the simplest way is to use a balanced fertilizer each year. This assumes that the nitrogen will be used up during the season and the phosphate and potassium, if not used up, will remain in the soil for future crops. An established well-worked vegetable garden is seldom deficient in either of these nutrients. Adding plenty of organic matter will help keep everything at the right levels, too.

Nitrogen Requirements

The amount of nitrogen a vegetable needs depends on the type of plant. Below are listed the vegetables and their needs for nitrogen:

HIGH:
Beet, broccoli, Brussels sprouts, cabbage, cauliflower, Asian greens, leek, potato, spinach, Swiss chard

MEDIUM:
Asparagus, chicory, eggplant, garlic, lettuce, onions, pepper, squash, sweet corn, tomato

LOW:
Carrot, cucumber, fava bean, parsnip, pea, radish, rutabaga, turnip

Note: Fruit-bearing vegetables, such as cucumber, eggplant, melon, pepper, and tomato, initially need nitrogen to build up a strong plant, but need a high-potassium fertilizer when the fruit is forming.

Cover crops

These inedible crops are used as a temporary ground cover for land that would otherwise be vacant, especially over winter. They are also known as "green manures," because when dug into the soil they add organic matter and nutrients. They are worth building into your cropping plan and have several benefits:

- They keep the soil covered during periods between vegetable crops, preventing soil erosion or a hard surface crust from forming.

- They mop up any nutrients left over from fertilizers applied during the summer or released from organic mulches, which would be lost into the groundwater.

- Their roots keep the soil open, preventing compaction, and as they rot they provide openings for vegetable roots.

- Some root deeper than vegetables and extract nutrients from deep in the subsoil. Members of the legume family hold atmospheric nitrogen in nodules on their roots. This is available to subsequent crops when these rot down.

- The bulk of leaves and stems can be chopped up and dug in to add bulk to the soil before sowing or planting a crop.

Green manure ready to be dug into the soil.

Sowing cover crops

As soon as you clear the last vegetable, loosen the soil surface roughly. Scatter the cover crop seeds evenly and thickly, and work them into the soil with a rake. Water thoroughly, especially at the end of a dry summer.

Some cover crops are winter hardy, but if left to flower the following spring, they will set seed and become a nuisance. Dig them in as soon as they start to flower. Use a sharp spade to chop the foliage; then dig or till the area, inverting each clod to bury the cover crop. Even immature cover crops that won't survive the winter will improve the soil, though not as much as mature crops.

Cover Crops

You can grow these plants as a cover crop:

Alfalfa (legume): Sow in spring.

Bean, field or fava (legume): Sow in fall.

Buckwheat (tender): Sow in spring or summer.

Clover, crimson (legume): Sow in fall.

Lupin, field (legume): Sow in spring.

Mustard (fast-growing): Sow spring to fall.

Rye, winter (deep rooting): Sow in fall.

Rye, annual: Sow in spring or fall; dig in before it seeds.

Mulching & Weed Control

retaining moisture, keeping weeds at bay

WEEDS COMPETE WITH CROPS, especially newly sown or planted ones, for water, nutrients, and space. Mulching—covering the soil surface around and between vegetable plants—is one way of controlling weeds, but there are other methods, and mulching has other positive points. The three main benefits are:

- It starves weeds of light, prevents weed seeds from germinating, and physically stops weeds from competing with your crops.

- It stops moisture in the soil from evaporating in hot weather, reducing the need for watering. However, some impermeable plastic sheets can also make watering more difficult.

- Mulches help to moderate extreme temperatures. Some mulches help warm up cold soils in the spring by absorbing heat from the sun; others insulate the soil in summer, keeping it cooler on hot days.

Organic mulches

Homemade compost is the best mulch of all. It's free and nutritious and the quickest form of recycling you can do. The problem is that you can never make enough to cover more than a small part of the vegetable garden each year. It may also contain weed seeds or seeds from a previous

Transplants can be planted through slits made in a black plastic sheet.

crop—tomato and squash are capable of surviving the composting process.

Try to avoid adding any uncomposted organic matter because as it decomposes it can remove nitrogen from the soil. This is mainly a problem if you dig it into the soil. If necessary, you can counter this effect by adding a nitrogen fertilizer.

Other excellent sources of organic mulches include fallen leaves—chopped or shredded so they don't form a mat—hay or straw, grass clippings (as long as the lawn hasn't been treated with an herbicide), composted animal manures, bark chips, and pine needles (which are good for acidifying lime soils). If you can get these in bulk and for little or no cost, pile them around crops in a 2-inch (5cm) layer.

Be on the alert for slugs and snails, which will enjoy the shelter of organic mulches, and take precautions if they threaten your plants. (See "Controlling Pests," pages 54–57.)

Sheet barriers

There are several types of plastic sheets that can be used to warm the soil, and some will also conserve moisture and block weeds:

- Clear plastic sheets will help warm the soil in spring, but they will also produce a flush of weed seedlings, which can still receive sunlight.

- Black plastic sheets will prevent weeds and conserve soil moisture, but they will not warm the soil.

- Infrared transmitting mulches are green or brown and let heat from the sun through to warm the soil but not light that weeds need to grow; they are more expensive.

- Landscaping fabric is sheeting made from tightly woven plastic fibers. It prevents weeds, conserves moisture, and also lets rain or irrigation water through.

Use a hoe to remove small weeds that sprout near your vegetables.

Using plastic sheets

Put plastic sheets in place before the crop is sown or planted. Stretch the material taut and bury the edges by pushing them into the soil with a spade. Temporary plastic sheets can be weighed down with stones or lumber. Once the soil is warm, remove the sheet.

If you intend planting widely spaced vegetables, you can leave the sheet in place to control weeds. Cut an X in the material just wider than the plant's root ball, and fold the flaps underneath. Use a trowel to plant through the hole.

What are weeds?

Any unwanted plant is a weed. Persistent weeds are specialists at exploiting the opportunity presented by bare soil and the resources for vegetables, most of which are not naturally able to compete.

Perennial weeds are those that survive as deep taproots or underground roots or rhizomes and come back year after year. Where fruit or perennial vegetables are to be planted, perennial weeds can become a real nuisance unless they are destroyed before planting. If you recognize any perennial weeds in your vegetable garden, spend the necessary time it takes to remove every piece of root before you plant permanent crops—it will mean a lot less work later.

Annual weeds have a cycle of flowering and setting seed in the same year. Most soil is full of dormant seeds from annual weeds. As soon as you disturb the soil, weeds get a chance to germinate and start their cycle. You can weaken this cycle each year when you grow annual vegetables. Any tactics you use against annual weeds will gradually reduce them over a few years.

Weeding methods

There are a number of different methods you can use to control weeds. The ones you choose will depend on how many weeds you have and when they appear.

- Mulching is an effective technique, especially if your soil is full of perennial weeds. Cover an area for at least a year with a black plastic sheet to clear it of weeds before you start cultivating it.

- Flush out annual weeds by covering the soil in early spring with a clear plastic sheet. This will warm the soil and bring on a flush of weed seedlings. Hoe these off and there should be fewer to compete with your vegetables during the growing season.

- Hoe regularly—choose whichever type of garden hoe that works for you. Keeping the blade sharp by using a metal file will make for less effort when it comes to using the tool. Choose a warm, dry day so that hoed weeds shrivel up and die quickly. Keep the blade parallel with the soil surface or just below it and aim to sever weeds neatly from their roots. Annual weeds won't regrow, and perennial ones will be set back but will resprout. You may find a short-handled weeder is a better tool for raised beds.

- Hand weed among rows of crops, where hoeing will cause too much damage. This may sound like hard work, but if you combine it with thinning seeded rows, eventually the crop will shade out any new weeds.

- Weeding with a flame weeder is best confined to uncropped areas before you start sowing or planting. The trick is to pass the flame steadily over the soil surface to boil the weeds' sap without actually setting fire to anything.

- Weed killers are best kept out of the vegetable garden. The one exception is to use a systemic weed killer to kill the roots of perennial weeds before you lay out the garden. This will save a lot of work later, especially if you garden organically from then on.

Preventing Diseases

growing healthy plants

KEEPING YOUR VEGETABLES HEALTHY is the best approach to avoiding diseases. Once a plant is infected by a disease, there's not a great deal you can do about it. Preventive measures are the best solution. However, there is a handful of cures that are acceptable to organic gardeners.

The best approach is to remove the conditions that diseases need to flourish as much as possible. This may sound obvious, but as with people, sickly, struggling plants tend to be more susceptible to diseases than healthy, vigorous plants. If you make sure your vegetables get off to a good start and always have sufficient—but not too much—water, nutrients, and space, they will have the best chance of thriving. However, if your plants run out of water or any one of the essential nutrients—apart from showing deficiency symptoms and suffering an interruption to growth—they'll be vulnerable to fungal spores that attack weak plant tissues.

Good garden hygiene

If plants show the first symptoms of diseases, such as potato blight or mildew, pick off the affected leaves or shoots and destroy them. If you act quickly enough, you may stop its spread. If a plant is beyond saving, pull it up and you may confine the disease, especially if that plant was the source of the disease. If you are trying to encourage beneficial insects, remember that this doesn't apply to plants that have suffered from any kind of disease. (See "Controlling Pests," pages 54–57.) Remove the diseased plants and any plant debris, particularly any fallen leaves, and dispose of them in the trash.

At the end of the season, gather up crop remains, even if they show no disease symptoms, and add them to the compost pile to rot down. In a well-made pile, many minor diseases will be killed as the material heats up in the decomposition process. However, don't put obviously diseased plants on the compost pile because if the bacteria or fungal spores are not killed, you can help spread the disease next year.

Clean seeds

Always buy seeds, seed potatoes, sweet potato slips, and onion and garlic sets from a reputable source. Accepting them from friends can mean accepting diseased seeds. These should at least start free of disease. Be careful if you save your own seeds—take them from the healthiest-looking plants, and reject any seedlings that aren't growing normally.

Air and water

Some of the most common plant diseases, such as powdery and downy mildews, are made worse by humid conditions. Plants that are crowded are particularly vulnerable, so giving plants plenty of room, especially in late summer, can help.

Other diseases, such as blight, are spread by rain splash. Keeping the foliage dry by watering the soil carefully will help slow the disease's spread.

When planting transplants, allow plenty of room for air circulation.

Crop rotation

When it comes to diseases that attack plant roots, crop rotation is one way to prevent it from recurring next season. (See "Crop Rotation," pages 22–23.) By growing vulnerable crops on a different piece of ground over a four-year period, the fungi, bacteria, or other organisms that attack them are deprived of the hosts. Although some diseases may be persistent in the soil—for example, clubroot—they won't have a chance to build up to damaging levels.

Even if you don't follow a crop-rotation plan, if any vegetable develops a soil disease, remove and destroy the remains of that crop. Next year grow that vegetable and any closely related crops in a different part of the garden. It is important to try to avoid transferring infected soil from one part of the garden to another, even on your gardening tools or boots.

Resistant varieties

Modern vegetable varieties and hybrids have often been bred or selected to resist major diseases that trouble vegetable growers, such as wilts, leaf spots, mildews, and various viruses. Look for the term "resistant" on the label. The variety can tolerate the presence of the disease longer than other varieties without succumbing to it. If your crops regularly develop a particular disease, check the seed brochures for resistant types. Or look for "tolerant" varieties that do well in your local area. If these grow vigorously in your area—even, for example, in dry heat—they will be less susceptible to disease.

Virus diseases

Diseases caused by a virus are difficult to control once established in a crop. Look for the telltale signs— yellowing, crinkled, or distorted leaves—and remove and destroy affected shoots or plants. They can be spread on seeds or by sap-feeding aphids or other insects, so buying from a reputable seed company and keeping aphids off your plants will help. (See "Controlling Pests," pages 54–57.)

Discolored plants are a sign of disease, such as tomato blight.

Fungicides

Some of these simple chemcials have been used for centuries in some cases as preventive measures:

- Make a baking soda solution by dissolving 1 tablespoon of baking soda plus 1 tablespoon of vegetable oil in a cup of warm water, then add to a gallon (3.8L) of water as a spray for powdery mildew.

- Compost tea is a stimulant rather than a fungicide, but many organic gardeners swear by it as a disease preventive. (See "Compost Tea," page 48.)

- Copper, added as copper sulfate or Bordeaux mixture (originally for controlling vine diseases), helps control damping off in seedlings, blight, and gray mold. Because it is toxic to fish, do not use near ponds.

- Sulfur, available as either green or yellow sulfur dust, can help control powdery mildew, black spot, scab, and some other fungal diseases. Use it carefully: sulfur is an irritant and can damage plants if used when temperatures are above 85°F (30°C) or if used with horticultural oils that are used to control insects.

Controlling Pests

encouraging the good, keeping out the bad

AS SOON AS YOU CONGRATULATE yourself on producing a fine crop of vegetables, you can be sure some critter will want to dine on it. Pests come in many forms, from hungry deer to minute spider mites. If you wait for the pests to strike, there may be little you can do except reach for a spray. However, if you prepare your defenses in advance, you can outwit most of them.

Fence them out

The only real defense against larger pests, such as deer and rabbits, is to erect a wire fence around the vegetable garden. Make sure this is high enough so that larger animals cannot jump over it—that means 8 feet (2.4m) high if deer are a problem—and if rabbits are a nuisance, bury the fence in a trench 12 inches (30cm) deep. An alternative for particularly tempting crops is to cover the bed with temporary hoops of stiff wire mesh.

Netting supported by a wooden frame protects these vegetables.

Net them out

With flying pests, such as birds, and larger insects, such as cabbage butterflies, the best protection is to cover beds with netting—match the mesh size to the pest you want to keep out, and keep in mind that insect pests can lay eggs through the mesh if crop leaves are touching it. Use hoop supports made from stiff wire or flexible plastic piping to support the net and secure the edges all around. This works fine for strawberries, but for larger berry fruit you may need to construct a taller wooden frame or cage to support the mesh.

Floating row covers

This lightweight fabric made from spun polyester is doubly useful—it insulates crops against cold and frost and it has such tiny holes that even the smallest insects cannot get through, although air and water can. (See "Extending the Season," page 39.) Lay it loosely over a newly sown or planted crop and weigh down the edges to prevent insects from getting underneath. As the plants grow, you may need to loosen the edges occasionally. Here are some points to keep in mind:

- Use it in combination with a crop-rotation plan because some pests overwinter in the soil under a previous crop—you don't want them hatching under the cover! (See "Crop Rotation," pages 22–23.)

- Remove the cover in the evening (when insects are less active) to weed the crop—weeds will enjoy the conditions under the cover, too.

- Remove the cover when fruit-bearing crops, such as squash, start to flower to allow pollinators in. You can also remove the covers when the pests are no longer a threat or when you start harvesting.

- For root crops, such as carrots and onions, you can leave the floating row covers in place until harvest, but the plants may scorch in hot weather, so during this time remove them.

A floating row cover can be set up over vegetables quickly, and is easy to remove when you want access to your vegetables.

Traps

Most mollusks live in the sea, and even their terrestrial cousins, the slugs and snails, cannot survive without moisture. They feed at night, returning to a damp sheltered spot by day. Use upturned pots, pieces of lumber, or damp burlap around the vegetable garden to attract them. Check these daily and destroy any slugs or snails sheltering there. You can drop them in a bucket of soapy or salty water to kill them.

Another trick is to position beer traps around your vulnerable crops. Bury a plastic cup or metal can so the lip is level with the soil surface. Fill the container with diluted beer, and collect the drowned slugs each day—recycle the beer for the next day.

Collars and barriers

Individual young plants can be protected from slugs and cutworms by surrounding them with a barrier or collar made from 4–6-inch (10–15cm) open-ended sections cut from plastic beverage bottles. Push the collars into the soil to anchor them in place. Or spread diatomaceous earth, the ground skeletons of tiny ocean creatures, around the plant. Protect raised beds and containers from marauding slugs with a continuous band of copper tape, but first trap any slugs inside the bed.

Collars made from thick, black plastic will help protect young cabbage family plants from cabbage root maggots. Cut a 4-inch (10cm) circle; punch a hole in the center for the plant; and make a slit from the edge to the center so it will fit around the plant's stem and lie flat on the ground.

Handpicking

Larger leaf pests, such as cabbage worms and beetles, are big enough to see as soon as they appear on your plants. If you notice nibbled leaves, look for the culprits on the underside of leaves or in the soil near the plant. Look for clusters of eggs, too, and rub these off to prevent the next wave of attack. Put the caterpillars on a bird table to encourage birds to do the job for you.

Biological controls

If soil pests, such as root weevil, European cranefly, grubs, or cutworms, are a real problem in your garden, look for beneficial nematodes. These are sold as a powder that is diluted in water and spread onto the soil. Follow the instructions on the package precisely and the invisible worms will kill the pests underground. The best approach is to treat the whole vegetable garden all at once, along with the surrounding area, to prevent a new invasion.

Attracting beneficials

Fortunately, few species of insects are actually bad, and even they are only doing what comes naturally—eating your vegetables. Most others are neutral and some are good, in the sense they eat or infect the pests with parasites. In the past, gardeners have indiscriminately used man-made pesticides to kill pests—and unwittingly killed the good guys, too. These days, and especially if you garden organically, maintaining a balance has become the main goal. Even if pests do appear, you can be sure their predators will find them, probably before you do. There are several steps you can take to help attract beneficial animals and insects.

A little untidiness can be helpful. Leaf litter or organic mulches will provide cover for as many spiders, ground beetles, and millipedes as it does slugs and snails. As long as you can stop the slugs and snails from eating your vegetables, the predators will take care of soil pests and the odd slug, too. A patch of weeds in a corner of the garden will provide a refuge for beneficial insects over winter. A pile of rotting logs or the compost pile will harbor beetles, spiders, and toads that eat insects.

Mix a few bright, open flowers into the vegetable garden or in nearby borders. Hover flies are attracted to flowers—and their larvae are voracious aphid eaters. Lacewings are attracted to carrot-family flowers, such as fennel, and both they and their larvae eat aphids. Daisy-type flowers are especially good at attracting bees to pollinate your fruit-bearing vegetable plants, too. There

are also pest killers, such as the parasitic wasps. These are easy to attract as long as you have a flourishing garden with a good mix of plants.

Be willing to accept low levels of pests on your vegetables. Nothing attracts predators, including birds and amphibians, into your garden better than a good supply of live food. Insect-eating birds in your garden will make short work of aphids or cabbage loopers. Provide them with shelter, nesting sites, and fresh water in return. A pond, even a short half-barrel sunk in the ground, should attract toads and frogs—they'll spend their time eating up pests for you.

The trick is not to lose your nerve too soon. If you spot aphids, look for ladybugs; if you spot loppers or caterpillars, look for parasitic wasps or birds. They may take a few days to find their new food supply, but if you can live with a little damage and give them time, they will find it. Even spider mites are preyed on by predatory mites you may not notice.

Only if pests are starting to get completely out of control do you need to take action. Before you reach for the insect spray, think about all the beneficials you might harm if you aren't careful.

Ladybugs can keep plants free of aphids.

Effective natural insecticides

There are several natural insecticides that you can try:

- *Bacillus thuringiensis* (Bt for short) is a powder that contains bacteria. The toxins they produce kill only caterpillars. Dilute and apply it as a spray. It will kill pest caterpillars, such as cabbage worm, but also other caterpillars it contacts, so target sprays carefully. Another type of Bt targets the grubs of Colorado potato beetles.

- Garlic and pepper sprays repel small insect pests, such as aphids, mites, lacebugs, and leafhoppers.

- Horticultural oil is an emulsion of petroleum or vegetable oils that smothers soft-bodied insects, such as aphids and caterpillars. It also prevents some fungal diseases.

- Insecticidal soap is a short-lived, contact killer of aphids and other soft-bodied pests.

- Milky spores are spores of a bacteria that are sprayed onto lawn areas to kill the underground grubs of Japanese beetles (which attack grass roots) and reduce the population of beetles (which attack vegetables).

- Neem oil is extracted from the seed of a tropical tree. It disrupts the feeding and life cycle of many leaf-eating pests but does not harm bees or predatory insects.

- Pyrethrum, a chemical extracted from a tropical daisy, paralyzes many pests on contact but breaks down rapidly. Don't confuse it with pyrethroids, man-made chemicals that are similar but more toxic.

The last resort: sprays

Even if you are not a strictly organic gardener, you may not like the idea of covering fruit and vegetables with man-made poisons. Fortunately, there are less persistent sprays made from natural ingredients that are effective. These should be the last step if prevention and beneficials have failed and insect pests are gaining the upper hand. Before using any spray:

- Remember that even natural or "green" insecticides are still poisons. Most are indiscriminate and will kill beneficial insects as well as pests.

- Don't use old sprays. When you need them buy sprays in small quantities and use them within a season or two.

Caterpillar droppings are a sign of insect problems.

- Read the label carefully and follow any precautions. Make sure a spray is recommended for the crop and pest you have in mind.

Effective spraying

If you decide to use a spray, do so on a warm, calm day; avoid windy days so you can control the spray. The early evening is better because beneficial insects are less active, and spraying in full sun can scorch plants, too. Most insecticides will kill on contact, so make sure you cover the undersides of leaves and the growing tips (where most pests are likely to be) thoroughly. If your sprayer has a variable nozzle, set it to give the finest spray and aim to cover the plant with only a light misting. If the spray starts running off the plant, you know you are applying too much.

If you use a natural contact spray, one spray may not be enough and you may have to repeat the treatment a couple of times to kill the survivors; check the label for the recommended intervals. For some pests, such as whiteflies, the immature stages are impervious to sprays and will hatch out at intervals—time repeated sprays to catch them when they do.

If the crop is ready to harvest, observe the safe interval between spraying and eating, and make sure you wash the crop well. Avoid breathing the spray drift, and wash your hands after spraying.

Staking & Supporting

a helping hand for climbers

SOME VEGETABLES AND FRUIT are climbers by nature and will grow up trees or through shrubs. Others will happily sprawl across the ground, although there are advantages to you to encourage them upward. You can use a variety of materials to support these plants, including wood or lightweight metal or PVC (polyvinyl chloride) pipes to make frames for supporting wire, string, or plastic mesh.

With all support systems, erect them before you sow or plant the crop. Not only will you be able to do so more quickly, but you will avoid damage to the crops that can occur if erected while they are growing.

Permanent supports

Berry fruit, such as summer-fruiting raspberries, blackberries, and their hybrids, are a long-term investment, and grape vines even more so. Therefore, it is well worth your effort and time to build an appropriate structure to support them. After all, the structure will have to carry 6–7 foot (1.8–2.1m) canes and pounds of berries, as well as stand up to gusts of wind.

Use stout posts at least 3 inches (7.5cm) across made from naturally durable lumber, such as redwood, or treat the part that is to go in the ground with a nontoxic wood preservative. The posts should be at least 5 feet (1.5m) tall above ground and extend 2 feet (60cm) below it. For additional strength, brace the end posts with a diagonal to counter the effect of the wires pulling them together.

Space the posts 6–8 feet (1.8–2.4m) apart. Nail strong wire around the outside of each post at the top and another halfway up so that the wire wraps around the post and is parallel on each side. You can use this "double wire" system to tuck new shoots between the wires during the summer to keep them out of the way, before tying them in during the fall.

Annual supports

Climbing vegetables, such as the pole bean, need something to climb. There are several approaches:

- Tepees are groups of poles—bamboo poles are best—arranged in a circle and tied together at the top. The circle should be 2–3 feet (60–90cm) wide and the point 6–7 feet (1.8–2.1m) high, so you'll need 8-foot (2.4m) poles pushed well into the soil. Pole beans will twine up them, although they may need help getting started.

- Make a trellis to support rows of climbers. You can make the whole structure out of bamboo poles, although in windy gardens additional bracing will be required—for example, two rows of poles tied together at the top and strengthened with horizontal poles across them at the top. Use vertical strings at 6-inch (15cm) intervals for the beans to climb.

Tepees are ideal supports for beans and peas.

- Or use stout posts or even fence posts at each end of the row. Run strong wires between these and tie vertical bamboo poles, strings, light wire, or plastic mesh to them. Vine crops, such as cucumber and melon, climb using tendrils rather than by twining, so horizontal strings or plastic mesh will help support them.

- Indeterminate tomatoes can be trained with a single stem and no side shoots. These aren't natural climbers and need to be tied to a support, either a single stake per plant or a trellis structure for rows of plants. Construct these from bamboo poles and string, allowing wider spacing than for beans.

Crops That Need Support

Some vegetables definitely need support, but there are others that can benefit from it, too:

VEGETABLES THAT NEED SUPPORT

Pole bean (tepee, trellis)

Runner bean (tepee, trellis

Pea (except dwarf varieties)

Tomato (stake, trellis, cage)

FRUIT THAT NEEDS SUPPORT

Brambles (blackberry and its hybrids and raspberry)

Grape vines

VEGETABLES THAT CAN BENEFIT FROM SUPPORT

Asparagus (posts and string)

Broccoli, purple sprouting (staking)

Brussels sprouts (staking)

Cucumber (trellis)

Eggplant (staking)

Fava bean (posts and string)

Jerusalem artichoke (posts and string)

Malabar spinach (trellis)

Melon (trellis)

Pepper (posts and string)

Squash, small-fruit winter types

Sweet potato (tepee, trellis)

Caging

Tomato plants that are not trained as a single stem can become unruly, and the tomatoes will be vulnerable to pests and disease if they lie on the soil. The easiest way to support untrained indeterminate varieties or bush varieties is to grow them inside a wire cage. You can buy store-bought tomato cages, but these may not be strong enough for large vigorous plants. You can make your own from a square of concrete reinforcing mesh with 6-inch (15cm) mesh. Roll it into a cylinder 2 feet (60cm) in diameter and about 4–5 feet (1.2–1.5m) tall, and push it into the ground to anchor it firmly. One extra advantage of wire cages is you can wrap them in a clear plastic sheet to protect the newly planted tomatoes during cold spells.

Staking

Tall plants that may need some temporary supporting, depending on how sheltered your garden is, include Brussels sprouts and purple sprouting broccoli. If they start to lean over before you've started picking, hammer a stake in beside each plant and tie them to it.

Perennial vegetables, such as asparagus and Jerusalem artichokes, usually get by without support, but if there are strong wind gusts, these can topple the stems or loosen the plant in the ground. If necessary, hammer pairs of stakes along the rows and surround the plants with string.

To tie a stem to a support, use a soft material such as garden twine.

Harvest

ONE OF THE MAIN REASONS FOR GROWING YOUR OWN VEGETABLES is so that you can harvest them at their peak, when they are more full of flavor and freshness than anything available from a supermarket. With many vegetables, the flavor, particularly the sweetness, and texture will start to deteriorate soon after picking them. So the secret for the best vegetables possible is to pick little and often, and to eat seasonal vegetables the same day you harvest them. Knowing exactly when to harvest each kind of vegetable takes experience, but there are pointers to help you, depending on whether it is the leaf, stem, root, or fruit you intend to eat.

Even with careful planning and successional sowing, a glut of certain vegetables during the season is often unavoidable. For most people, having too much fresh produce is not a problem, especially because most vegetables, herbs, and fruit can be stored or preserved for use in winter. As when harvesting for fresh eating, you will have to act promptly to retain as much flavor and goodness in your stored produce. If you are faced with a surplus of zucchini and tomatoes in the same week, the trick is knowing which to take care of right away, which to leave, and which to put in temporary storage until you can deal with them.

Deciding When to Pick

harvesting vegetables at their peak

EACH VEGETABLE HAS A PERIOD when it is at its best. Some have a relatively short window and, if you miss it, the produce will spoil. However, others have a much longer season and you can pick them anytime up to full maturity. When it comes to leafy vegetables, for example, remember that they are trying to build up reserves to produce flowers or storage organs. Your aim is to pick and eat them before they reach this stage.

Lettuce and other greens eaten fresh

Many leafy greens, including lettuce, arugula, endive, chicory, and all Asian greens are eaten fresh. They will remain in good condition on the plant and can be harvested over several weeks. Head lettuce and Chinese cabbage should be left until the head feels firm when squeezed lightly. However, as soon as leafy greens show signs of bolting, or producing flower stalks, use them immediately or discard them.

You can sow all these crops successively to maintain a constant supply during the summer. (See "Using Space Efficiently," pages 40–41.) Most loose-leaved lettuce and greens respond to the cut-and-come-again approach.

When cutting tough leaves, such as Swiss chard, use a sharp knife.

This is a simple method where you cut off the entire plant close to the ground; it will regrow to produce a fresh crop of leaves a few weeks later.

Leafy greens that are cooked

Spinach, Swiss chard, and other greens that are cooked can be cut anytime the leaves are large enough. Either cut the whole plant or cut individual leaves from the outside. Old leaves can be tough and stringy; discard them. Any vegetable eaten like spinach can be frozen.

Cabbages form dense hearts and most stand for weeks before they start to bolt (produce flower stalks). Cut and eat them anytime during this period. Some are bred for winter storage and will not bolt until the following spring. You can store these in a cool place indoors.

Kale and Brussels sprouts last longer than most other greens. This is because they are biennials and will flower naturally in their second year. In their first year, they build up huge plants and then slow down in fall. This means you can generally leave them in the vegetable garden until you need them, especially because they are hardy, too.

Broccoli and cauliflower

When it comes to broccoli and cauliflower, the immature flower heads are the edible part. Each head consists of a lot of tight green or white buds. These are the trickiest of crops to harvest, because you have a short time between the head reaching full size and the buds starting to open into flowers. Getting the timing right takes practice, but you can cut the head as soon as it reaches a good size and give priority to any heads where the individual buds are becoming large. Cauliflower produces only a single large head; broccoli continues to produce edible smaller sideshoots after the main head has been cut.

Snap or cut Brussels sprouts, working from the bottom up.

Roots, tubers & bulbs

You can start to harvest roots as soon as they are large enough to eat and continue until they reach full size. Then you can store them for winter use. Some types or varieties are best eaten fresh, while others are best grown for storing.

- Immature roots are suitable for eating fresh. Choose early varieties and make several sowings to extend the harvest of small, tender roots. You can harvest beets, carrots, kohlrabi, and turnips as small "baby" vegetables if you grow them closely together; pull them up in bunches like radishes.

- Leave roots for storage in the garden until the tops die off; then store indoors and eat anytime during the winter and early spring. Root vegetables are natural storage organs and help the plant survive unfavorable conditions over winter, which is why you can store them for so long. However, all will start to sprout, or regrow, sometime during spring, so aim to eat them before this occurs.

In areas with milder winters, you can leave beets, carrots, parsnips, turnips, and rutabaga in the ground until you need them. An alternative in areas with severe winter frosts is to store them in boxes in a cool building or basement. (See "Other Storage Strategies," pages 68–69.) None of these roots should be allowed to completely dry out during storage.

You can dig potato tubers as soon as they are large enough or leave them until the tops die off. Dig the tubers; let the skin dry; and store them indoors.

Leeks are best left where they are until you need them. The plants will stop growing when the cold weather starts and are hardy. There's nothing to stop you from starting to dig them early when they resemble oversized scallions. Lift bulbs, such as onions, shallots, and garlics, after they thoroughly ripen and dry in the fall, and store in a cool, dry, airy place indoors.

Fruit-bearing vegetables

A lot of vegetables, such as peas and beans, are really fruit that are grown for the edible seeds. Some are used when immature, such as cucumbers and summer squash, and some when ripe, such as tomatoes and melons.

- Immature fruit is best picked young. No one will want to eat a ripe cucumber or eggplant or an oversized zucchini or summer squash. Pick cucumbers and eggplant when they reach nearly full size, but before the seeds start to develop. A change of color often indicates that ripening has started. You'll quickly learn to discard overmature fruit and pick them when they are just right. Summer squash and zucchini can be picked as small as you like, and this is a good strategy to avoid a glut. Don't let any of the fruit set seed or cropping will start to decline—as far as the plant is concerned, its job is done!

- Pick tomatoes, melons, pumpkin, and winter squash when these are fully ripe to enjoy their full flavor. In the case of melons, pumpkins, and winter squash, the seeds are discarded (although some can be roasted and eaten). Tomato seeds are eaten unnoticed. The downside is that once the first flush of fruit has formed, the plant won't produce much more. The exception is the tomato varieties known as indeterminate—more tomatoes will form even after the first ones have fully ripened.

Leave beets in the ground until you are ready to use them.

When it comes to peppers, you can pick both sweet and chili types as green, immature peppers or let them ripen to their full color—these will be sweeter. Picking some green will help extend the season because once they start to turn color, no more young ones will form.

Peas and beans

Peas and most beans can be eaten as immature pods. In this case, wait until the pods reach a good size and the immature peas or beans inside are still small. Leave them too long and the pods can become stringy. There's no lower size limit, and you can pick bush beans and snow peas as small as you like. If a glut is looming, start picking smaller pods.

If the aim is to harvest immature seeds, as with garden peas or fava beans, you should leave the pods to reach their full size—when the peas in the pods are ready, you should feel some resistance when you squeeze them. Alternatively, pick and shell a few pods and use them to gauge when the rest of the crop will be ready. If you pick over the plants frequently, you will encourage more cropping.

Some bean types are grown for the dry mature seeds, such as soy bean and shelling varieties of bush beans or pole beans. You can store dry beans for use during the winter. Remember to soak dry beans and to rinse them before cooking them.

Asparagus and rhubarb

The two crops you harvest as young shoots, asparagus and rhubarb, are best cut for only a limited period so you don't exhaust the plant. Cut asparagus when the spears are still tight, and cut rhubarb before the leaves start to enlarge. Asparagus has a short harvest season, but it freezes well.

Herbs

There are two strategies for annual herbs: pick sprigs and dry them, or freeze tender leaves at their peak, right before the flowers open. (See "Freezing & Drying," pages 66–67.) You have another option for perennial herbs. Continue picking during the winter in mild areas or grow in pots and bring them indoors in cooler areas.

Harvesting methods

The ideal time to pick most fresh crops is early in the morning when they are cool and fresh. To harvest a leafy crop, especially those with a head, such as certain lettuce cultivars and cabbages, use a sharp knife. A knife or scissors are suitable for cutting individual leaves from leaf lettuce and other leafy greens, kale, Swiss chard, or spinach. If you pick a leaf by hand, hold the stem of the plant as you carefully pull with the other hand—but there is a risk you could pull out the whole plant.

Handpick fruit-bearing vegetables. Avoid damage to the plant as you harvest them because any opened areas can be an entry point for disease. When you handpick, hold the stem in one hand as you pull with the other. Some vegetables should be picked with part of the plant still attached. Peppers and eggplant should have a short piece of stem attached, and you may need a knife or pruning shears to harvest them. For tomatoes, keep the green calyx attached, which should come away with the fruit if you snap the stem at the "knuckle." Cut cucumbers, zucchini, and other squash at the stem just below the bottom of the fruit, using a sharp knife.

Root vegetables are often lifted with a garden fork, but avoid spearing them with the fork's prongs. For potatoes and Jerusalem artichokes, use the fork to first loosen the soil, but then use your hands to collect the crop. Long-root crops, such as carrots and parsnips, will require you to push the fork down to a good depth before lifting. Leeks, celery, and onions can also be lifted with a fork.

Short-term storage

As a general rule, pick only what you'll eat that day to enjoy vegetables at their best. The exception is crops that will spoil if you leave them unpicked. If you can't use them immediately and don't have time to preserve them right away, you can always give them away.

Most crops will stay fresh for a few days or a week in the refrigerator. For leafy greens, put them in unsealed plastic bags to stop them from wilting and cool them immediately in the refrigerator to preserve their flavor. For other vegetables, keep them cool, which will help to slow down their deterioration; dry them on paper towels; and store in the refrigerator. Don't wash the vegetables until just before you cook or serve them—they won't store as well. (For longer term storage, see "Freezing and Drying," pages 66–67, and "Other Storage Strategies," pages 68–69.)

Storage Strategies and Good Yields

Below are the average yields of vegetables and the storage methods that you can use for them:

	YIELD 1 FT./30CM ROW	YIELD PER PLANT	FREEZE	DRY	STORE INDOORS	LEAVE IN GARDEN**
Asparagus	1 lb. (450g)		•			
Bean, bush	1 lb. (450g)		•	•		
Bean, pole	1½–2 lb. (680–900g)		•	•		
Beet	1½–2 lb. (680–900g)				•	•
Broccoli		1 lb. (450g)	•			
Brussels sprouts		1½ lb. (680g)	•			•
Cabbage		5–6 lb. (2.3–2.7kg)				•
Carrot	1½ lb. (680g)		•		•	
Cauliflower		2–3 lb. (900g–1.4kg)	•			
Celery	1½–2 lb. (680–900g)					•
Corn		1–2 cobs	•			
Cucumber*		3 lb. (1.4kg)				
Eggplant		2 lb. (900g)	•			
Kale		1–2 lb. (450–900g)				•
Leek	2 lb. (900g)					•
Melon		4–6 lb. (1.8–2.7kg)	•			
Okra		1–2 lb. (450–900g)	•			
Onions	1 lb. (450g)				•	
Parsnip	1½–2 lb. (680–900g)				•	•
Pea, snow	1½–2 lb. (680–900g)		•			
Pepper		1–2 lb. (450–900g)	•	•		
Potato		5–6 lb. (2.3–2.7kg)			•	
Spinach and Swiss chard	1½–2 lb. (680–900g)		•			
Squash, summer		5–6 lb. (2.3–2.7kg)	•			
Squash, winter		8–9 lb. (3.6–4kg)			•	
Tomato		4–5 lb. (1.8–2.3kg)	•	•		
Turnip	1–1½ lb. (450–680g)				•	•

* Not usually stored, but smaller types can be pickled.

Freezing & Drying

preserving vegetables for the long term

FREEZING IS A GOOD WAY to preserve certain fruits and vegetables if you have too many, and a few vegetables are worthwhile growing just for the freezer so that they are available outside of the harvesting season. However, many vegetables don't freeze well and will lose their essential texture as well as a lot of flavor. The vegetables suitable for freezing can be found in "Freezing Vegetables," opposite.

The trick with freezing is to harvest crops young and sweet and process them as quickly as you can to preserve all that flavor. If you intend to eat frozen vegetables within a couple of months, you don't have to blanch them first. However, if you think you will keep them frozen for a longer period, blanch them. Blanching, or plunging vegetables into boiling water, kills bacteria and inactivates enzymes that can taint the produce with unpleasant tastes.

Try to pick, blanch, and freeze your crop on the same day. In fact, before you harvest, have the water in a saucepan on the stove top ready to boil to speed up the process,

along with anything else you'll need for blanching. You'll need a steamer basket with a handle or handles that fits into a large saucepan of boiling water, along with another container filled with water and plenty of ice and a cutting board and sharp kitchen knife.

Prepare the vegetables as you would for eating fresh— for example, by removing any inedible parts and slicing larger ones. Load them into the wire basket, but don't overload it. Make sure the water is boiling vigorously and plunge the basket into it for a few minutes. (See "Freezing Vegetables," opposite, for the length of the blanching time.)

Remove the basket and pour its contents into the second container filled with cold water. (Add ice from time to time to keep it cold.) Let stand for about as long as the blanching time. Drain well; divide into meal-size portions; and fill plastic storage containers or plastic bags; seal; and place in the freezer.

Aim to eat frozen fruit and vegetables within a year of harvest and preferably sooner. If you still have stored produce from the previous year when you are ready to harvest again, you are freezing too much—or you need to be more adventurous in turning them into meals during the winter.

A bowl of cold water will stop the blanching process.

Freezing Berries

Smaller berries, such as currants and blueberries, will freeze well, but raspberries, blackberries, and, in particular, strawberries lose their texture. However, if you intend to use these fruit for jam, sauces, or smoothies, freeze them; once they have been blended into their new form, their texture won't be a problem.

Freezing Vegetables

	BLANCH (MINUTES)	NOTES
Asparagus	2–4	Discard tougher stalks and pack in containers large enough to avoid damaging the tips; use within 9 months.
Broccoli	3–5	Break into florets and pack into containers to preserve their shape.
Bush bean	2–3	Freeze smaller ones whole, larger ones sliced; eat within 4 months if not blanched.
Carrot	5	Choose small roots, or slice larger roots; will also last a year if not blanched.
Cauliflower	2–3	Break heads into pieces; add lemon juice to the blanching water to preserve color.
Pepper	3	Remove seeds and slice; no need to blanch if eaten within a month.
Pole bean	2–3	Freeze smaller ones whole, larger ones sliced; eat within 4 months if not blanched.
Snap/snow pea	1–2	Pick young, before any strings develop; eat within 6 months if not blanched.
Spinach/ Swiss chard	n/a	Cook to soften leaves; squeeze out any excess water; and freeze in portion-size balls.
Sweet corn	4–6	Freeze whole ear or carefully scrape off kernels; eat within 6 months.
Tomato	n/a	Freeze small ones whole; halve or quarter large ones, or puree; then freeze.
Zucchini	2–3	Pick small and freeze whole; use within 6 months.

Hang chili peppers upside down if you want to dry them.

Drying chili peppers and tomatoes

Chili peppers can be dried easily for winter use. Let them ripen fully on the plant for as long as possible. Cut the whole plant and hang it upside down in a warm, dry, airy place until the fruit is leathery and the seeds rattle inside.

You can have sun-dried tomatoes if you live in a hot region. Lay fully ripe fruit on metal racks in full sun until they turn leathery. Store them in a warm, dry place, or pack them in jars and cover with olive oil. If your climate is not suitable for drying tomatoes in the sun, dry them in the oven. Halve them and place in a single layer on a cookie sheet. Place them in an oven at 200°F (95°C) with the door propped open for 24 hours.

Freezing & drying herbs

A good way to preserve fresh herbs is to pack them into ice-cube trays; cover with water; and freeze. Once frozen, pop the cube out and transfer to plastic freezer bags. Use them anytime you want herbs in winter. This method can also be used for chili peppers.

Most herbs can be picked when mature—just before they start to flower is the best time—and hung up in bunches to dry. Pick on a hot day, and hang in a warm, dry, airy place to dry off completely. Strip leaves off the stalks as needed.

Other Storage Strategies

storing late-season vegetables, seeds, and dry beans

LONG-TERM STORAGE METHODS are worth considering in certain situations. If you have a small vegetable garden, you should make the best use of your space by growing only fresh summer vegetables—these will be more flavorful than any store-bought vegetables—and buy the bulky winter vegetables. However, if you have a large vegetable garden, you can include additional vegetables to store through winter. Even if you aren't aiming for total self-sufficiency, there's nothing more satisfying than a heart-warming winter roast or stew made with homegrown vegetables.

Store dry potatoes in a dark place.

Storing indoors

You may have read about storing vegetables in a root cellar. This is one of the techniques that dates from the days before domestic freezers and supermarkets stocking every kind of vegetable year-round. If you have a basement, it is a good place to store vegetables for winter. If not, a cool but frost-free unheated building, such as a garage or shed, will also be suitable.

You can store root vegetables dug up during the late fall in a cool place indoors. These include potatoes, sweet potatoes, main-crop carrots, beets, rutabaga, and parsnips. Make sure the potatoes are dry—lay them in a dry, airy place indoors—and remove any damaged tubers first; then store them in the dark. It is important that they are not exposed to light, or they will turn green and become inedible.

Store beets, carrots, parsnips, and rutabaga in deep wooden boxes containing moist sand. Start with an inch (2.5cm) of sand—this should be just moist, not wet. Carefully lay a single layer of roots on the sand so they are not touching. Add more sand until all the roots are covered; then repeat with more layers until the box is full.

Store onions, garlic, and shallots dry, otherwise they will rot or sprout. The old technique of braiding them into strings works well because hanging them allows plenty of air circulation. Alternatively, place them in single layers on trays with openings (for ventilation) or hang them up in plastic mesh vegetable bags. They don't need to be kept in the dark. Check them regularly and discard any soft or sprouted bulbs.

Store pumpkins and winter squash in a cool, dry basement or unheated building. They don't need to be kept in the dark. Check regularly; discard any fruit that become soft.

Leaving the crop outdoors

In milder areas, the simplest storage strategy of all for some vegetables is to leave them in the garden. Some vegetables are hardy enough to survive outside until you eat them. Provided the soil doesn't freeze solid, kale and Brussels sprouts will cope with moderate frosts—in fact, frosts are said to improve the flavor of Brussels sprouts.

The same is true of parsnips. These and main-crop carrots can be left in their rows over winter. As a precaution against hard frosts, cover the row with a layer of straw or leaves. Spinach and argula can also persist under a leafy mulch. Beets are less hardy but, in milder areas, you can leave them in the garden in milder areas covered with a straw blanket.

Seed crops

Some crops are grown for their seedpods or dry seeds. Apart from the obvious soy, bush, and pole bean varieties, there are edible sunflower seeds and popcorn. In all these cases, leave the pods, ears, or seed heads on the plant as long as possible to dry in the sun. If necessary, continue drying them indoors and then shake out the dry seeds. Make sure they are completely dry before storing them in airtight jars.

Seed saving

While on the subject of saving seeds, it is worthwhile to leave a few pea or bean plants unpicked so that you can save their seeds to plant next year. Do this only with open-pollinated, or non-hybrid, varieties so they will be more or less the same as their parent plant. If you grow a lot of beans, you may get slight variations the following year, but by repeatedly choosing the best plants each year you will be selecting a strain that suits your garden. However, never save seeds from a crop that has been affected by any obvious disease, and pick the most vigorous and heaviest cropping plant for seeds.

Other vegetables from which is it easy to save seeds

Onions are traditionally braided for storage.

include all the fruit-bearing vegetables. Tomatoes and peppers are easy because they have seeds when you harvest them. If you let one eggplant fruit ripen, it will produce seeds, too. You can also save seeds from cucumbers, melons, and squash. However, in these cases, you will need to hand-pollinate a female flower (these have a small swelling at their base) using a male flower from the same plant (using a small paintbrush); then seal it to exclude pollinating insects. Otherwise, the resulting seeds can be a mixture of any other varieties growing nearby.

Don't save seeds from F1 hybrids because the offspring won't be like the parent. (See "Starting From Seeds," pages 28–29.) Although you can save seeds from root or leafy vegetables in their second year, or after they have bolted, this involves more effort and it is easier to buy fresh seeds of a named variety each year.

5

Salad Greens

IF THERE'S ONE GROUP OF CROPS that is really worth growing at home, it's salad greens. You can eat them absolutely fresh, literally straight from the garden to the salad bowl, secure in the knowledge they have not been sprayed with pesticides.

Lettuce and leafy greens, such as spinach, are fast-growing and extremely versatile. You can fit them around other slower-growing crops to fill space early in the year—before later crops get going and need room—then plant them again later in the season after early crops have been harvested. These plants will also benefit from the shade created by other summer crops. Many varieties of lettuce and Swiss chard are decorative enough to justify a place in the ornamental garden, and most grow well in containers and window boxes, too.

Lettuce forms the heart of most green salads, but you can try adding some extra spicy or bitter flavors with arugula and chicory. For the ultimate salad experience, try growing mesclun mixes or, better still, mix your own with your favorite flavors. This is an ideal crop for growing in containers close to the kitchen door. Finally, remember to choose some hardier greens, such as endive or corn salad, for winter use.

Arugula

a quick grower with a lively peppery flavor

ADD A REAL ZEST TO YOUR SALADS by mixing arugula with other salad greens. You'll appreciate its peppery flavor even more if you grow your own to eat fresh straight from the garden. Wild (or rustic) arugula has narrow, finely divided leaves. It is slower growing but will have a finer flavor. Salad, or cultivated, arugula is bulkier, grows more quickly, and has a milder flavor.

 SOW

Sow seeds directly into a well-prepared seedbed. Sow thinly in short rows 6 inches (15cm) apart. Or if your soil is free of annual weeds, broadcast the seeds thinly into small patches. Because the leaves taste hotter as they age, sow small amounts every two weeks to produce a constant supply of tender young leaves.

 grow

Grow arugula in fertile soil that has had plenty of organic matter worked into it, or in containers of sterile seed-starting mix. Water regularly to keep the soil constantly moist, especially in hot spells. Lack of moisture will intensify the peppery flavor. Keep weeds down by hoeing between rows. Flea beetles are attracted to arugula and may cause severe damage, especially in hot weather.

 harvest

Start cutting as soon as the plants reach 3 inches (8cm) high. Use scissors to cut the plant 1 inch (2.5cm) above soil level, leaving a stump to regrow and produce fresh leaves. Keep cutting each batch until the flavor of the leaves becomes too hot; then move on to the next batch. Harvest just before you need the leaves for maximum freshness. Rinse quickly in cold water; drain well; and serve right away. If you can't eat all the leaves immediately, store in a refrigerator for up to a few days in a plastic bag.

FAQ

Q Why are my plants all stem and flower with tough leaves?

A Your plant has "bolted," or produced flowers instead of young leaves. This often happens in hot weather or if there is insufficient moisture. Keep the soil moist, and avoid sowing in summer in hotter regions. The flowers are edible, and the seeds can be collected for a free crop.

Cultivated arugula has rounder leaves than wild arugula.

 Use a well-secured floating row cover to protect the leaves from flea beetles.

Endive

a popular European salad green

THIS BITTER GREEN can be grown in North America, too, to add to salads from summer to winter. There are two types: frisée endive and broad-leaved endive, or escarole. Their bitter taste adds piquancy to lettuce-based salads.

 ## sow

For a succession of summer and fall leaves, sow small amounts of seeds from spring to early summer. For a winter crop, start in late summer by sowing seeds directly into a seedbed or into small pots to be planted in the soil in early fall. For loose leaves, sow seeds directly in rows into a well-prepared seedbed; thin to 6 inches (15cm) for frisée endive or 12 inches (30cm) for escarole. For large hearts, start the seeds in small pots or divided flats. Sow a few seeds per pot or division; then remove the weakest seedling. Transplant 10 inches (25cm) apart.

 ## grow

Endive is trouble-free if the soil is kept moist. If it dries out and growth is stunted, the leaves will taste bitter. Even well-grown endive is too bitter for some tastes, but you can produce paler, sweeter-tasting leaves by blanching them while still in the ground. Place a plate over the center of frisée endive once it reaches full size.

 ## harvest

Pick leaves as you need them, or cut off a whole head about 1 inch (2.5cm) above the ground level. Frost will make the flavor less bitter. The outer leaves will be more bitter than the heart. Store in plastic bags in the refrigerator for up to 10 days.

Varieties

- **BROAD-LEAVED ESCAROLE** has rosettes of broad leaves. It is hardy and will provide a supply of leaves all winter if given some protection in colder areas. A good reliable variety is 'Batavian Full Heart' (90 days).

- **FRISÉE ENDIVE** is a more attractive plant, but it is less hardy than the broad-leaved variety and is better suited for summer production. The tight hearts are self-blanching to some extent, and they can be blanched to reduce the bitterness. Good varieties include 'Pancalleri' (82 days) and 'Salad King' (95 days).

FAQ

Q Why is my endive rotting in fall?

A While endive is a hardy vegetable, it can rot if there is a lot of fall or winter rain or if the ground is waterlogged. Protecting the plants with hot caps can help. As insurance in future years, you can dig up some plants and plant in a bucket of moist sand. Keep them in a cool, dark place, and harvest in a couple of months.

Chicory

ADD FLAVOR AND COLOR TO SALADS with chicory, a cool-weather leafy green with a bitter flavor that will add bite to a bland salad. Cutting chicory, which includes rosette and loose-leaved types; the upright head of blanched greens known as Belgium endive; and radicchio, which has a striking red-and-white heart, are all members of this family.

1 SOW

You can sow cutting chicory in spring for an early harvest, but it may turn bitter in hot weather, or sow in late summer for a fall harvest. Sow the hearted types, such as radicchio and Belgium endive, in late summer for a late fall or winter crop. Sow roughly three months before the first frost in your area. In mild winter areas, the plants should survive over winter without protection.

- Sow the seeds of all types directly in rows 12 inches (30cm) apart and ¼ inch (65mm) deep.

- Thin seedlings to 10–12 inches (25–30cm) apart for large hearts or Belgium endive. For cutting chicory, thin the seedlings to 9–10 inches (23–25cm) apart.

Varieties

- **'GRUMOLO'** is a cutting type that forms rosettes of dark green leaves (55 days).

- **'INDIGO'** is a fast-growing, round-headed radicchio cultivar with bright red leaves (72 days).

- **'SUGARLOAF'** is a pale green loose-leaf cutting cultivar with a firm heart (55 days).

- **'WITLOOF'** is a Belgium endive type that will produce pale green, upright plants with firm hearts (110 days).

Belgium endive has a tight, upright head of leaves.

PEOPLE HAVE USED CHICORY SINCE BEFORE CLEOPATRA'S TIME, MORE THAN 4,000 YEARS AGO.

 Remove slugs and snails by picking them off by hand.

② grow

Keep the soil well watered in dry periods, or the plants will become too bitter. Mulch with organic matter to retain soil moisture and suppress weeds. Slugs and snails can be a nuisance. Radicchio will start to develop its distinct colors as the temperature drops in fall.

- For cutting chicory grown as a perennial, remove the mulch in early spring and cut the plants to about 1 inch (2.5cm) above their crowns. If a plant bolts—sends up a flower stalk—cut the plant back and it will resprout.

grow: forcing

The roots of Belgium endive are dug up in the fall and forced indoors during the winter to produce sprouts, which the French call "chicons." The leaves are blanched—they are grown without exposure to light.

- Dig up the roots when at least 1 inch (2.5cm) wide at the top in late fall and trim to 6–9 inches (15–23cm); cut the leaves 1 inch (2.5cm) from the top. Store the roots in boxes of moist sand in a cool but frost-free place until you are ready to force them. Plant three or four roots at a time in a large pot filled with potting mix so the cut stumps are just visible. Cover the pot with another upturned pot to exclude all light and store in a dark, cool place with a temperature of about 50°F (10°C).

FAQ

Q What is causing the leaves of my radicchio to have brown edges?

A The most likely cause is heat damage (this is known as tip burn). If you cut off the brown portions, the leaves will still be edible. In the future, adjust the planting time to avoid hot weather or find a cooler spot, perhaps shaded by taller plants, to grow them.

The red-and-white leaves of raddichio are protected by green outer leaves.

③ harvest

These are hardy plants that will keep in the garden well into winter, especially if protected with a mulch.

- Pick individual leaves of cutting types as needed when about 4 inches (10cm) tall, or cut off whole heads. If you leave the stump, it may regrow to produce fresh leaves.

- You can leave radicchio in the ground until needed. When the heads feel firm, remove the outer green leaves to reveal the red-and-white hearts.

- Belgium endive will be ready to harvest about four weeks after forcing, when the chicon is 6 inches (15cm) high. If you return the pot with the roots to the dark, cool room, it may resprout a second or third time.

Alternatively, use barriers, such as crushed eggshells, to keep slugs and snails away.

Lettuce

the ultimate salad green

LETTUCE IS THE MAINSTAY OF A GOOD SALAD, and growing your own allows you to appreciate it at its freshest. There are many types available—from crunchy icebergs, to sweet crisp romaines, to bright red loose-leaf types. Lettuce is a quick and easy crop to grow, is ideal for growing in containers, and is decorative enough for the ornamental garden, too.

Varieties

- **BATAVIAN 'MERLOT'** is a red-leaved Batavian cultivar (50–65 days).

- **BUTTERHEAD 'BUTTERCRUNCH'** is a reliable older cultivar (65 days).

- **BUTTERHEAD 'CASSANDRA'** is a modern cultivar that has developed better resistance to fungal diseases (70–85 days).

- **CRISPHEAD 'ICEBERG'** is a reliable older variety (75 days).

- **GREAT LAKES** produces crisp, tender heads (85 days).

- **LOOSE-LEAF 'LOLLO ROSSA'** is a decorative Italian cultivar that has bright red, frilly leaves (55 days).

- **LOOSE-LEAF 'SALAD BOWL'** is a typical green cultivar with deeply indented leaves. There's a red version, too (45–50 days).

- **ROMAINE 'LITTLE GEM'** forms a small romaine head that is ideal for closer spacing during summer (54 days).

- **ROMAINE 'WINTER DENSITY'** is a hardier cultivar for fall sowing and may survive over winter in milder areas. 'Chartwell' is a good modern hybrid (54 days).

▲ Romaine is a tall pointed lettuce with a paler firm heart. It is sweet and crunchy and slow to bolt, and it has a long shelf life.

▲ The butterhead has a round head with soft, buttery-textured leaves and yellow hearts. It is best grown late in the season but doesn't keep well.

1 SOW

You can sow seeds directly into a well-prepared seedbed. Or start seeds in small pots or seed-starting trays, or buy started plants and plant as transplants.

- To sow lettuce directly into a seedbed, sow thinly about ½ inch (1.5cm) deep in rows 12 inches (30cm) apart. Thin gradually to 12 inches (30cm) apart for larger types, 9 inches (23cm) for small romaine types. Use the thinnings in salads, and leave the remaining plants to produce firm heads.

- If starting seeds off in small pots or a seed-starting tray, grow these until they have about four leaves; then plant in their final positions 12 inches (30cm) apart for mature heads but closer if you intend to pick as loose leaves.

- Give started plants a good soak before planting them in their final positions 12 inches (30cm) apart.

- Sow batches of lettuce regularly throughout the year for a succession of crops. In cooler areas, you can grow lettuce almost year-round.

- In areas with cold winters, wait until the danger of frost has passed and use a plastic sheet to warm the soil before sowing or planting.

- Lettuce germinates erratically when temperatures reach 70°F (21°C), so in warmer regions sow in spring and fall. Try hardier varieties in areas with mild winters.

Allow enough room for lettuce heads to develop.

▲ The crisphead lettuce is a large plant with crinkled outer leaves and a firm, pale crisp heart.

▲ The Batavian lettuce looks like a crisphead but has a looser heart and better flavor.

▲ Loose-leaf types, as the name implies, produce a lot of leaves but little in the way of a heart.

GROWING IN CONTAINERS

Choose an interesting-looking cultivar, such as 'Freckles', or one of the red-leaf types for a colorful display. Sow several dozen seeds; then thin out in stages to leave three or five plants to grow to full size in a 12-inch (30cm) or 2-gallon (7.5L) container. Water regularly, and if necessary, add a high-nitrogen liquid feed occasionally. Harvest individual leaves from the outside to prolong the display.

Lettuce is an ideal vegetable for growing in a raised bed.

FAQ

Q Why is my lettuce stunted and crinkled?

A Greenfly (aphids) are the most likely cause. To confirm their presence, examine the leaves, particularly the undersides and leaf bases. Spray with an organic pesticide based on pyrethrum or insecticidal soap. Follow the instructions on the package carefully.

Q What causes whole plants to suddenly wilt and die?

A Cutworms or root aphids may be responsible. Dig around the dead plants to investigate. Cutworms are rarely visible, but they will sever the stems at ground level. Hoeing between rows will expose cutworms to the soil surface, making them vulnerable to natural predators. Root aphids can be seen on plants—these are difficult to destroy, but because they are more likely to attack in late summer, adjusting the sowing times can help.

Q Why are the leaf edges turning brown?

A This is known as tip burn and is caused by calcium deficiency due to sudden hot weather. Keep plants well watered in hot, dry spells, or grow lettuce in semishade in hot areas.

Q How can I prevent the white downy mold on my lettuce?

A Downy mildew occurs mostly in cool, wet weather. Remove affected leaves, and avoid wetting the leaves when watering.

If there aren't too many aphids, try blasting them off the leaves with a strong jet of water.

② grow

Lettuce requires a fertile soil and a good supply of nitrogenous fertilizer. In poorer soils, work in organic matter before sowing or planting to help retain moisture. Scatter a little high-nitrogen fertilizer, such as blood meal, along the rows as plants develop.

- Make sure you water regularly in hot, dry weather to maintain rapid growth.

- Seedlings and young plants are particularly vulnerable to slugs and snails. Use traps or barriers if necessary.

- Keep weeds down by pulling them out by hand until the lettuce is large enough to successfully compete with them.

③ harvest

You can harvest lettuce any time from the first baby leaves to big firm-hearted plants. This means each planting can be used over a long period.

- Hearting lettuce types, such as butterheads and crispheads, are best left until they produce firm hearts. Check their progress by pressing gently with the back of your hand. When the heart feels solid, cut the plant and remove the outer leaves. Whole lettuce hearts should keep for at least a week in a refrigerator.

- Loose-leaf varieties are best picked as needed and used straight away. Gather individual leaves, discarding tougher outer ones; rinse in cold water and shake dry.

- If you want baby leaves for salads, see pages 80–81.

Use a sharp knife to cut a head of lettuce just above soil level.

Mesclun & Others

a melody of young, tender greens

INSTEAD OF USING ONLY MATURE SALAD GREEN LEAVES, you can sow a mix of salad green seeds and cut the immature leaves as needed. These immature leaves are known as mesclun. The choice is between using prepared seed mixes or mixing your own seeds using your favorite flavors. If you buy a prepared mesclun seed mix, check the packet to make sure it includes your favorites. Whichever way you do it, the result is a fresher and tastier salad than anything you can buy.

The advantage of buying the seeds separately and creating your own mix is that you can adjust the ratio to produce your ideal mix. However, make sure they have a similar sowing-to-harvest time. An alternative approach is to grow batches of individual seeds and mix the leaves together when they are ready to be harvested. Try adding herbs such as cilantro, basil, or chervil, each with its own distinctive taste.

SOW

Sow small amounts of seeds about two or three weeks apart from spring until late fall. During summer, particularly in the warmest areas, many of the constituents of a mesclun seed mix will go to seed rapidly or the flavor will become hot or bitter, so avoid sowing during the hottest weather. Mesclun seed mixes are best sown in patches or bands rather than rows. It is a great crop for containers (see "Growing in Containers," right) or raised beds.

- If you buy a prepared mesclun seed mix, shake the packet well before you sow the seeds to ensure a uniform spread.

- In raised beds or the garden, sow a series of short rows 3 inches (7.5 cm) apart—or better, sow thinly in wide bands or patches, scattering the seeds so they are about ½–1 inch (1–2cm) apart.

- Water the furrows thoroughly before sowing, then cover with soil to keep the seeds moist.

 GROWING IN CONTAINERS

A 12-inch (30cm) pot should provide enough greens for two decent servings. If you cut with scissors and allow the plants to resprout, they should provide two more harvests a few weeks later. Sow thinly to space seedlings ½–1 inch (1–2cm) apart. Position the pot in partial shade, and water regularly. If you use a compost-based soil mix, feeding won't be necessary until after the second cut; then you can use a high-nitrogen liquid fertilizer to give the plants a boost.

A mixture of mesclun leaves adds interesting textures and colors.

When ready to harvest, use scissors to snip the leaves.

 grow

Baby leaf crops will be ready to harvest only six to eight weeks after sowing. Most of the plant varieties used in mesclun seed mixes will regrow when cut, and with care you should get three or more crops from each sowing.

- Water regularly, especially in hot, dry weather, to keep the soil surface moist at all times. Lack of moisture will cause plants to go to seed prematurely.

- Protect the plants from pests, such as slugs and snails. You can use barriers to protect areas of raised beds or raise containers off the ground.

 harvest

Baby leaves can be cut as soon as they grow to about 2 inches (5cm) high, but ideally they should be about 4 inches (10cm) high. Leaves this small will be sweet and subtle. As they get bigger, the flavor of the more exotic types will intensify, so you can adjust the flavor to suit your own taste.

- Harvest just enough for a meal and serve right away for maximum flavor and freshness.

- Use sharp scissors to cut the leaves about ½ inch (1cm) above soil level, leaving the stumps to regrow. Plunge into a bowl of cold water and rinse thoroughly.

Varieties

- **ARUGULA** adds a distinctive peppery flavor but can outgrow lettuce in the mix. It is also prone to bolting in hot weather and is a magnet for flea beetles.

- **CORN SALAD** is slow-growing and can be overwhelmed by faster-growing leaves in summer, but is worth adding to winter mixes.

- **CHICORIES,** including radicchio and endive, add a bitter note, as well as color and texture.

- **KALE,** such as 'Black Tuscany', or the red types, such as 'Red Russian', are mild and tender as young leaves.

- **LOOSE-LEAF LETTUCE** makes a good choice, especially the red kinds that add color and interest.

- **ORIENTAL GREENS,** such as bok choy and mizuna, add a mild peppery flavor. Chinese mustards and cress, such as 'Wrinkle Crinkle', add a more distinctive heat to the mix.

- **PICK AND MIX** Any type of lettuce can be picked as baby leaves, although the best by far are the romaines, which produce sweet, meaty leaves.

- **SPINACH,** with its soft, buttery leaves, is good for adding bulk to a salad and for adding a different texture.

- **SWISS CHARD,** especially the red or yellow stemmed kinds, and the young leaves of beet, such as red-leaved 'Bull's Blood', add color.

Spinach & Swiss Chard

quick-growing greens

SPINACH can be added to salads when harvested as young leaves or cooked as mature leaves. Swiss chard is easier to grow and more colorful. The leaves can be used in the same way as spinach, and the succulent stems make a useful additional vegetable.

1 SOW

Spinach bolts readily during the summer and is best grown in either early spring or fall. Sow spinach as soon as soil conditions are suitable in the spring. Use a plastic sheet to warm up the soil in colder regions. Fall sowing will provide the most success in the majority of areas.

- Make several sowings of spinach between four and ten weeks before the first fall frost date in your area. The latest sowing should survive over winter to provide a crop the following spring.

- Sow spinach ½ inch (1 cm) deep in rows 12 inches (30cm) apart. The large seeds are easy to handle and space at 2 inches (5cm) apart.

- Thin spinach seedlings later to 6 inches (15cm) apart, using the thinnings in salads.

Swiss chard grown in cooler areas is best sown in spring, as soon as the soil conditions allow. In warmer areas, make several sowings through the spring and summer because the older leaves may become tough in hot weather.

- Swiss chard "seeds" are actually corky fruit containing several seeds. Like beet, each "seed" will produce a clump of seedlings. You can separate these later, thin them out, or leave them to grow as a clump.

- Plants may overwinter to produce a crop the following spring before bolting—it is a biennial.

- Sow seeds for Swiss chard as for spinach, but thin the plants in stages to 12 inches (30cm) apart.

GROWING IN CONTAINERS

Choose a multicolored mix of Swiss chard, such as 'Bright Lights'. Sow three or five seed clusters to a 12-inch (30cm) or 2-gallon (7.5L) container. Cover the seeds with about ½ inch (1cm) of sterile seed-starting mix. Each seed cluster may produce more than one plant, so thin out if necessary. Alternatively, plant started Swiss chard plants in the container. Water regularly, and liquid feed with a high-nitrogen fertilizer when the plants start to fill the pot. Pick off tender stalks from the outside of each plant as needed.

FAQ

Q Why is there a white, furry growth appearing under the leaves?

A This is downy mildew, which thrives in cold, wet conditions. Remove the affected leaves as soon as it appears. Thin out the remaining leaves or plants to increase air circulation.

Q Why did my Swiss chard produce tall shoots instead of just leaves?

A Swiss chard may bolt prematurely the first summer if it was sown too early in the year. Try sowing later in spring.

② grow

Both crops need moist soil and are greedy feeders.

- Spinach bolts quickly if it doesn't have enough moisture, whereas Swiss chard will become tough. If growth starts to slow down, side-dress with a general purpose or high-nitrogen fertilizer.

- Both crops are attractive to slugs and snails—use barriers or traps to protect the crop from damage.

③ harvest

Both spinach and Swiss chard leaves can be eaten raw as a salad green when small and tender. Larger leaves are best cooked.

- Pick individual spinach leaves, or cut whole plants. Strip off larger stalks, and cook the leaves whole.

- Cut the whole of young Swiss chard plants, but leave a stump, which should regrow. Or cut leaves when they reach 10 inches (25 cm) long, starting from the outside of the plant. More leaves will grow from the center.

- Rinse the leaves thoroughly in cold water to remove dirt.

- Cook Swiss chard stalks by steaming or stir-frying.

Varieties

- **'BRIGHT LIGHTS'** is a vibrant Swiss chard mix with white, yellow, red, and intermediate-color stems (60 days).

- **'BRIGHT YELLOW'** is a Swiss chard cultivar with golden yellow stems and green leaves (60 days).

- **'RHUBARB CHARD'** is a Swiss chard cultivar with bright red stems and leaf veins (70 days).

- **'SPACE'** is a smooth-leaf spinach suitable for salads or for cooking (40 days).

- **'TYEE'** is a spinach with crinkled leaves, better for cooking (45 days).

Orach

Also called mountain spinach, orach is a warm-weather alternative to spinach. It grows rapidly into a large plant, up to 4 feet (1.2m) high, but it doesn't become bitter if it bolts. Sow the seeds directly once the soil has warmed up, 1–2 inches (2.5–5cm) apart in rows spaced 12–18 inches (30–45cm) apart, and thin later to 6–10 inches (15–25cm) apart. Thinnings and young leaves can be added to salads. For spinach, cut the plants when they reach 12–18 inches (30–45cm) high. There are green, white, and red selections; red orach is the most common and makes a spectacular ornamental border plant.

Swiss chard may have attractive red stems.

Edible Flowers

a splash of color

YOU CAN ADD COLOR AND INTEREST to your salads and other dishes by scattering in a few fresh flower petals, but choose edible flowers that add flavor and texture as well as color. Many flowers have a distinctive flavor of their own—but make sure you choose blossoms that are known to be edible.

1 sow

Sow annual flowers directly. You can use them as edging to flower beds or interplant them among rows of vegetables. To make weeding easier, sow them in short rows or patterns so you can distinguish them from weed seeds. Simply scratch a line in the soil; scatter the seeds thinly; and cover with soil.

2 grow

Annual flowers are often tough and will thrive on any irrigation or fertilizer aimed at adjacent vegetables. If you let some flowers go to seed, most will spread around the garden. Once you learn to identify them, you can simply leave a few each year or transplant them if they start to stray too far.

3 harvest

The best time to pick flowers is in the early morning, once the dew has dried. You don't need to wash them, but make sure you check for insects. To keep the flowers fresh until needed, place the stems in a jar of cold water, or bag the flowers and store them in the refrigerator. The central disk of the flowers can be bitter, so just use the petals.

Varieties

- **BORAGE** has blue cucumber-flavored flowers good in salads or floated in summer drinks. It is also a good plant for attracting bees.

- **CALENDULA** is an original marigold and has bright orange, slightly nutty petals; modern varieties come in a wider range of colors.

- **NASTURTIUM** has flowers with a distinct peppery taste, and they come in a huge range of bright colors.

- **PINKS** (dianthus) has petals that have a sweet taste with a hint of clove.

- **VIOLA** provides delicate little flowers that come in a rainbow of colors but add little flavor.

Other Flowers You Can Eat

If you already have these in your vegetable garden you can eat the flowers, too.

- **HERBS** such as basil, chives, cilantro, and thyme, which have culinary uses (pages 178–187), have flowers with a more subtle flavor than the leaves, but with added color.

- **ZUCCHINI** (pages 175–177) has huge flowers that are great for stuffing and frying in batter. Use the male flowers (with no bulge underneath), or pick the female flowers when the zucchini are tiny.

 Edible flowers will attract beneficial bees and predatory insects to your garden.

Other Salad Greens

SEVERAL OTHER CROPS are grown to add to salads, and the hardier types, such as corn salad (also known as lamb's lettuce or mache), miner's lettuce (also known as claytonia), and upland cress, are good alternatives to lettuce during winter in colder areas.

1 sow

Corn salad, miner's lettuce, and upland cress are good follow-on crops after summer crops are harvested.

- Sow them in late fall to crop through the winter.

- Sow directly into the ground ½ inch (1cm) deep in rows 6 inches (15cm) apart. Thin in stages to leave plants every 6 inches (15cm). You can use the thinnings in salads.

2 grow

All of these crops can withstand several degrees of frost, but if it gets really cold, cover them with hot caps. Otherwise, they require little attention during winter.

- In mild spells, slugs may be a nuisance and may need removing; pull out weeds by hand, or hoe them away, to prevent them from swamping these slow-growing plants.

- Miner's lettuce, which is a native plant, may self-seed readily. Keep offspring in check.

3 harvest

Pick individual leaves or cut whole plants as required for winter salads. Rinse thoroughly to remove dirt. Corn salad has a mild flavor, miner's lettuce has round, succulent but bland leaves, and upland cress has a peppery flavor reminiscent of watercress.

Corn salad leaves are ideal for adding to salads.

Varieties

- Corn salad is sold as unnamed seeds, although named cultivars, such as 'Cavallo' and 'Vit', are also available (50 days).

- Miners' lettuce has no named cultivars (40 days).

- Upland cress is sold as unnamed seeds, although a variegated form has recently become available (50 days).

6

Beans, Peas & Sweet Corn

BEANS AND PEAS ARE MEMBERS OF A GROUP OF PLANTS KNOWN AS *LEGUMES,* and they are usually planted together as part of a crop-rotation system. (See "Crop Rotation," pages 22–23.) These plants are particularly useful because they can convert atmospheric nitrogen into nitrate, which they—and other plants—can use. Examine the roots of the plants at the end of the season, and you'll see nodules, or lumps, that contain nitrogen-fixing bacteria. If you sow legumes in an area that has not been cultivated before, first inoculate the seeds with *Rhizobia* bacteria to ensure they can convert the nitrogen—simply shake the seeds with this black powder in a bag to coat them. If you leave the roots to rot in the soil in the fall, they will add nitrogen to the soil, which will benefit greedier crops the following season. Beans and peas are delicious when eaten fresh from the garden, but any surplus can be frozen. Some types of beans are easy to dry.

Although sweet corn is actually a grass, we've grouped it with the legumes because these crops have a long association. Native Americans often grew the two crops together, along with squash. Growing corn and beans together works well with modern varieties, whether you choose the taller varieties or simply plant bush beans under the taller corn.

Fava Bean

MOST FAVA BEANS, which are also known as broad beans, are much hardier than bush beans and are worth considering for an early crop. However, some people may have a serious reaction to fava beans. If you are of African, Mediterranean, or Southeast Asian descent, make sure you only consume fava beans that have been cooked.

 ## sow

Sow seeds directly in the ground in early spring as soon as the soil can be prepared. Choose a sunny position, or if temperatures will rise, one with partial shading. Germination will take place within two weeks at 50°F (10°C) average temperature.

- Sow the large seeds 1–2 inches (2.5–5cm) deep and about 6 inches (15cm) apart. You can sow a few extras to allow for loss and to transplant into gaps later.

- Alternatively, grow fava beans in double rows with plants 3–4 inches (7.5–10cm) apart. Make wider paths between the double rows for picking.

- In areas with mild winters, you can sow fava beans in the late fall and let them overwinter. As long as the young plants are about 6 inches (15cm) tall before they stop growing, they will survive frosts and continue growing the following spring.

Allow 6 inches (15cm) between plants if growing in normal rows.

grow

Dwarf varieties will not need support, but taller varieties may lean even when grown in blocks. Support them using posts and string around blocks or along rows to keep them upright.

- Mulch to keep weeds down.

- When the plants are in full flower, pinch off the growing tip to encourage pod formation.

- In dry weather, give the plants a good soaking once a week after the flowers fade and the pods start to form.

Varieties

There are two main types of fava bean. Longpods, as the name suggests, have long pods with up to eight beans. These are the hardiest and can be sown in fall. Those with short pods have fewer beans.

- **'EXPRESS'** is a good longpod type (50–60 days).

- **'IMPERIAL GREEN LONGPOD'** is another good longpod type (60–70 days).

- **'THE SUTTON'** produces a good yield of white beans with a good flavor (84 days).

- **'WINDSOR'** has short pods with four round beans; it is better for spring sowing (75 days).

You can use string or twine to provide support for taller plants.

Lima Bean

In warm regions, lima beans are a better option. Homegrown ones have more flavor than store-bought beans. The plants need dry weather and warm soil (at least 65°F/18°C) and are sensitive to cold. Depending on the variety, grow them like bush beans (pages 90–92) or pole beans (pages 93–95).

FAQ

Q Why is there yellow stippling on the leaves?

A The plants are hosting spider mites; spray insecticidal soap on the undersides of the leaves.

Q What is causing the leaves to disappear?

A Japanese beetles and Mexican-bean beetles can skeletonize the leaves; cover the beans with floating row covers to keep out these insects.

3 harvest

The first young pods should start to form in early summer. You can pick these and eat them as whole immature pods. If you let the pods reach full size, wait until the beans inside are fully formed.

- Remove the pods by pulling sharply downward or by cutting them, or you may damage or uproot the plant.

- The beans should be plump and soft before picking. The scar where the bean joins the pod should be green or white, not discolored.

- Older beans have a tougher skin, which can be removed after cooking if you prefer.

- You can blanch and freeze surplus beans.

Feel the pod to check whether or not the beans are fully formed.

Bush Bean

low-growing, undemanding plants

THE BEANS IN THIS GROUP ARE EASY AND QUICK TO GROW. You can eat the pods green, wait for the beans in the pods to fill out and eat them, or dry and store the beans for winter use. As crops, bush beans need little or no support and provide most of their own fertilizer, too. Although each crop is short-lived, you can sow several times through the year for a succession of fresh beans, or sow once for a crop of dry beans.

 sow

Bush beans are very sensitive to frost. Wait until after the last spring frost date in your area before sowing or planting them outside. They also resent being transplanted, so it's not a good idea to try starting indoors to get a head start on the season.

- To ensure a regular supply of green beans, you can make several sowings, starting from early spring in milder areas and continuing until fall.

- The seeds germinate best when the soil temperature exceeds 55°F (13°C). You can use a soil thermometer to check the soil's temperature at ½ inch (1.5cm) deep in early morning.

- In colder areas, you can have an earlier crop of beans by sowing them under a floating row cover. Put the cover in place a week or two before sowing to warm up the soil.

- Before sowing the seeds, make a seed furrow about 1 inch (2.5cm) deep; dribble water into the bottom of the furrow and let it soak in.

- Because seed quality will deteriorate quickly, sow only fresh seeds for the best results.

- Aim to sow the seeds 3 inches (7.5cm) apart in rows about 2 feet (60cm) apart. Thin to 5–6 inches (12.5–15cm) apart.

- You can also grow bush beans in blocks, with 6 inches (15cm) between plants each way.

 grow

Bush beans don't require much fertilizer because nodules on the roots convert atmospheric nitrogen, which can then be used by the plant. When the flowers start to appear, make sure the plants never run out of water to ensure a continuous crop of fresh beans.

- As a general rule, a thorough soaking once a week is better than more frequent light watering, because the water will penetrate deeper into the soil.

- The last sowing might struggle to reach maturity in colder areas. Cover with a floating row cover when the temperature starts to drop in the fall.

- Grown in blocks, bush beans should be self-supporting, although taller types in exposed gardens may need support. Use posts and string along each side of the row.

Most bush beans grown in blocks won't require staking.

 When the harvest is over, cut the tops for the compost pile, but leave the roots in the

Dried and Shelling Beans

Beans grown for drying are usually even easier to harvest because you can leave all of them to mature and dry before picking the whole crop at once. If it is dry, watering when the pods are forming will increase the crop. However, once the pods are maturing, let the plants dry off. When the plants appear dead and the pods brown and dry, uproot whole plants and hang them in a sunny spot or an airy room to dry completely. When fully dried, remove the pods and shake out the dried beans. Discard any damaged or discolored ones, and store the rest in airtight jars to use in winter dishes.

For something between fresh and dry beans, try "shelling" beans. Leave the pods to swell; then shell the mature beans before they start to dry. Large round beans will taste good like this. Use them fresh or freeze them if you have a surplus.

'Borlotti' is a large variety ideal for shelling.

GROWING IN CONTAINERS

Push about 18 seeds into a 12-inch (30cm) or 2-gallon (7.5L) container, thinning if necessary to leave around 12 plants. Choose a variety with yellow or purple pods for ornamental value. Water regularly and pick over the plants every other day to keep them bearing—and to prolong the display.

Varieties

There are several main types of bush beans.

- **FILET** types produce a lot of long thin beans with a round profile. Pick them frequently before they reach 4 inches (10cm). Good cultivars include 'Triomphe de Farcy' (48 days) and 'Maxibel' (50 days).

- **PURPLE** types produce round, bright purple beans that turn dark green when cooked. Good cultivars include 'Royal Burgundy' (60 days) and 'Purple Teepee' (75 days), which holds its pods above the plant.

- **ROUND-POD** types have long, plump pods up to 6 inches (15cm) long. Reliable cultivars include 'Blue Lake' (45–50 days), 'Contender' (45–50 days), and 'Tendercrop' (56 days).

- **SHELLING BEANS** can be produced from any of the larger seeded green varieties. Good cultivars include 'Borlotti'—do not confuse this with the pole types of the same name—(70 days) and 'Vermont Cranberry' (65 days).

- **WAXPODS** have round yellow pods that are crisp (waxy is a misnomer). Cultivars include 'Pencil Pod Wax' (52–60 days).

Soybean and Edamame

They are often used dried, but soybeans are also eaten as fresh beans, known by the Japanese name "edamame." You can grow and harvest soybeans like bush beans, but they are more tolerant of dry conditions and less reliable in regions with cooler summers. Soybeans produce numerous small pods, each with only two to four seeds. 'Envy' produces bright-green seeds (75 days); 'Green Pearls' is a quick-maturing edamame type (65 days).

③ harvest

Pick green beans for eating fresh regularly, twice a week; they grow quickly. If you let the beans in the pods mature, flowering will stop. Pick beans when they are a few inches long to full size, depending on the variety. The flavor develops as the pods mature, but they should snap cleanly when bent, and the seeds should be immature.

- Pick by snapping each bean off using your finger and thumb to avoid uprooting the whole plant.

- To enjoy the beans at their best, eat straight after picking, cooking lightly to retain a slight crunch.

- You can freeze the thin filet-bean types whole with little preparation. For the larger flat-pod types, cut them into sections; blanch them in boiling water; and cool and freeze quickly.

The beans in these pods are immature, so they are ideal for eating as fresh green beans.

A surplus of green beans is ideal for freezing.

FAQ

Q What is causing the speckled leaves on my plants, and why are they covered in fine webbing?

A Spider mites are barely visible but multiply rapidly in hot weather to eventually cause serious damage. Spray with an insecticide based on soft soap.

Q Why do the leaves look more like lace?

A Mexican-bean beetles and their larvae can skeletonize the leaves. Spray with an insecticide that disrupts insect reproduction, such as neem. Avoid the problem by planting early.

Q Why are plants yellow and stunted?

A Look for colonies of aphids (these are small, round insects), particularly at the growing tips. Spray with an insecticide based on soft soap, and repeat as necessary.

Pole Bean

attractive plants with maximum yields

THESE BEANS REQUIRE MORE WORK TO GROW than bush beans, but because pole beans climb, they make better use of limited garden space—and each plant produces a huge crop of beans over a much longer period than bush beans. Many have colorful flowers or pods and are useful for adding height and interest to a vegetable garden or even as an ornamental flower border. For even greater variety, consider the more unusual runner and asparagus beans.

SOW

Pole beans are sensitive to frost, so wait until after the last spring frost date in your area before sowing. The soil temperature should be at least 65–70°F (18–24°C).

- For the best results, choose seed cultivars based on your climate. Look for types that do well in cool conditions if you live in a cool climate; however, if you normally have long, hot summers, heat tolerance and disease resistance will be important factors to consider.

- These beans are always grown using supports. (See "Bean Supports," page 95.) Push two or three beans about 1 inch (2.5cm) deep into the soil near the bottom of each support.

grow

Pole beans can easily reach 7 or 8 feet (2.1 or 2.4m) tall in a season and need a structure to climb.

- Although beans require little feeding—in fact, they manufacture their own nitrogen fertilizer from nodules on their roots—they do benefit from a moisture-retentive soil. You can either work plenty of organic matter into the soil before sowing the seeds or mulch the surface once the plants are established to help retain soil moisture.

- When the lead shoots of the plants reach the top of the supports, make sure you nip them off—this will encourage sideshoots to form lower down and give you a greater yield of beans.

New shoots will cling to the supports as the plant grows.

- Watering is important for seeds forming inside the pods. When flowers start to form, make sure the plants never run out of moisture—a thorough weekly soaking is more effective than more frequent, but lighter, watering.

- In areas that have a long growing season, you can try a second midsummer sowing. This crop should grow quickly and will take over when the spring crop starts to flag in early fall.

Tepee supports are one of the easiest ways to support pole beans.

Varieties

There are many kinds of pole beans:

- **FLAT-POD** types have wide, flat, green pods. The immature beans are clearly visible. Good varieties include 'Kentucky Wonder' (65 days) and 'Romano' (70 days).

- **PURPLE-POD** beans are decorative, with pale purple flowers and round, dark purple pods. Unfortunately, the color is lost when cooked because they turn dark green. Cultivars include 'Blauhilde' (64 days) and 'Purple King' (75 days).

- **ROUND-POD** types have long, plump pods. The beans are not visible until the pods are too mature. Reliable cultivars include 'Blue Lake' (60 days) and 'Fortex' (60 days).

- **SHELLING BEANS** are produced from the large bean types. One of the most interesting cultivars is 'Borlotto Firetongue' (70–80 days), a green-and-red pod variety from Italy with plump, speckled beans.

- **YELLOW-POD** types make unusual ornamental plants. The pods are flat and pale yellow. Cultivars include 'Marvel of Venice' (75 days) and 'Goldfield' (60–70 days).

Runner Beans and Asparagus Beans

White or red flowers and long, flat pods are produced by runner beans, which are vigorous climbers. The beans have a coarser texture than pole beans, but some people like their more robust flavor. Unlike pole beans, they are pollinated by insects or hummingbirds—in fact, they are popular for attracting these birds—so they can fail to set pods. 'Scarlet Runner' (90 days) is a popular variety.

The asparagus bean (or yard-long bean) is a vining bean that grows best in areas with long, hot summers. Under ideal conditions, it is very vigorous, so make sure you provide sturdy supports. The beans can grow very long but are best picked up to 18 inches (45cm). There are no named cultivars (75 days).

Yellow types have flat pods.

grow: bean supports

There are many traditional methods used to support pole beans:

- Tepee poles should be at least 8 feet (2.4m) tall, set out in a circle at least 3 feet (90cm) across, with poles spaced 6–8 inches (15–20cm) apart. Push the poles well into the ground, and tie the tops firmly, or use a special tepee clip to hold them together.

- In windy areas, create double rows of poles 2–3 feet (60–90cm) apart, tied and braced with horizontals where they cross at the top. You can substitute wire or string for some of the vertical supports. Vertical supports should be 6–8 inches (15–20cm) apart.

- Pole beans will also grow up chain-link or timber fences, trellises, or arches. If you don't have one that is suitable, you can use plastic or nylon mesh with a 4–6-inch (10–15cm) grid, available from seed and garden suppliers.

Double rows of supports are ideal in windy areas.

These long plump pods belong to a round-pod type variety.

 harvest

When beans start to form, you'll need to pick them regularly. If beans are left to mature, flowering will slow down—and so will your production of new beans. If picked regularly—at least twice a week—the plants should continue cropping all summer.

- There's no lower limit to bean size. However, the smaller they are the more tender they'll be, and larger beans will have a stronger flavor.

- As a general rule, once the beans start to become visible the pods are ready to eat. Any larger and they'll start to become tough and stringy.

- Most pole beans can be left to dry and harvested as shelling beans or dried for winter storage. (See "Dried and Shelling Beans," page 91.)

Pea

FROZEN PEAS ARE SO UBIQUITOUS that it is easy to forget the simple pleasure of shelling pea pods and eating fresh, sweet peas straight from the vegetable garden. If you find shelling peas too labor intensive, you can try snow peas or snap peas instead; you eat the pods whole so there's less work—and less waste, too.

 SOW

Peas are hardy plants, so they are a useful early crop. In cold areas, start them off under floating row covers if there's a chance of frost.

- In cooler areas, you can make several sowings through the spring and summer for a succession of fresh peas. However, in hotter areas they will suffer in the heat, so confine yourself to early spring and fall crops.

- In areas with mild winters, a sowing in late fall should survive over the winter for an extra-early crop the following spring. As long as the plants are around 6 inches (15cm) high, they should be able to survive the occasional frost.

- Peas are usually sown in furrows about 6 inches (15cm) wide. Scatter the seeds so that they fall roughly 2 inches (5cm) apart each way.

- Sow peas directly into seed furrows 1 inch (2.5cm) deep. If the soil is dry, water the bottom of the furrow thoroughly before sowing.

- An alternative is to sow double rows with seeds 2 inches (5cm) apart in rows 6 inches (15cm) apart. Allow 2 feet (60cm) between double rows for access.

- Dwarf varieties can also be sown broadcast in blocks. They will support themselves, but you may have to pull up the whole crop and harvest them all at once. This is an option if you grow peas for the freezer.

- Peas do not like soil that is both cold and wet, so if your soil is very wet, sow them into a raised bed, or on a south-facing slope, where the soil will have the most sun exposure to help reduce moisture in the soil.

Pea seedlings are cold hardy but won't appreciate very wet soil.

 Spray peas weekly with a solution of baking soda to help control powdery mildew.

② grow

Peas require no fertilizer, but you should work plenty of organic matter into the soil to help retain moisture around the roots.

- Dwarf varieties are more or less self-supporting, especially the semi-leafless types. However, taller varieties will definitely need supports, and mid-height varieties can be kept under control by running strings on either side of the rows between 4-foot (1.2m) stakes. Old-fashioned climbing varieties can be trained on tepees, plastic mesh, or fences, like pole beans. They should attach themselves to the supports using their tendrils, but you may need to tie in stray shoots occasionally.

- Do not water peas until the first flowers start to form. As the pods start to swell, regular watering in dry spells should increase the yield.

Once you see flowers beginning to form, you can water the plants.

Using twiggy branches for pea support is an old traditional method.

 GROWING IN CONTAINERS

Push 16–24 peas about 1 inch (2.5cm) deep into a 12-inch (30cm) container. Snap peas, which you can add raw to salads, are best—don't expect a huge crop at each picking. Add a few twiggy branches, about 2 feet (60cm) high, for the peas to scramble up. Water regularly, and pick pods every other day to prolong the harvest. Feeding is unnecessary.

Varieties

- **SHELLING PEAS** have plump pods with thin walls and are harvested after the peas have reached full size but are still sweet. Good cultivars include 'Green Arrow' (70 days), 'Little Marvel' (65 days), and 'Maestro' (60 days), which are all vine types.

- **SNAP PEAS** have thick, fleshy pods and are picked before the peas inside develop. They are sweet and crunchy when cooked or eaten raw. 'Sugar Snap' is a reliable older cultivar that grows up to 6 feet (1.8m) tall (68 days). Good modern cultivars include 'Cascadia' (3 feet/ 90cm; 60 days) and the compact 'Sugar Ann' (55 days) and 'Sugar Bon' (56 days).

- **SNOW PEAS** have flat pods and are picked before the peas inside develop. They are best lightly cooked. 'Oregon Sugar Pod II' grows to about 30 inches (75cm) and does not usually need support (68 days). 'Mammoth Melting Snow', an heirloom type, grows to 5 feet (1.5m) tall (75 days).

Leafless Peas

Apart from the pods and the peas themselves, the tendrils on pea plants are also edible, and these have become a trendy salad ingredient in recent years. All pea varieties have tendrils to help them climb, but some varieties have no leaves—just loads of tendrils. These dwarf varieties are self-supporting, producing a mass of tendrils. Pick young, tender shoot tips with their tendrils for a delicate pea flavor, and leave the plants to produce a crop of peas. 'Sugar Lace', a snow pea, grows 30 inches (75cm) high (68 days), while 'Survivor', a shelling pea, reaches only 24 inches (60cm) high (70 days).

▲ Flat pods with undeveloped peas indicate that these are snow peas. Both the peas and the pods are eaten and are ideal in stir-fry dishes and salads.

▲ The pods protecting shelling peas are not eaten— only the sweet tender peas inside them are.

To remove aphids from the plants, you can try spraying them off using a strong stream

▲ Pick snap peas young and eat as snow peas or harvest with slightly more mature peas.

FAQ

Q Why are my peas covered in white powder?

A This is powdery mildew, a disease that strikes in warm, humid weather with cooler nights. The best solution is to sow early in spring or look for resistant varieties.

Q What is causing the plants to become mottled or distorted?

A Several viruses attack pea plants and cause various symptoms, including yellowing, mottling, and distortion of the leaves. Most are spread by aphids, so try to prevent these from attacking by spraying with insecticidal soap or covering the crops with floating row covers.

Q Why are my plants turning yellow and dying?

A This is caused by either Fusarium wilt or root rot. In the future, grow peas in well-drained soil; plant resistant varieties; and follow a crop-rotation plan.

③ harvest

For the maximum harvest, pick pods regularly to encourage more flowering and more pods to form. Nip off the pods using your index finger and thumb to avoid uprooting the plant.

- Shelling peas should reach full size, usually 4–5 inches (10–12cm). Check that the peas inside are full size and still sweet; they turn starchy with age. After a while, you'll be able to tell the right stage to pick them. If you don't eat them right away, keep them in their pods and shell at the last minute for maximum freshness.

- You can pick snap peas either when they are immature or when they reach full size but before the peas have formed. If left too long, they will become stringy. Overly mature snap peas can be shelled.

- Snow peas have flat pods, and you can usually see the immature peas inside. Pick as soon as they reach about 2 inches (5cm) up to their full size. Eat these raw, stir-fried, or lightly steamed. Snow peas may have a string, which can be removed before or after cooking.

- If you have a surplus of any kind of pea, they freeze well. Blanch briefly in boiling water; cool quickly; and freeze on a metal tray. Separate and transfer to plastic bags or plastic containers when frozen.

- You can pick pea shoots or tendrils when young and tender and add them to salads. They will have a mild pea flavor.

of water.

Sweet Corn

freshly picked for the freshest flavor

IF YOU LIKE CORN ON THE COB, you will really appreciate it straight off the plant and into the saucepan. With today's many varieties to choose from, even if you have a short growing season, you will still be able to grow sweet corn. Choose varieties suitable for your area. If you want corn for popcorn, make sure you choose a variety that has been specifically developed for that use.

 1 SOW

Wait until all danger of frost is past and the soil is reasonably warm—at least 55°F (13°C)—before sowing corn. It needs at least 70–100 days of warm weather from seed to harvest. In short-season areas, choose an early variety. Because all the ears will mature at the same time from each sowing, make several sowings through the spring and summer, planting your last crop 3 months before the first fall frost date.

- Grow at least 12 or 16 plants, sowing in a block instead of in rows—for example, three or four rows of four plants each—to ensure good pollination. (See "Grow," page 102.) Space plants 14 inches (35cm) apart each way.

- Sow seeds in the ground 1–1½ inches (2.5–4cm) deep. Either space seeds 6 inches (15cm) apart and thin out later, or better still, sow two seeds at each position and nip out the weaker one later.

- In areas with a cold spring and a short season, start seeds in pots where you can maintain a temperature of at least 59°F (15°C). Deeper pots will be best because the roots are easily damaged. Gradually acclimatize the plants to life outside before planting them outdoors.

- In colder areas, warm the soil with plastic sheets before sowing or planting.

If you sow two seeds together, leave only the strongest plant standing.

CENTRAL AMERICAN CIVILIZATIONS WERE CULTIVATING SWEET CORN 5,400 YEARS AGO—AT THAT TIME IT HAD MORE STARCH AND WASN'T AS SWEET.

 To prevent birds from snatching a newly emerging seedling, protect freshly sown

Grow corn close together in blocks to ensure pollination.

SOW: three sisters

This is a traditional method of growing corn, beans, and squash together. It is a practice used by Native Americans that allows the plants to be grown together using the space wisely.

- This practice is based on using heirloom drying beans and taller corn instead of modern sweet corn varieties. Today's modern pole beans may be too vigorous for the shorter sweet corn and can get in the way of harvesting. Choose your varieties carefully, selecting corn varieties that are harvested at the end of the season.

- If you lack space and like the idea of three sisters, you can adapt the concept by interplanting sweet corn and bush beans or letting squash or pumpkins trail underneath the corn plants. At least you'll have two of the three elements growing together.

Varieties

Because sweet corn is pollinated by the wind, it is easily pollinated by other corn nearby, so it is best to stick to one type.

The earliest varieties mature in around 60 days from sowing; others take as long as 90 days. You can choose from varieties with white, yellow, bicolor, or even multicolor kernels.

There are three main types of sweet corn:

- **ORDINARY VARIETIES**, which include heirlooms, contain a small proportion of sugar that rapidly turns to starch after harvesting. These are arguably the tastiest if you get the harvest time right, are easier to grow, and are more tolerant of colder summers. Good cultivars include 'Golden Bantam' with yellow kernels (75 days), 'How Sweet It Is' with white kernels (87 days), and 'Silver Queen' with white kernels (92 days).

- **SUGAR-ENHANCED VARIETIES** are slightly harder to grow, have more sugar to start with, and lose it less quickly. Cultivars include 'Kandy Korn' with yellow kernels (84 days), 'Quickie', which are small plants with bicolored kernels (65 days), and 'Sugar Buns' with yellow kernels (72 days).

- **SUPERSWEETS** are the sweetest and retain their sugar longer. The downside is that they are harder to germinate, need ideal growing conditions, and you must isolate them from other types to prevent cross-pollination (the odd chewy kernels in an otherwise succulent cob are the result). Cultivars include 'Early Sunglow' with yellow kernels (63 days), 'Northern Xtra Sweet' with yellow kernels (72 days), and—a good choice for northern gardens—'Indian Summer' with multicolor kernels reminiscent of heirloom Indian corn.

- **EXTRA-TENDER VARIETIES** are the latest development; these are exceptionally sweet and have such thin skins you can eat them raw straight off the plant. 'Xtra Tender and Sweet' is a good cultivar with yellow kernels.

The spiky tassels of the male flowers appear on top of the plants.

② grow

Sweet corn needs a position in full sun but with shelter from winds. The soil should be deep, and raised beds will help to warm the soil in spring. Work an inch or so of organic matter into the soil before planting, and apply a balanced fertilizer.

- Provided the soil is moist at planting time, the plants should not need regular watering. In very dry weather, a thorough soaking when the ears start to form should increase yields.

- Corn plants produce offshoots, or tillers, around the base. Although these are unlikely to produce ears, leave them to help feed the main plant.

- As the plants grow, hill up the soil around the bottom of the plant. This will prevent them from blowing over.

- Sweet corn is pollinated by the wind. Each silk sticking out of the developing cob is attached to a female flower, and all need to be pollinated to produce a perfectly filled cob. Planting in blocks instead of rows helps ensure that pollen from the male flowers (the spiky tassels at the top of each plant) falls on the silks lower down. Choose a still day and tap each plant gently when the flowers are fully developed—you'll see clouds of pollen being released.

③ harvest

Plan on an average of one-and-a-half ears per plant. Although more may start to form, they may not all reach maturity.

The cobs should be ready to harvest when the silks turn brown and start to dry up, about 20 days after the silks first appear. To check, carefully peel back the leaves covering the ear and push a thumbnail into a kernel. If the juice is watery, it's not ready, and if it is starchy, it may be too old. However, milky juice is just right, so pick and eat straight away.

- Be careful to avoid damaging the plant by pulling the ear downward to snap it off.

- Ideally, cook the corn immediately, or store in a refrigerator to slow the conversion of sugars to starch.

- Older ears can be husked and the kernels frozen.

- It isn't worth saving seeds of modern varieties—many are hybrids and the results will probably be disappointing.

Brown, dried silks are a sign this cob is ready to be picked.

Popcorn

One type of corn has hard kernels that "pop" when heated rapidly—of course, this is popcorn. You can grow popcorn exactly as you do sweet corn. The major difference is you leave the ears until the stalks turn brown. Cure the ears in a warm dry place for up to five weeks. Test the kernels at weekly intervals by stripping some from an ear and trying to pop them. When this is successful, strip the remaining kernels and store them in sealed jars somewhere cool. Popcorn varieties are available in a range of colors, including red and blue. 'Strawberry' has small decorative reddish ears. Most need at least 100 frost-free days to mature.

FAQ

Q What is eating my ripe ears of corn before I have a chance?

A Many wild animals, especially raccoons and deer, have a sweet tooth and know when corn is just perfect for eating. Use repellents or other deterrents; if this fails, you may have to use a high fence or an electric fence.

Q Why are some plants stunted?

A This may be an infestation of corn rootworm. Look for the small grubs that burrow in roots and kernels. The adult beetles eat corn tassels. Rotating crops and thorough cultivation may help. Or drench the soil with a parasitic nematode.

Q My corn ears are being attacked by worms. What can I do?

A European corn borers are beige wormlike creatures that feed beneath the corn husks and may burrow through stalks. Crop rotation and careful destruction of the crop residue should help. Or spray leaves and tips of the ears with Bt (*Bacillus thuringiensis*).

Sunflower Seeds

Drought-tolerant sunflowers enjoy the same growing conditions as sweet corn. In most areas, wait until the last spring frost and sow directly into the soil 1 inch (2.5cm) deep. Sow 6 inches apart (15cm) in rows 2 feet (60cm) apart. Thin seedlings to 18–24 inches (45–60cm) apart. When the heads droop and the backs turn brown (in about 90 days), bring indoors to dry, or protect them from birds. When fully dry, rub the seeds off the head and store. Choose cultivars selected for edible seeds, such as 'Mammoth Russian'.

7

The Onion Family

ONIONS AND THEIR RELATIVES are essential vegetables for the cook. Just think of how many recipes call for onions or garlic—or both! Scallions add a bite to leafy salad greens, while leeks are one of the main ingredients of many warming winter dishes. One advantage to growing onions and their relatives is that there is no need to worry about when to harvest them. They'll stay fresh in the ground until you need them, and when fall comes you can dry them off and store them for winter use. This means you'll have fresh onions, garlic, leeks, and scallions when called for in a recipe—and fresh ingredients always result in a more delicious dish.

In general, these are easy plants to grow. You can grow onions from seeds, or you can take a shortcut and start them from onion sets, which are basically bulbs already half-grown. Garlic is unique in not ever producing seeds. Instead, simply plant a clove and it will multiply into a bulb containing a dozen or so new cloves by the end of the season. Shallots and multiplier onions do produce seeds, but you can treat them the same as garlic. Leeks will require a little more effort. Along with scallions, they are grown from seeds.

Garlic

a distinctive, flavorsome bulb

GARLIC IS UNIQUE AMONG VEGETABLES. It never produces seeds, so the only way to propagate it is by saving cloves from the previous season. Fortunately, each clove you plant divides into a bulb containing 12–15 new ones. It is easy to grow enough for the most adventurous of cooks who use garlic in almost every recipe.

sow

You can plant garlic from the supermarket, but there's a risk of introducing viruses and other diseases. It is safer to start with certified disease-free stock from a reputable supplier. Plant garlic in fall in most areas. Although it grows slowly, if at all, during winter, the plants should thrive in spring. Garlic plants need a period of cold to start bulb formation. In very cold regions, plant as soon as you can work the soil in early spring.

- Break the bulbs apart and plant the individual cloves.
- Push them gently into the soil so the pointed tops are just covered.
- Space the cloves 6 inches (15cm) apart in rows about 12 inches (30cm) apart.

Varieties

- **HARDNECK**, or rocambole, types produce a false flower shoot, which hardens by late summer. Around this a single layer of cloves forms. Hardneck types grow well in areas with cold winters, producing larger bulbs than the softneck types. These bulbs have a stronger flavor and are easier to prepare, but they will not keep well. Cultivars include 'German Red' and 'Spanish Roja'.
- **SOFTNECK**, or artichoke, types produce several layers of small cloves and keep well for winter use. Reliable cultivars include 'California Late' and 'Early Italian Red'.

grow

Garlic requires little attention, apart from keeping weeds down. Watering in dry spells when the leaves are actively growing should increase the size of the bulbs.

- When the tops start to dry off, excavate around the base to reveal the bulbs and expose them to the sun.

harvest

When the tops have died off completely, lift the bulbs carefully with a fork and let them bake in the late summer sun for as long as possible. Keep them dry, if necessary, by completing the drying process in a greenhouse or on a sunny windowsill.

- When completely dry, braid the remains of the tops and hang them in a cool, dry airy place.

FAQ

Q Why do all my garlic produce tall stiff shoots?

A Softneck types shouldn't produce a flower stem, but they may do so if there is an interruption to growth, for example, in a dry spell. Hardneck garlic will produce a false flower shoot, or scape. Cut this while it is soft and green to use in cooking. A ring of cloves will form around the bottom of this stalk.

Shallot

a sweet "multiplier" onion

A PLANTED SHALLOT SET OR SMALL BULB will multiply into a bunch of a dozen or so shallots during the season, hence it being referred to as a multiplier onion. Although shallots are smaller and harder to prepare than onions, they have a sweeter taste and are prized by chefs. The Egyptian walking onion is a perennial multiplier onion that is fun to grow.

1 sow

You can grow shallots from seeds, but the easiest way to start them is with sets. (If you opt for seeds, follow the sowing and transplanting instructions for "Onions" on pages 110–113.) Seeds will produce a large single bulb that may not divide by the end of the season.

- In the North, wait until the soil is workable, two to four weeks before the last spring frost date, and add a little general-purpose fertilizer. In the South, plant in fall.

- Simply push each set into the ground until the tip just disappears. Space them about 6 inches (15cm) apart in rows 12 inches (30cm) apart.

2 grow

Keep weeds down with mulch, hoeing between rows, or weeding by hand as necessary—be careful not to disturb the bulbs. Shallots do not need watering unless it is very dry. In this case, a thorough soaking every week or two will increase the size of the bulbs.

Varieties

- **SEEDS:** 'Ambition' is an attractive red-brown-skinned cultivar with white flesh.

- **SETS:** These are usually sold as red or gray, but you may come across named cultivars, such as 'Pikant'.

3 harvest

When the tops have dried off and the skins on the clumps of bulbs have started to set, lift the clumps with a fork. Let them bake in the sun. In wet weather, bring them indoors to cure. Well-ripened shallots should store well through winter. Keep them somewhere cool and dry; check occasionally for rot.

Egyptian Walking Onion

Also known as tree onions, Egyptian walking onions are perennials that should last in the garden for many years. They bear tiny bulbs at the top of their flower stems. If you leave the shoots, they will bend down to the ground, planting the aerial bulbs—this unique trait has led to the term "walking onion." You can use the bulbs from the flower stalk or lift and divide the underground bulbs and use them as pickling onions or for cooking.

Leek

LEEKS DO NOT MAKE LARGE BULBS LIKE ONIONS, but some cultivars are hardy enough to leave in the ground into the winter until needed. They have a mild flavor suitable for many dishes, and you can use them instead of onions in many recipes. The white base of the stem is particularly prized compared to the coarser green leaf. Fortunately, the proportion of white base can be increased by following these growing techniques to blanch them.

 SOW

Leeks are slow growers, so the earlier you start them the bigger and better they'll be. In mild areas, you can sow directly into the ground eight weeks before the last spring frost date. Elsewhere, start them in seed-starting trays in early spring. Alternatively, buy started plants.

- Sow directly in the ground thinly in a furrow ½ inch (1cm) deep or in wide trenches the width of a hoe, aiming for a seed every ½ inch (1cm).

- In trays, aim for the same density. When the seedlings straighten out and resemble grass, you can tease them apart and replant individually in divided trays.

 grow

When the seedlings are about the thickness of a pencil, they are ready to be transplanted to their final position.

- Prepare the site with a fork to loosen the soil and work in a general-purpose fertilizer. Create a trench 4 inches (10cm) wide and deep with a hoe. This will make hilling to blanch the stem bases easier.

- For plants raised in a seedbed, water them to loosen the soil and lift and separate the individual plants. To make transplanting easier, clip off about half the roots and cut some of the leaves to compensate, too.

- Plant the leeks in the bottom of the trench using a dibble or trowel so that just the tip of the leaves is visible.

Varieties

- **'AMERICAN FLAG'** is a popular fall and winter cultivar (140 days).

- **'KING RICHARD'**, an early maturing cultivar, can be used as baby leeks or left until it reaches full size (75 days).

- **'LINCOLN'** is also an early maturing cultivar that can be used as baby leeks or left until it reaches full size (50 days).

- **'PANDORA'** is a modern cultivar for fall harvest (90 days).

Use scissors to trim the roots of transplants.

 Remove slugs and snails by picking them off by hand. Alternatively, use barriers,

Space the plants 6 inches (15cm) apart for medium-size leeks. Don't fill the hole, but water the bottom of the trench well to settle the plants.

- As the plants grow, gradually fill in the trench. You can increase the blanched portions by drawing soil up against the bottom of the plants.

- Alternatively, use a dibble or trowel to plant leeks in individual holes deep enough so that just the tips of the leaves are exposed. Space the plants 6 inches (15cm) apart with 12 inches (30cm) between rows. Hill soil around the plants as they grow to blanch the stems.

- Leeks prefer moist soil. Make sure you avoid wetting the leaves when you give the plants a thorough soaking, which should be every week in dry spells.

- Take precautions against slugs if they are a problem.

FAQ

Q What is the reason for my leeks producing a tall thick stem?

A Like other members of the onion family, leeks are biennials, maturing over two years. However, if they receive any interruption to their growth—such as lack of moisture, pest damage, or excessive heat—they may bolt. This means they will form a flowering shoot in their first season of growth.

Q Why are the leaves of my plants covered in reddish brown spots?

A Leek rust is a fungal disease that often looks worse than it really is. Although the leaves are affected, the white base of the plant is still edible. Destroy severely affected plants (making sure they don't end up in your compost pile), and follow a crop rotation to minimize the effects of rust. (See "Crop Rotation," pages 22–23.)

Elephant Garlic

Although elephant garlic looks like a giant version of regular garlic, it is actually related to the leek. However, like garlic, you can plant one clove and, by the end of summer, you will have a huge bulb with a delicious mild flavor. It is particularly useful if you like roasted garlic.

The white bases are exposed when the outer leaves are removed.

3 harvest

You can harvest leeks at any stage. When they reach pencil thickness, they are a good, milder substitute for scallions in recipes.

- To harvest mature leeks, use a garden fork to carefully lever them out of the ground without damaging them. Remove a couple of the outer leaves to reveal the white base and trim off excess green leaf tops.

- Leeks will keep for a week in a refrigerator. However, it is easier to leave cultivars in the ground until needed or as long as you can. To extend the harvest in cold areas, draw straw up against the stems to protect them.

such as crushed eggshells, to help keep slugs and snails away.

Onions

BY GROWING YOUR OWN ONIONS, you'll have a greater selection from which to choose. It's easy to produce a supply of onions for year-round enjoyment—as long as you have a fertile, well-drained soil. One sowing, or planting, should provide fresh onions all summer and enough to dry and store through the winter, too. Onions are easy to grow from seeds, but you can save time and effort by starting with onion sets or started plants. Onions are mostly trouble free, and you can grow a surprising number in even a small garden.

 SOW

You have two options when growing onions from seeds: either sow them directly into the ground or start them in seed-starting trays and transplant later. Whichever method you choose, remove all weeds and rake the soil to produce a seedbed.

- Sow directly in spring when the soil temperature reaches 50°F (10°C). Make seed furrows ½ inch (1cm) deep and 6 inches (15cm) apart. Sow thinly, aiming for a couple of seeds every inch of row. Thin them out later to leave a seedling every 1–2 inches (2.5–5cm). You can use these thinnings as you would scallions.

- To give them an early start in areas where springs are cold, plant the seeds in seed-starting trays about eight weeks before the last frost date. Fill a divided seed tray with seed-starting mix and sow a couple of seeds per cell. Cover with ½ inch (1cm) of mix and keep somewhere warm and sheltered. Seedlings can be slow to grow, but at least they will reach a good size when planted in the garden.

- A technique known as multiseeding works well with onions. Sow 3–6 seeds per cell in a divided seed tray, and let all the seedlings grow. Plant them out as a clump; as they grow, they will push apart to create a group of perfect round onions. Space the clumps about 6 inches (15cm) apart.

AS FAR BACK AS THE ANCIENT EGYPTIANS, PEOPLE BELIEVED THAT ONIONS COULD ABSORB "INFECTIOUS MATTER."

▲ Yellow onions often have a thicker skin than other types, making them less prone to infection and attack by insects. These are good all-purpose onions.

Varieties

For spring sowing in the North, choose a long-day variety. These won't start to form bulbs until there is daylight for at least 14 hours. In the South, choose short-day varieties, which require 12-hour days to begin forming bulbs. In mild winter areas, you can also start short-day varieties in fall. These will survive over winter, start growing again in spring, and produce bulbs in late spring or early summer.

If you want named cultivars, choose seeds; these may also be available as transplants.

- **'AILSA CRAIG'** is a popular long-day cultivar that produces large brown-skinned onions with a mild flavor (105 days).

- **'CANDY'**, a modern yellow cultivar, should do well in all states (85 days).

- **'SNOW WHITE'** is a white-skinned cultivar for all areas (90 days).

- **'WALLA WALLA SWEET'** is a good choice if you want a mild sweet-flavored onion. It is best for northern states (115 days).

- **'YELLOW GRANEX'** is a popular short-day sweet onion, best for southern areas (165 days).

Onion Sets and Transplants

Small onion bulbs grown from seeds the previous year are known as onion sets. Because they were sown close together, they do not get big enough to produce a flower in the second year—as onions normally do. When you plant onion sets, they will continue to grow, producing a full-size onion by the late summer. Sets are easier to grow than seeds—simply push the sets into the soil so the tops are just buried. However, they are more expensive than seeds, and there is less choice of variety. They are usually available as unnamed red, white, or yellow types. You can also buy onion transplants that are ready to plant, which will save the time and effort of growing onions from seeds.

▲ White onions are available as large bulb types, which are suitable for slicing, and as small bulb varieties, which are ideal for boiling and pickling.

▲ Red onions have red skin, but the flesh may be white, red, or bicolored. Red Bermuda types are a good choice for serving raw in salads or sandwiches.

② grow

Onions are shallow-rooting plants, so they do best in fertile, moisture-retentive soil. They do not need much fertilizer—a little balanced fertilizer is enough. Too much nitrogen will produce excessive leaves.

● Keep weeds down by hoeing carefully between the rows, being careful not to nick the bulbs or disturb the roots. Hand weed as necessary within the rows.

Bulbs grow just below the soil's surface.

FAQ

Q Why are some of my onions producing a tall thick shoot?

A This is known as bolting—the bulb is producing a flower shoot. This normally happens in the second season after the mature bulb has survived the winter. Sometimes immature bulbs will try to flower in the first year. There are a number of causes, such as lack of moisture, high temperatures, root damage, or not storing sets correctly before planting them. You can still use the bulbs, but eat them fresh because they won't be suitable for storing.

Q Why are some leaves turning yellow and wilting?

A This could be due to onion root maggots burrowing into the bulbs, causing them to rot. Destroy all damaged bulbs and any crop debris at the end of the season. Practice crop rotation. (See "Crop Rotation," pages 22–23.)

Q What can I do about onions that are rotting and covered in mold?

A Several diseases, including downy mildew, attack onions. This disease is worse in periods of warm days and cool, humid nights. To minimize its effects, practice crop rotation, keep weeds down, and don't crowd maturing onions.

Q Why have rusty stripes appeared on the leaves of my onions?

A Especially during hot, dry weather, thrips will feed on the leaves. You can spray the plants with an insecticidal soap or with neem.

To keep onion root maggots away from onions, cover them with a floating row cover.

③ harvest

You can start to pull fresh onions for using in the kitchen as soon as the bulbs are large enough. However, remember that young bulbs won't store for more than a week or so at this stage. Allow the bulk of the crop to fully mature.

- When the tops start to dry and fall over, the bulbs will not grow anymore. Carefully lift them out of the ground with a fork, and lay them raised off the ground to bake in the sun for up to 10 days. If rain is in the forecast, cover the bulbs or move them indoors into a well-ventilated area to cure. Let the bulbs dry off and finish curing before storing them.

- Use any damaged bulbs, ones with thick necks, or any that have bolted (produced a flower shoot) first.

- Store only sound bulbs. The tops should be brown and dry, and you can braid these together to form strings. Alternatively, store loose bulbs on trays. Store in a cool dry place until needed, checking occasionally and removing any that are starting to rot.

Make sure the onions are completely dry before putting them in storage.

You can use fresh, young bulbs right away, or wait for them to mature.

Scallion

SCALLIONS, OR GREEN ONIONS, AND BUNCHING ONIONS are quick and easy crops that you can fit in any spare ground. You can grow them most of the year, and because they take only 10 to 12 weeks from sowing to harvest, it is worth sowing small amounts regularly. There are two types: normal garden onions that are harvested when immature; bunching, or Japanese, onions that produce thin stems but never make much of a bulb. Some multiplier onions are perennials that can be divided and harvested every year as scallions.

SOW

Make the first sowing about eight weeks before the last spring frost date. For a constant supply, make several sowings through the spring and summer at roughly monthly intervals. In mild winter areas, make a fall sowing for a winter and early spring harvest.

- Because they are harvested small, scallions are best grown densely. Use a hoe to make a furrow 4–6 inches (10–15cm) wide and ½ inch (1cm) deep. Scatter the seeds thinly, aiming for a seed every ½ inch (1cm); then cover with soil. (It is not worth starting scallions in seed-starting trays for transplanting.)

- For clumping types, after the first harvest, replant sections of the clumps to continue your crop. In the following years, the clumps may produce flower stalks and become dormant. However, when temperatures turn cooler, they will produce new stems.

GROWING IN CONTAINERS

Scatter the seeds thinly over the surface of the potting mix, and cover with a ½-inch (1cm) layer of potting mix. Aim for a seedling every ½–1 inch (1–2cm) apart each way, but don't worry too much about spacing because the plants will push apart as they grow. Water regularly. You can begin to pull individual plants carefully as they reach pencil thickness, leaving the remainder to continue growing.

Varieties

Scallions are biennials and will produce a small bulb in their first season. You can use any garden onion variety and harvest immature plants that can be used in the kitchen as scallions; however, it is better to use a variety that has been specifically bred for this purpose.

- **'RED BARON'** is a modern cultivar with bright red bulbs and green leaves (65 days).

- **'WHITE LISBON'** is a reliable older cultivar that produces small white bulbs (60 days).

Bunching onions produce single stems but insignificant bulbs. Others will eventually split to produce clumps of stems and can be treated as perennial onions.

- **'EVERGREEN HARDY WHITE'** is a hardy perennial clump-forming cultivar (65 days).

- **'ISIKURA IMPROVED WHITE'** is a single-stemmed cultivar that grows to 12 inches (30cm) tall (50 days).

- **'TOKYO LONG WHITE'** is also a single-stemmed cultivar that grows to about 12 inches (30cm) tall (65 days).

② grow

Water regularly in dry weather to keep the plants growing rapidly and to prevent an interruption to their growth.

- Keep weeds down by hoeing between the bands, and by hand-pulling any weeds among the crop.

- You can harvest bunching onions as an annual crop, or let them overwinter in milder areas. In cooler regions, cover them with straw or floating row covers. In very cold regions, plant divisions in pots and bring indoors for the winter; replant outdoors in early spring. You can keep bunching onions going by splitting the clumps and replanting individual stems. If you follow a crop rotation plan, plant them with other onions.

③ harvest

You can start pulling scallions as soon as they reach pencil thickness. Loosen the soil with a fork or trowel to avoid damaging them. Either lift clumps together or gently pull individual plants to give the remainder space to develop. They keep well in the ground, so simply pick as much as you need for a meal.

Once the scallions reach pencil thickness, they are ready to harvest.

Some scallion varieties have red skin.

The Cabbage Family

THE CABBAGE IS AN OLD-WORLD VEGETABLE WITH A LONG HISTORY. In fact, its history is so long that many common vegetables share its heritage—the leaves of kale, the buds of Brussels sprouts, the immature flowers of cauliflower and broccoli, the roots of the turnip, even the stems of kohlrabi. Members of the cabbage family are cool-season crops that vary from easy to grow to challenging, and no vegetable garden would be complete without a few of them.

Because all members of the cabbage family are attacked by the same pests and diseases and prefer rich soil, they have their own place in the classic crop-rotation plan. (See "Crop Rotation," pages 22–23.) If you find the European types too bulky for a small plot, their Asian relatives are smaller and faster to grow, making them better suited to busy lifestyles and smaller plots.

Broccoli

LIKE CAULIFLOWER, BROCCOLI IS UNUSUAL because it is the immature flower buds that are eaten—leave one unpicked and it will burst into a mass of bright yellow flowers. These flower-bud heads are packed with vitamins and nutrients, which are claimed to help prevent cancer and heart disease. Broccoli is easy to grow and, thanks to the sideshoots that form after the main head has been cut, it crops over a long period. Broccoli is also a cold-tolerant plant, so you can produce a succession of heads through three seasons. Two relatives of the green broccoli are worth trying: purple sprouting broccoli and broccoli rabe.

 ## SOW

You can raise broccoli from seeds indoors if you want a lot of plants; otherwise buy transplants. When buying them, make sure they are healthy and vigorous, about 3 inches (7.5cm) high, and are not rootbound.

- Transplant after the last spring frost and again in late spring or early summer for a fall crop.

The heads of flower buds are the most delicious part to eat.

 ## grow

Broccoli likes rich firm soil. Dig in plenty of organic material or a generous dose of plant-starter fertilizer before planting.

- Set the plants 12 inches (30cm) apart each way. This will allow room for decent main heads and a small follow-on crop of sideshoots. Spacing closer, about 6 inches (15cm) apart in 12-inch (30cm) rows, will provide only main heads. Wider spacing, up to 18 inches (45cm) each way, will produce a longer and larger crop of sideshoots.

- Pat the transplants in well, burying them so the lowest pair of leaves just rests on the soil surface. Tread the soil firmly to prevent the mature plants from falling over later.

- Water the transplants well until the plants are established; then water regularly to keep the soil moist to a good depth.

- Broccoli is a magnet for all the pests that attack the cabbage family. To keep them away, cover the new transplants with well-secured floating row covers. Otherwise, be prepared to spray the plants regularly with an organic insecticide.

- When the main broccoli heads start to form, side-dress the crop with a seed-starter fertilizer to encourage additional cropping, and keep the soil uniformly moist.

- Mulch to conserve moisture and keep weeds down.

 You can fit a root collar around the stem of each plant to prevent cabbage root flies

A main head appears on a stem, with smaller sideshoots underneath.

Varieties

- **MODERN CULTIVARS**, which include 'Green Goliath' (55 days), 'Gypsy' (56 days), and 'Packman' (50 days), are all quick maturing with large, solid heads.

- **OLDER CULTIVARS**, including 'Green Sprouting' (60–90 days), 'De Cicco' (65 days), and 'Waltham' (79 days), bear over a long period.

Broccoli Alternatives

Broccoli rabe enjoys the same growing conditions as broccoli but is a much faster crop. Sow seeds directly in seed furrows ½ inch (1cm) deep and 6 inches (15cm) apart. Thin in stages to 6 inches (15cm) between plants. Make several sowings from early spring until about a month before summer temperatures are expected to exceed 95°F (29°C). Start again from six weeks before the first fall frost and continue through fall in mild areas. Pick the plants when they reach 6 inches (15cm) tall and have loose flower buds. They taste slightly bitter and are popular in Asian cooking. (See "Other Asian Greens," pages 128–129.) There are a few named cultivars of broccoli rabe, such as 'Sessantina' (35 days) and 'Zamboni' (50 days), or grow the unnamed 'Spring Raab' (42 days).

Purple sprouting broccoli produces plants with a lot of small, purple heads. It is hardy, and in milder areas, it's ready for harvest in early spring from a midsummer sowing. There are no named varieties.

Purple sprouting broccoli produces edible leaves.

from laying their eggs.

THE FIRST-CENTURY ROMAN WRITER PLINY THE ELDER WROTE ABOUT BROCCOLI, BUT IT WASN'T INTRODUCED TO ENGLAND UNTIL THE EIGHTEENTH CENTURY. THOMAS JEFFERSON GREW IT AT MONTICELLO.

3 harvest

Cut the main head when it reaches full size, usually 3–4 inches (7.5–10cm) across, and the buds are still tight and green.

- Unlike cauliflower, you can leave the broccoli plant in the ground after harvest. Once the main head is cut, smaller sideshoots will start to appear and may continue for weeks or even months. These may get smaller, but they are still worth collecting regularly.

- If you haven't sprayed or covered the crop, check for cabbage worms deep inside the head before preparing it to eat.

- Broccoli heads should keep for a week unwashed in the refrigerator. It is also an easy crop to freeze if you have a surplus.

FAQ

Q Why does my broccoli only produce small heads?

A Any interruption in early growth will cause heads to form prematurely. Try to avoid planting rootbound or stressed transplants, and don't plant them until the soil temperature reaches 50°F (10°C).

Q Why are the stalks hollow?

A This may have occurred due to a minor nutrient deficiency or excess nitrogen. Use a seed-starter fertilizer and mulch with garden compost.

Q Why have my broccoli plants suddenly wilted?

A Broccoli and all cabbage crops are attacked by cabbage maggots. The grubs burrow into the roots and may cause enough damage that the plants wilt on warm days. This pest can be prevented by covering the crops with floating row covers, or placing foam rubber or tar paper beneath each transplant, resting it on the soil.

Q The leaves of my young plants are peppered with tiny holes. How can I prevent them?

A Flea beetles target all members of the cabbage family, especially in hot weather. Severe attacks can set back the plants, but they often outgrow the danger. Spray with neem oil or apply beneficial nematodes. In future seasons, cover the crop with floating row covers to keep them off.

Q How can I stop caterpillars from getting into the heads and destroying them?

A Cabbage caterpillars or loopers belong to butterflies or moths that home in on members of the cabbage family. You can prevent them from getting anywhere near your crops by covering them with floating row covers or fine mesh. Handpick any caterpillars you see, examine the leaves, and crush any eggs you find. Alternatively, you can spray with neem oil soap or the biological control Bt (*Bacillus thuringiensis*).

 If you find cabbage worms, soak the broccoli heads in salted water to expel the worms.

Brussels Sprouts

wintertime treat

BRUSSELS SPROUTS ARE A USEFUL CROP FOR COLDER AREAS, and they are harvested during the fall and winter. After the first frosts, the sprouts hold well on the plants, and the taste becomes sweeter and less harsh. They can be grown during cooler periods in warmer regions, but the sprouts will probably be looser. If you don't like sprouts because of their bitter taste, maybe you haven't tried homegrown sprouts—these sweet bundles may change your mind.

sow

Unless you want a lot of plants, buying transplants is much easier than sowing your own.

- Don't buy too many transplants—these are large, greedy plants. Plant them 2 feet (60cm) apart each way.

- In the North and cooler regions, plant in midsummer. In the South, plant in the fall for a spring harvest

 grow

Prepare the soil by digging in plenty of compost or well-rotted manure the previous fall. Don't dig into the soil because the plants need a firm footing. Tread the soil before planting to firm the plants in well.

- Mulch around the plants during warmer weather to keep the roots cool. Feed monthly with a fertilizer. Water during dry spells to keep them growing steadily.

- Brussels sprouts are tall, top-heavy plants, so they are susceptible to leaning. This is because their root system is close to the surface. If you planted in firm soil and your yard is sheltered, the plants should be fine. If not, pile soil up around the stems or stake individual plants.

- Snap off the lower leaves as they become old and brown, leaving just a stump or stem below the developing sprout.

- A month before the first hard frost is due, cut the leafy topknot—you can cook this like cabbage—if you want the sprouts over a short period. If not, leave the tops until last.

harvest

You can start picking the sprouts from the bottom of the stem upward once they reach about 1 inch (2.5cm) in diameter. They should snap off cleanly if you push hard with your thumb.

- After the first few frosts, the quality of the sprouts' flavor should improve.

- If temperatures below 20°F (-6.5°C) are predicted, cut a couple plants at ground level; trim off the leaves and excess stem; and store them outside the back door.

- You can store harvested sprouts in the refrigerator for a couple of days, and they will freeze reasonably well. However, Brussels sprouts will always have the best flavor if cooked after being freshly picked.

Varieties

- **'JADE CROSS'** is a dwarf and relatively quick-growing cultivar; it is good for northern regions and also warm areas with a short cool period (88 days from transplants).

- **'OLIVER'** is another dwarf cultivar; however, it takes slightly longer to mature from transplants (95 days).

- **'TRAFALGAR'** is a tall cultivar at 3 feet (90cm) suitable for cooler areas (up to 130 days).

Cabbage

a versatile vegetable with smooth or crinkly leaves

CABBAGE TAKES UP PLENTY OF SPACE in the vegetable garden, but you can't help but admire a well-grown red cabbage or crinkly leaf savoy. It is a cool-weather crop; however, in warmer regions, you can still grow cabbage as long as you avoid hot summer temperatures. Choose several varieties for a mixture to eat raw or cooked.

 sow

You can raise your own seedlings indoors for transplanting outside later, or buy started cabbage plants.

- Start the seeds in individual small pots from early spring to midsummer, depending on your region and the variety.

- Plant transplants outdoors to avoid maturing in temperatures above 90°F (32°C). In cool areas, plant in spring and harvest in summer and fall. In warmer areas, plant in early spring and harvest before hot summer days; plant again in late summer for a fall crop. In hot areas of the country, plant in late summer for a fall

harvest and in late winter for a spring harvest.

- Space early varieties 12 inches (30cm) apart and late varieties 18 inches (45cm) apart each way. If you find conventional cabbages too large, try planting them closer together. This works well for the smaller varieties. Reducing the spacing each way to 10 inches (25cm) or closer should produce heads about 4 inches (10cm)

 grow

Like all members of this family, cabbage plants prefer a fertile soil that is well supplied with organic matter and nutrients, and constant moisture.

- If you want to grow cabbage plants successfully, you'll need to take time to dig or till plenty of compost or well-rotted manure into the plot, preferably the previous fall to let the soil settle. A cover crop will retain nutrients. (See "Cover Crops," page 49.)

- Larger types of cabbage can take a while to reach full size, so make use of the space between them with a quick crop. (See "Using Space Efficiently," pages 40–41.)

- Keep weeds down by mulching or shallow hoeing.

- Keep the soil evenly moist by giving it a good soaking once a week during dry spells. A mulch will help conserve soil moisture. If you allow the soil to dry out and then give it too much water at once, the heads may split.

- Insect pests, such as flea beetles in the early stages, aphids, cabbage worms, and cabbage maggots, can be a nuisance. Keep them off your cabbage plants by protecting them with a floating row cover.

- Give the plants a side-dressing with a high-nitrogen fertilizer three to four weeks after transplanting.

Varieties

- **EARLY GREEN** cultivars include 'Dynamo', which has compact round green heads that stand well and are resistant to splitting (65 days), and 'Earliana', which is an early round, green cabbage that can withstand light frost (60 days).

- **LATE GREEN** cultivars include 'Savoy King', which has dark green crinkled leaves (80 days from transplants). 'Storage No. 4' has large firm heads for fall harvest and storage into spring (80 days).

- **RED** cultivars include 'Ruby Perfection', which forms dense, medium-size heads that hold and store well (85 days). 'Super Red 80' has medium-size dark red heads resistant to splitting, and stores well, too (78 days).

Close spacing between cabbage plants will produce smaller heads.

③ harvest

Cut the whole head when it reaches full size. Usually a cabbage head will keep fresh in the ground for a few weeks or even months in cooler weather. Once the shape of a head starts to change and it becomes looser, it is about to bolt; use it immediately.

- Cut the head to leave a couple of inches of stalk. After a few weeks a baby cabbage will sprout from the stump. If you make a cross-shape cut in the top of the stump, you'll get four baby cabbages as a bonus.

- If the wrapper leaves are diseased or damaged by pests, peel off a few layers until you reach unblemished leaves.

- You can cut and store winter cabbage in a root cellar or cool garage.

FAQ

Q Why are my cabbages wilting?

A Dig up a severely affected plant to check. If the roots have been mined and nibbled by grubs, these are cabbage maggots. (See "Frequently Asked Questions," page 120.) If the roots are swollen and resemble fingers, clubroot disease is the problem. This persists in the soil for a long time. Destroy the affected crop and plant cabbage plants in a new part of the vegetable garden, being careful not to transfer soil, even on your boots. Crop rotation should help prevent clubroot, as should adding lime to increase the soil pH to 7.0. (See "Finding Out About Your Soil," pages 16–17.)

Q What makes the heads split?

A This can be caused by changes in soil moisture or because the heads have grown too fast. If the soil has dried out, add only 2–3 cups (475–700ml) of water per plant daily. If the plant is growing too quickly, twist the plant to break some of the roots and slow down their growth. Some types are less prone to splits.

Use a sharp knife to cut a cabbage head from the stem.

Cauliflower

a finicky vegetable that's worth the trouble

TO GROW THE BEST CAULIFLOWER HEADS, YOU NEED TO BE DEDICATED, but there's nothing more rewarding. The sweet, white curds taste much better straight from the garden than they do from the supermarket. There's also the boost to your reputation as a gardener. However, to get to this stage, you have to fight off all kinds of pests, protect the heads from the sun, and provide plenty of food and water. Cauliflower plants are also sensitive to frost, hate hot weather, and bolt at the least provocation. But if you can pull it off, you'll be glad you made the effort.

 sow

Start with transplants. Because any interruption to growth can affect the quality of the heads, make sure store-bought transplants are fresh and undamaged and have not been allowed to dry out. Or start from seeds indoors; sow them four to five weeks before you plan to transplant them outdoors.

- Harden off transplants well and plant outdoors after the last spring frost date for a summer crop and again in early summer for a fall crop. Be careful to avoid disturbing the roots, and bury the plants so the first pair of leaves sits on the soil surface.

Varieties

- **WHITE STANDARD** cultivars include 'Early White' (52 days), 'Fremont' (62 days), and 'Snow Crown' (50 days).

- **ROMANESCO** cauliflowers have unusual green spirelike heads. 'Veronica' is a modern cultivar (85 days).

- **COLORED** cultivars are now available, including 'Cheddar', with pale orange heads—the color is retained on cooking—(68 days), and 'Graffiti', which has bright purple heads that fade to pale blue when cooked (80 days).

 grow

Cauliflower plants need a rich soil and plenty of water. Work a generous amount of organic matter into the soil or apply a seed-starter fertilizer before planting.

- Cauliflower plants grow best when planted in firm soil, so tread on it to firm in the transplants.

- For conventional-size heads, space the plants 18 inches (45cm) apart each way.

- Water the transplants well until they are established. Afterward, don't let the soil dry out—check that the soil is moist 6 inches (15cm) below the surface, even if the surface is dry.

- Apply a fertilizer either as a side-dressing or as a liquid feed when the plants reach full size.

- Cauliflower plants are prone to all the usual cabbage family pests, and there's nothing worse than caterpillars inside the heads. (See "Frequently Asked Questions," page 120.) Cover the plants with floating row covers buried around the edges; practice crop rotation.

- Some varieties are self-blanching in that the inner leaves protect the curds. Blanching prevents exposure to the sun, which causes the head to become coarse and yellow. For non-blanching types, check weekly and when the head reaches 2 inches (5cm), if it is exposed, break some of the outer leaves and fold them over the top of the plant to shade the head. If necessary, tie or peg the leaves together to keep them in place. A week or so later, the curds should be ready.

Like all cabbage family plants, provide protection to keep insects away from cauliflower.

grow: baby cauliflowers

Cauliflowers respond well to close spacing to form small heads, provided the soil is fertile and they never go short of water. Choose a small, fast-maturing variety.

- Plant transplants 6 inches (15cm) apart in blocks. This spacing will produce heads about 3 inches (7.5cm) across.

- Or sow seeds directly into the ground so they can grow rapidly and without interruption. Sow ¾ inch (1.5cm) deep in short furrows 6 inches (15cm) apart and thin later to every 6 inches (15cm).

- The heads may all mature at the same time, so sow several small batches.

3 harvest

Judging the optimum time to harvest cauliflower heads takes some practice. The ideal is when the head has reached full size and the individual buds are still tight and white. If you leave them too long, the buds will become loose and eventually turn into flowers.

- Cut the stalk below the head and remove all the outer leaves except a couple of wrapper leaves, which will help protect the curds.

- You can store cauliflower in the refrigerator for several weeks. It also freezes reasonably well. Break it into pieces; blanch in boiling water; cool; and freeze on a metal tray so pieces remain separated when bagged.

The white curds of cauliflower are a delicious treat.

FAQ

Q My cauliflower plants are producing only tiny heads. What's wrong?

A Any interruption to early growth may cause small flowers to form prematurely. This is known as buttoning. Be careful when transplanting; avoid planting until the soil temperature reaches 50°F (10°C).

Chinese Cabbage

quick-growing exotic cabbage

THIS IS ONE OF A GROUP OF LEAFY VEGETABLES—which includes bok choy and the other Asian greens discussed on the following pages—that have little in common except that they all originated in the Far East. Most are members of the ubiquitous cabbage family, and all are worth growing in the modern vegetable garden. Unlike the Old-World cabbage and its relatives, these are quick-growing, space-efficient crops. They suit modern lifestyles and adventurous cooks alike. Chinese cabbage can be used in place of iceberg lettuce in salads.

 SOW

Chinese cabbage is a crop for cool weather and is usually sown after midsummer—when the days are shorter—for a fall crop. Modern varieties are less prone to bolting and can be sown in early spring in cooler areas.

- Start the seeds in pots about six weeks before the last frost and plant them outdoors 12–15 inches (30–36cm) apart just before the last frost.

- Sow fall crops directly in the ground about 90 days before the first fall frost date. Thin in stages to 12–15 inches (30–36cm) apart.

Varieties

- **'BLUES'** is a quick-growing, barrel-shape cultivar, good for spring or summer sowing (55 days).

- **'MICHIHLI'** is an older cultivar with a cylindrical head up to 18 inches (45cm) tall (73 days).

- **'ORIENT EXPRESS'** is an older quick-maturing, barrel-shaped cultivar (45 days).

- **'TWO SEASONS'**, a squat cultivar that is bolt-resistant, can be sown spring or fall (65 days).

- **'WONG BOK'**, an older squat type about 9 inches (23cm) tall, is best for a fall or winter harvest.

 grow

Chinese cabbage really benefits from well-dug soil loaded with plenty of organic matter.

- It is a magnet for the cabbage family pests, such as flea beetles, cabbage caterpillars, and slugs. (See "Frequently Asked Questions, page 120.) Cover the crop with floating row covers; use traps or barriers to protect from slugs.

- Keep the soil constantly moist. A drip irrigation system is worth considering for this crop.

- Keep weeds down by shallow hoeing to avoid damaging the root system.

- Mulching with organic material before the weather starts to warm up in late spring will help retain moisture, suppress weeds, and keep the soil cool.

- Give a high-nitrogen liquid fertilizer every other week.

 harvest

Chinese cabbage can be used at any stage, from seedling to fully formed heads. Young plants and thinnings are also best cooked lightly. The mature plants produce tight heads and can be used in salads or shredded and lightly cooked.

- Cut the whole plant at soil level, and remove the outer leaves until you reach clean leaves that are tightly wrapped around the pale, tender heart, which is the part to eat.

Bok Choy

a cabbage with tender leaves

BOK CHOY NEEDS REASONABLY RICH SOIL AND PLENTY OF MOISTURE in order to produce a crop of tender leaves. Any interruption to growth may make it bolt. These plants also attract the whole range of cabbage family pests; flea beetle can be a real nuisance unless you cover crops with floating row covers.

 ## sow

Bok choy grows best in cool conditions. In cooler areas, sow in early spring and again in late summer for a fall crop. In milder regions, sow in late summer to fall for a winter crop.

- In cold areas, sow seeds in divided seed-starting trays about four weeks before the last frost to plant outdoors after hardening off well.

- Sow in late summer in seed furrows ½ inch (1cm) deep and 8–12 inches (23–30cm) apart. Thin the seedlings in stages to 8–12 inches (23–30cm) apart, depending on the size of the variety.

Varieties

- **'JOI CHOI'** is a taller cultivar, at 12 inches (30cm), with white leaf stalks (50 days).

- **'MEI QUING'** has pale green stalks (45 days).

- **'RED CHOI'** is a new and unusual cultivar with reddish leaves when full size (45 days).

- **'TATSOI'**, or rosette bok choy, is a looser version of fleshy, light green stems and rounded leaves. It is hardier than bok choy and worth considering as a winter crop (45 days).

- **'TOY CHOI'** is a dwarf version, with heads 4–5 inches (10–12cm) tall (30 days).

- **'YUKINA SAVOY'** has crinkled leaves (45 days).

 ## grow

Bok choy grows quickly in rich, moisture-retentive soil. It is also a good candidate for containers filled with a rich potting mix. Whether growing in pots or the ground, water regularly and feed with a plant-starter fertilizer every other week.

 ## harvest

Like all Asian greens, you can pick bok choy as immature leaves. However, if you want the fleshy white or green stems, let the plants reach full size.

- You can cut individual leaves from the outside of the plant or pull up the whole plant.

- A good compromise is to cut the plant an inch (2.5cm) or so above soil level and leave the stump to resprout for a second flush of leaves.

 ## GROWING IN CONTAINERS

The Asian vegetables here and on the following pages are great for containers. You can sow them thickly and snip them as baby leaves. (See "Mesclun & Others," pages 80–81.) Let them grow bigger and use them for stir-fries or wilted greens. They will grow to full size in a container. You can sow the seeds thickly—about a seed every 1 inch (2.5cm)—and thin out in stages, adding the thinnings to salads or stir-fries, until you have a few plants left to grow to full size.

Other Asian Greens

THESE ARE ALL RAPID-GROWING, LEAFY GREENS that you can grow in the same way as bok choy. (See "Bok Choy," page 127.) Most, such as the Asian mustards, can be eaten as salads, wilted as greens, or added to stir-fries when they are immature. Surprise your dinner guests with some of these unusual vegetables.

Mizuna (above), like mibuna, produces leafy, rosette-forming greens.

Mustards are known for their spicy flavors.

Komatsuna is a
fast-growing crop.

Mibuna and Mizuna

Mibuna has rounded leaves, while mizuna has deeply serrated leaves. Both have a mild mustard flavor, which adds a gentle bite to salads. As the plants reach maturity the leaves become coarser and develop a stronger flavor; these are best cooked lightly. For full-grown plants (both take 40 days), thin the seedlings in stages to 12–18 inches (30–45cm) apart. You may come across named cultivars, but they have little to offer compared to unnamed types.

Mustards

Mustards pack a lot more punch and are good at spicing up a salad when the leaves are young and tender. They become hotter as they reach maturity, but steaming or stir-frying will mellow them. They are cold-tolerant and are best grown in cool and temperate regions. Sow in early spring and fall. Mustard varieties include 'Red Giant', with large round red leaves, while 'Miike Giant Purple' has large crinkled leaves (45 days).

Komatsuna

Komatsuna is also known as Japanese mustard spinach, which gives a clue to its flavor—a cabbage somewhere between mustard and spinach. It is tolerant of cold but also fairly resistant to drought, so it can be grown from early spring to fall in all areas. It reaches maturity in just 35 days. Sow directly in the soil. For full-grown plants, thin in stages to 12 inches (30cm) apart (35 days).

Chinese broccoli looks nothing like the traditional broccoli normally enjoyed by Westerners.

Both the leaves and flower shoots of choy sum can be eaten.

Chinese Broccoli

Chinese broccoli, also known as Chinese kale or gai lan, has glossy blue-green leaves and crunchy flower shoots. Sow in rows 4 inches (10cm) apart, and thin plants in stages to 4–6 inches (10-15cm) apart. Cut the main stem just before the first flower opens and many more shoots will form. It can be grown all year in warmer parts but is also suitable for colder areas as a summer crop. 'Green Lance' is a good cultivar (45 days).

Hon Tsai Tai

Hon Tsai Tai, or purple-flowered choi sum, is an attractive plant with purple leaves and flower stalks and green leaves with a mild mustard flavor. It produces a lot of flower shoots, which you cut before the buds start to open (37 days).

Choy Sum

Choy sum, also known as edible rape or yu choy, grows fast in warm areas and can be sown in spring or fall—it may bolt in hot weather. Pick the first flower shoot at 5–6 inches (8–10cm) tall and more should follow. Use the young leaves and immature flower shoots in stir-fries (45 days).

Hon tsai tai has a mild flavor.

Some Non-Cabbage Asian Greens

Here are some other Asian greens worth considering for your vegetable plot:

- **AMARANTH** is a warm weather crop. The young leaves and shoots can be added to salads, while slightly older leaves and stalks are harvested regularly to cook like spinach. It is easy to grow from seeds but can be propagated from rooted nonflowering sideshoots. There are both green- and red-leaved forms (50 days).

- **GARLAND CHRYSANTHEMUM**, shingiku, or chop suey greens have a slightly bitter taste. Grow it in mild or slightly cold areas in the early spring and fall—it goes to seed rapidly in hot weather.

- **MITSUBA** is a Japanese crop with leaves similar to parsley and long aromatic stalks. It is a perennial but is usually grown as an annual, maturing in 50 days or less in milder areas. Sow it in spring and fall.

Kale & Collard

KALE IS ONE OF THE CROPS THAT THRIVES IN COOLER AREAS and is hardy enough to survive hard freezes. It is more than just a delicious vegetable—the plants themselves are attractive enough to merit a place in the flower border. Collard has similar growing requirements, but it is more tolerant of heat than kale.

 sow

Sow seeds thinly into furrows ½–¾ inch (1.5–2cm) deep and 18 inches (45cm) apart. Thin plants to 18 inches (45cm) apart. Or buy transplants.

- Sow or plant in early spring and again in midsummer in cooler areas. In hot-summer areas, plant kale only in late summer for a winter crop.

Varieties

- **COLLARD 'GEORGIA'** has blue-green leaves that can withstand light frosts. It is a popular cultivar in the South (55 days).

- **COLLARD 'VATES'** is a quick-growing cultivar that is good for keeping in the ground over the winter (55 days).

- **KALE 'BLACK KALE'** is an old Italian cultivar of kale that is also known as 'Black Tuscany', 'Laciniato,' or 'Toscano'. This decorative plant is worth growing for its striking blue-green, strap-shaped leaves. It is also hardy—and it tastes good, too (125 days).

- **KALE 'REDBOR'** is a dwarf modern version with attractive, feathery leaves (55 days).

- **KALE 'RED RUSSIAN'** is an older cultivar with red leaves (55 days).

- **KALE 'WINTERBOR'** is a compact feathery-leaved green type (60 days).

 grow

Provided the soil has plenty of organic matter, kale and collard are easy crops to grow.

- Make sure the soil doesn't dry out, and apply a little plant-starter fertilizer monthly to encourage rapid growth and tender leaves.

 harvest

Pick the younger leaves as required. Discard the older ones because they may be tough. Rinse thoroughly to dislodge aphids or other insects.

- Leave kale to produce flower stalks in the spring. You'll get a flush of tender young leaves and you can use the stalks like purple sprouting broccoli.

Kale leaves are best prepared to eat as soon as they are picked.

Kohlrabi

YOU CAN ENJOY KOHLRABI NOT ONLY AS AN INTERESTING CONVERSATION STARTER but also for its sweet crunchy "roots." These are, in fact, swollen stem bases above the ground with leaves attached. This is one of the faster-growing members of the cabbage family, and it is worth growing as a space filler between slower crops. Purple kohlrabi are particularly attractive and unusual plants, and they make a good choice for a flower border.

 SOW

Sow seeds for transplants about four weeks before the last spring frost date. Or sow seeds directly into the ground when the soil can be worked in spring and again four weeks before the first fall frost date. In warm areas, sow until temperatures drop below 40°F (4.5°C).

2 grow

Kohlrabi grows rapidly.

- Lack of water will make them woody and give them a hot flavor, so water regularly during hot weather.

- Keep weeds down by mulching or by regularly hoeing between the rows, but be careful to avoid catching the bottom of the stem with the blade.

- Cover with floating row covers to prevent all the pests that attack members of the cabbage family.

3 harvest

Cut kohlrabi just below soil level when the swollen stems reach 1½–2 inches (3–5cm) in diameter. Trim off the lower leaves so that just a tuft of small leaves remains.

- The stems should stay fresh in the refrigerator for up to two weeks, but they have the most flavor when used just after being picked.

- Kohlrabi has a mild, sweet flavor and can be grated raw in salad or cooked like turnips.

Varieties

- **'EARLY WHITE VIENNA'** is actually pale green, but with white flesh (55 days).

- **'KOLIBRI'** is a newer cultivar with purple skin (50 days).

- **'PURPLE DANUBE'** is an older cultivar with bright purple skin (65 days).

- **'PURPLE VIENNA'** also has bright purple skin (60 days).

Root Vegetables

MOST ROOT CROPS HIDE THEIR TREASURES UNDERGROUND UNTIL FALL. However, once the vegetables are ready for harvesting, no gardener can fail to be excited by the prospect of digging a row of potatoes or sweet potatoes, or easing a well-grown carrot or parsnip from the soil. Root vegetables are the mainstay of the winter pantry.

There are also summer roots, which grow fast and are pulled young and tender, such as baby carrots, radishes, turnips, and beets. Unlike their winter cousins, these are quick crops that provide a good return for space in a smaller garden. It is worthwhile trying to grow summer root vegetables in containers, too.

Not all roots are subterranean. Some, such as Florence fennel and beets, actually grow above ground. We've also included celery in this chapter—it's not strictly a root but is related to carrots and parsnips. It goes well with the other roots in the garden—and in the stockpot, too.

Beet

refreshingly sweet, colorful roots

BEETS ARE ONE OF THE EASIEST CROPS TO GROW. The large seeds are easy to handle, and if the soil is moist and rich, they grow rapidly and resist most pests and diseases. They are also one of those easy-going crops that will just keep growing until you are ready to harvest. You can pick baby beets smaller than golf balls to serve whole, or let them grow to tennis-ball size for roasting or slicing. And if you think all beets are red, you'll be surprised to learn that colors such as gold, pink, and white will add variety to your meal.

1 SOW

Beet seeds are not true seeds but are, instead, corky fruit containing up to four seeds. This explains why several seedlings come up together no matter how carefully you space them. You can thin excess seedlings later or leave them to grow in clumps—they will push themselves apart as they grow.

- Some gardeners soak the seeds overnight in warm water to remove natural chemicals in the seeds that inhibit germination. However, as long as the soil is moist enough, the seeds will germinate anyway.

- Start sowing seeds in early spring as soon as the soil is workable and there's no chance of a frost. The soil temperature should be at least 50°F (10°C). For a succession of baby beets, make several sowings at intervals throughout the summer and into early fall. However, in warm areas stop sowing 60 days before you normally have extreme hot weather. (Beets are a good winter crop in warm areas.)

- For winter-storage beets, sow once in summer.

- Make seed furrows 1 inch (2.5cm) deep and 12 inches (30cm) apart. Space the seeds 1 inch (2.5cm) apart for baby beets or 2 inches (5cm) apart for large roots.

- Water the seeds regularly until the seedlings begin to emerge.

Varieties

Avoid "monogerm" varieties, which have been bred with a single seed in each cluster. Although these are good for commercial growers, they provide no real advantage for the average gardener.

- **BABY BEETS** can be harvested from a round, red, quick-maturing cultivar, such as 'Red Ace' (53 days), 'Red Cloud' (60 days), or 'Detroit Dark Red' (60 days).

- **'ALBINA'** is a white cultivar; it does not stain and is sweet and tasty (55 days).

- **'BURPEES GOLDEN'** has golden skin and flesh instead of the usual red. It tastes the same but has the advantage of not staining (55 days).

- **'CHIOGGIA'** is an heirloom cultivar with a pink skin and alternate pink-and-white rings when cut in half. The color bleeds when cooked, leaving it a pale pink (54 days).

- **'CYLINDRA'** is a long-root red cultivar; grow it if you like sliced beets (60 days).

- **'FORONO'** is another good choice if you're looking for a long-root cultivar (55 days).

 To prevent leafminer grubs from burrowing inside the leaves, cover crops with

GROWING IN CONTAINERS

Beets grow well in containers, but choose baby beets instead of big roots for slicing. Space the seed clusters 1–2 inches (2.5–5cm) apart each way—this spacing will limit the size of the roots—and cover with ¾ inch (2cm) of potting mix. Don't worry if more than one seedling grows from each "seed" because they'll push apart as they grow. Water regularly, and feed with a plant-starter liquid fertilizer biweekly. Start to pull individual roots as they reach 1–1½ inches (2.5–3.5cm) across, and leave smaller ones to grow.

 ## grow

Beets are greedy feeders, so be generous with compost when you prepare the bed, or add some plant-starter fertilizer before sowing.

- Apart from keeping weeds down while they are getting established, beets need little attention, especially if you apply a mulch. The root grows mostly above soil level, so if you don't use a mulch, hoe carefully to remove weeds.

- Beets shouldn't need watering unless the soil becomes dry at depth. If you don't water during periods of drought, the beets may split if heavy rain follows the dry spell.

A bulbous beet appears above ground.

③ harvest

You can start picking the young leaves to use in salads about four weeks after sowing the seeds, or prepare the older leaves in the same way that you would prepare spinach.

- You can start to harvest baby beets as soon as they reach 1–1½ inches (2.5–3.5cm) in diameter (these are suitable for pickling). Twist off the foliage and leave the thin taproot intact—this will help prevent the color from bleeding excessively when they are cooked. Don't peel the roots until after cooking for the same reason. When boiled and cooled, the skins will rub off easily.

- Leave later sowings to reach a good size—at least 3 inches (7.5cm) across—for use as a normal vegetable. Treat like the younger beets, twisting off the leaves and leaving the taproot attached.

- In mild winter areas, you can leave the beets in the garden until you need them. To extend the fall harvest, cover the rows with leaves or straw, or lift the crop and store the roots in boxes of moist sand. (See "Other Storage Strategies," pages 68–69.)

- For short-term storage, you can refrigerate beets for up to three weeks if you keep them in a plastic bag. The leaves will stay fresh in the refrigerator in a plastic bag for up to ten days.

FAQ

Q The leaves on my beet plants have transparent patches. Is this a disease?

A No, it's caused by leafminer grubs burrowing inside the leaves. They will not harm the roots, but severe attacks may reduce the plant's yields. Make sure you remove any severely affected leaves.

Q What is causing the brown spots on the leaves?

A This is cercospora leaf spot. The developed roots are still edible, but pick and destroy any diseased leaves.

floating row covers.

Carrot

crunchy, sweet, and nutritious

CARROTS ARE A TROUBLE-FREE BACKYARD CROP, as long as the soil conditions are right. The soil needs to be light (add compost if you have heavy soil), loose, deeply dug to 12 inches (30cm), and free of stones. For a gourmet treat, you can pull carrots as soon as the roots are as thick as a pencil, leave them a little longer for fresh full-size carrots, or keep them in the ground through fall. If you have a small space, harvest them young for the sweetest baby carrots you'll ever taste.

SOW

For fresh carrots, choose an "early" variety and make several sowings at intervals from very early spring (under floating row covers in cold areas) until early fall. For winter storage carrots, choose a "full-size" variety and make one sowing in early summer.

- Sow the seeds into the soil. Make a seed furrow ½ inch (1cm) deep. If the soil is dry, water the furrow; let it drain.

- Space rows 12 inches (30cm) apart. Scatter the seeds thinly to avoid having to thin out seedlings later. As a guide, aim for a seed every ½ inch (1cm).

- Carrot seeds are available as seed tape—thin paper tape with carrot seeds spaced at intervals. This is a really easy way to sow carrots. Simply make a seed furrow as above; lay down the tape; and cover with soil. Carrot seeds are also available as pelleted seeds—these are coated with a clay compound to make them easier to handle.

Varieties

You can harvest early carrot varieties in as little as 50 days after the seeds have been sown. They are best eaten when freshly harvested and make a good choice for growing in containers. Early varieties include:

- **AMSTERDAM** types, which grow rapidly to finger size; 'Minicor' (55 days) is typical.

- **CHANTENAY** types, such as 'Chantenay Red Cored' (70 days), are short and broad shouldered, better for shallow soils.

- **NANTES** types, such as 'Nantes Half-Long' (70 days) and 'Touchon' (65 days), produce slim, blunt-ended roots up to 6 inches (15cm) long. They can be left to grow as a full-size crop.

- **ROUND OR PARIS MARKET** carrots are a good choice if your soil is shallow or stony. 'Parmex' (50 days) and 'Thumbelina' (60 days) are typical cultivars.

Full-size carrots are slower growing but produce a higher yield by fall. These include:

- **DANVERS**, a type of large, broad-shouldered carrot, of which 'Danvers Half-Long' (75 days) is typical.

- **IMPERATOR** types have narrow pointed roots up to 10 inches (25cm) long. Cultivars include 'Canada Gold' (75 days).

- **UNUSUALLY COLORED** varieties include 'White Satin', with sweet white roots (65 days); 'Purple Haze', with purple skins and orange flesh (70 days); and 'Rainbow', a mix of white, pale yellow, and pale orange

GROWING IN CONTAINERS

Carrots do remarkably well in containers. Choose one at least 12 inches (30cm) deep to avoid restricting the taproots. Sow seeds thinly to avoid thinning later and cover with ½ inch (1cm) of potting mix. Ideally, the seedlings should be about 1 inch (2cm) apart each way, but don't worry—the roots will push apart as they grow. Choose a short, slim, early variety. Although the round ones will be okay in containers, you'll get more carrots with a thin, pointed variety. Keep the potting mix just moist, not wet, and harvest individual roots when they reach ½ inch (1cm) across the top.

2 grow

Keep weeds down until the carrot plants are well established by hoeing carefully between the rows—wait until the rows are clearly visible. You may have to weed the rows by hand until the carrots are bigger.

- Thin the seedlings to about 1 inch (2.5cm) apart. Wait until they are large enough to handle and avoid disturbing the remaining plants or you risk attracting carrot rust flies, which are attracted by their scent. One method is to snip off the tops with scissors.

- Water deeply once a week to keep the soil evenly moist at a good depth, which will encourage deep rooting. (Frequent watering encourages short, whiskery roots.)

Start harvesting carrots when they are the thickness of a pencil.

3 harvest

You can start pulling roots as soon as the tops of the roots reach ½ inch (1cm) across. Either carefully pull up the larger roots, leaving the rest to grow, or dig sections of a row together. Use a garden fork to loosen the soil and avoid breaking longer roots.

- If you don't use the carrots immediately, cut off the tops or the roots will wilt. They should keep for day or two in a refrigerator.

- The best way to store carrots is to leave them in the ground. If temperatures are expected to drop below freezing, mulch with straw or leaves to extend the season.

FAQ

Q Hardly any of my earliest sowings have come up. Can you tell me why not?

A Carrot seeds are generally slow to germinate, especially if the soil is cold. Wait until the soil temperature reaches 41°F (5°C) and sow the earliest crop at ¼ inch (6mm) deep.

Q Why are my carrots full of tunnels?

A They've been attacked by grubs of the carrot rust fly. These are attracted to the carrot smell when you thin or harvest carrots. The only sure way to prevent them is to cover the crop with floating row covers and thin or harvest in the evening when the flies are not active.

Q Is it safe to eat carrots with green tops?

A The tops of carrots go green if exposed to the light. Unlike potatoes, they are not toxic, but can taste bitter. Cut off the green top and eat the rest.

Celery

LIKE ONION, CELERY IS AN ESSENTIAL INGREDIENT FOR THE COOK. It is the basis of a good vegetable stock, and it is also good raw in a salad. It thrives in cool, damp conditions and needs a long growing period to produce its tasty, crunchy stems.

 SOW

Buy transplants, or raise your own from seeds.

- Soak the seeds in a compost tea for six hours before sowing into pots eight weeks before the last expected spring frost. The seeds need light to germinate—sow on the surface of the potting mix and cover very thinly. Regularly mist with water to keep the soil moist.Keep at 65°F (18°C) until germination occurs; then slowly harden off the seedlings until ready to plant outdoors.

 **grow**

Prepare the bed by digging in plenty of garden compost or well-rotted organic matter to help retain moisture.

- Plant outdoors when average daytime temperatures exceed 55°F (13°C). Space about 9 inches (23cm) apart each way in blocks instead of rows.

- Mulch around the plants with straw or organic matter to keep the soil cool and retain moisture.

- Water regularly to keep the soil consistently moist.

- Cover with floating row covers to prevent attack by carrot rust flies and other insect pests.

- Self-blanching varieties will mature more quickly and require less work than other varieties, which have to be blanched by covering the bottom of the plant with cardboard or newspaper collars or by growing in trenches like leeks. (See "Leek," pages 108–109.) Grow self-blanching types in blocks so they shade each other.

- Feed the plants weekly with a fish emulsion to keep them growing strongly.

Blanch some varieties of celery by placing a collar around the stems.

FAQ

Q What's causing the strange patterns in the leaves?

A Celery leafminers burrow between the leaf surfaces, leaving a pattern of tunnels. Remove severely affected leaves. Covering crops with floating row covers should prevent the insects from laying eggs.

Q Why is my celery starting to produce tall shoots?

A Celery is prone to bolting, or producing flower shoots early, in less than ideal conditions, such as dry soil or temperatures below 50°F (10°C).

 If your celery is being eaten by slugs, use an organic slug barrier to deter them.

Varieties

Self-blanching varieties are popular because they require much less work.

- **'GOLDEN SELF-BLANCHING'**, a compact variety with yellow stalks, is a good example of a self-blanching variety (115 days).

- **'TANGO'** is a fast-maturing green cultivar (85 days).

- **'UTAH 52-70'** is a green cultivar with a mild flavor (105 days).

3 harvest

You can cut off individual stalks from the outside of the plant as soon as they are large enough for your needs, or wait and dig up the whole plant.

- Use a sharp knife to cut a stalk—or the entire plant—just above the soil surface.

- Because celery is very sensitive to cold, harvest the plants before the first hard frost in the fall.

- You can store celery in the refrigerator in a plastic bag for a couple of weeks.

Celeriac

a taste like celery, with a hint of nuttiness

THE FLESHY ROOT OF CELERIAC is a good alternative to celery, its close relative.

1 sow

Celeriac needs a long season of 110 days or more from sowing, so start with transplants or raise your own.

- Sow seeds into small pots before the last spring frost. Cover the seeds lightly—they need light to germinate. Harden off the seedlings gradually and plant outdoors when 2–3 inches (5–8cm) tall. In warm areas, you can start celeriac in summer for a winter crop.

Celeriac's large knobby root has a distinctive celery flavor.

2 grow

Work plenty of organic matter into the soil before planting transplants to help retain moisture. Give plants plenty of room, about 12 inches (30cm) each way.

- Keep the soil uniformly moist by regularly soaking the soil to a good depth. Keep weeds down with regular hoeing, being careful not to nick the roots with the blade. In hot weather, keep the soil cool and moist by mulching, which will also keep weeds down.

3 harvest

Start to dig roots when 4 or 5 inches (10–13cm) across.

- You can store the roots by leaving them in the ground until needed. Cover them with straw to protect them from frost.

- In late fall, before the soil freezes, lift the roots; pull off all the leaves except the innermost tuft to prevent rotting; and store in boxes of barely moist sand.

Parsnip

A wintertime treat

PARSNIPS ARE SLOW-GROWING CROPS. Underground, the white roots are waiting for winter, when they really come into their own. Although you can harvest young tender roots earlier, this is one crop to leave until after the first fall frosts. If you like unusual root crops, there are some rarely grown alternatives to savor, such as salsify, scorzonera, and Hamburg parsley.

 sow

Parsnip seeds are attached to a flat membrane and can blow around. Their viability can be low. As a precaution, sow several seeds together.

- Dig and loosen the soil to at least 18 inches (45cm) if you want long, straight roots. Sow once in late spring when the soil is warm and moist.

- Make furrows ½ inch (1cm) deep and 12 inches (30cm) apart, and water the bottom if the soil is dry.

- Sow seeds 1 inch (2.5cm) apart. When the seedlings are 4–6 inches (10–15cm) tall, thin to 4 inches (10cm) apart.

- Because the seedlings can be slow to appear, an old-timers' trick is to sow radish seeds in the same furrow. These will appear quickly, marking the row so you don't accidentally hoe it. You can harvest the radishes long before the parsnips need the space.

Varieties

- **'ANDOVER'** is an older, canker-resistant cultivar with slender roots (120 days).

- **'GLADIATOR'** is a modern cultivar, resistant to canker (110 days).

- **'HARRIS MODEL'** is a well-established, medium-sized cultivar (120 days).

- **'JAVELIN'** is a modern canker-resistant cultivar, good as a baby vegetable (110 days).

 grow

In the early stages, hoe regularly between the rows to keep weeds down, but be careful to avoid damaging the seedlings.

- When the seedlings reach a few inches tall, apply a mulch of chopped leaves to suppress weeds and conserve water.

- Provided the soil is moist before sowing, they should not need additional watering. However, do not let the soil dry out at depth; drought followed by rain will cause the roots to split.

- Apply a general fertilizer as a side-dressing or spray with compost tea in midsummer.

Keep your parsnips in the ground until the first fall frost.

③ harvest

The flavor improves after a frost. The best way to store the crop is by leaving them in the garden. A thick mulch will extend the harvest season in cold regions.

- Dig the roots as they are needed with a garden fork.

- Leave the final cooking preparations until the last minute; the internal tissues will discolor when exposed to the air.

Unusual Roots

All three of these root crops are grown in the same way as parsnip and can also be left in the garden until needed.

- **HAMBURG PARSLEY** is a type of parsley bred for its parsniplike roots. You can use the leaves, but they are coarser than normal parsley. Roast the roots like those of parsnips (90 days).

- **SALSIFY** is a biennial, so it will flower in the second year. It has grasslike leaves, and the roots are long and thin and are said to taste like oyster. You can boil the roots in vegetable stock and roast the larger ones (100 days).

- **SCORZONERA** is a perennial, so if the roots aren't large enough after a year, you can let them grow for a second year. It has wider leaves and long, thin, black-skinned roots. The flesh discolors easily, so scorzonera is best cooked whole and peeled later (120 days).

Salsify has long, thin roots.

Use a garden fork to carefully lift parsnips out of the ground.

FAQ

Q What is causing the purple fungus that has appeared on my parsnips?

A This is parsnip canker, which is worse in wet conditions. Grow parsnips on a well-drained raised bed and practice crop rotation. (See "Crop Rotation," pages 22–23.) Choose a canker-resistant culitvar.

Q Why are my parsnip roots split and forked?

A Either the soil is compacted or stony, or you used fresh manure when preparing the bed. One solution is to dig a trench 18 inches (45cm) deep and fill with a mixture of well-rotted organic matter and stone-free soil; then make your seed furrow.

Potato

the great staple of the vegetable garden

POTATOES REQUIRE PLENTY OF SPACE, but few vegetables will reward you with such a prolific crop at the end of the season. Apart from the late-season varieties, which store right through winter, there are the fast-growing earlies, which can be ready to harvest after only a couple of months. Later cropping, but also good fresh out of the ground, are the waxy salad and the gourmet fingerling types. If you have limited garden space, try growing potatoes in containers—you'll be surprised at how easy and rewarding they are.

 SOW

Potatoes are not grown from seeds, but from "seed potatoes"—pieces of tuber each with a couple of buds, or "eyes." Buy seed potatoes from a garden center or mail-order seed company. Don't be tempted to try to grow potato plants from potatoes purchased from the supermarket. They may carry disease or be treated with chemicals to stop them from sprouting.

- Start by preparing a trench 6–8 inches (15–20cm) deep and the width of a spade. In light soil, make the trench 12 inches (30cm) deep and half fill with compost to help retain moisture. For heavy or poorly drained soil, grow potatoes in raised beds.

- Space the rows 30 inches (75cm) apart for mid- and late-season crops and 18 inches (45cm) for early-season crops.

- You can plant small seed potatoes whole or cut larger ones into sections, making sure that each section has two or three eyes (buds). Let the cut seed potatoes "cure" in a warm place for a few hours to two days.

- Plant the cured tubers or pieces about three weeks before the last expected spring frost.

- Lay the seed tubers at 12-inch (30-cm) intervals along the bottom of the trench and fill with soil.

The eyes of the seed potatoes will eventually sprout.

Varieties

- **EARLY-SEASON** cultivars include 'Caribe', which has purple skin and white flesh (70–90 days); 'Red Norland', which is very early with red skin and white flesh (90–100 days); 'Red Pontiac', an all-purpose variety with bright red skin and white flesh; and 'Yukon Gold', an early to mid-season variety with yellow skin and flesh (70–90 days).

- **MID- AND LATE-SEASON** types are numerous. Try 'Kennebec', a versatile yellow-fleshed cultivar that tastes good and stores well (100–110 days).

- **FINGERLINGS** are popular types with long, thin tubers, firm waxy flesh, and an unsurpassed flavor. 'Peanut Fingerling' has russet skin and firm, yellow, nutty flesh (105–135 days); 'Rose Finn Apple' has long, knobbly, pink tubers with firm, waxy flesh (105–135 days); and 'Russian Banana' is a gourmet variety with yellow skin and flesh (105–135 days).

- **UNUSUAL** varieties to try include 'All Blue', with blue skin and blue-and-white flesh (110–135 days), and 'All Red', with red skin and pink flesh (70–90 days).

GROWING IN CONTAINERS

You'll need a large container with a capacity of at least 2 gallons (7.5L), preferably more, half filled with a rich potting mix. Bury a sprouted tuber of an early or salad variety into the soil. As the tops grow, keep covering them with layers of potting mix until you reach the top of the container. Water regularly. If you used a rich potting mix, additional feeding will not be necessary. When the tops start to yellow and die off, usually after about two months for an early variety, you can start harvesting the potatoes. Either empty the pot and harvest the whole crop, or push your hand into the container and feel for tubers the size of an egg or larger, leaving any tiny ones to continue growing.

SIR WALTER RALEIGH, THE SIXTEENTH-CENTURY NAVIGATOR, WAS ONE OF FEW EUROPEANS AT THE TIME TO GROW POTATOES. HE HELPED TO SPREAD THE POPULARITY OF THE VEGETABLE.

Fingerling potatoes are one of many interesting varieties available.

grow

Potatoes will grow perfectly well on flat ground; however, because the tubers form near the surface of the soil, a proportion of them are often pushed out of the soil and, if exposed to light, they will turn green. Areas on potatoes that are green will become slightly toxic. Fortunately, the technique of "hilling," or piling up the soil in stages will prevent this. (See "Hill Sowing," page 32.) As a bonus, burying the bottom of the plant will encourage more tubers to form.

- A few weeks after planting the seed potatoes, shoots should emerge from the soil; protect these from any risk of frost with floating row covers.

- When the shoots reach 4–5 inches (10–12cm) tall, start to pile up the soil by drawing it around the bottom of the plants to form hills. Keep doing this as the plants grow until the hills are 12 inches (30cm) high.

- Water early varieties regularly throughout their growth. However, do not water late-season types until the flowers start to appear—tubers will be forming underground and plentiful water at this stage will increase the yield.

grow: heavy soil

If you have heavy and wet soil that is slow to warm up, instead of digging trenches simply put the tubers on the soil surface; then cover them with a layer of mulch. Straw or composted leaves are ideal.

- Make the first layer of mulch 4–6 inches (7.5–10cm) deep. Instead of hilling the soil, when the shoots are tall enough, add another layer of mulch.

- The mulch can make an ideal cover for slugs in the Pacific Northwest, so you'll need to make sure you provide slug protection if you live in the region.

Hilling the soil will prevent the tubers from turning green.

Dig up all the potatoes at once, or pull up a few at a time.

3 harvest

Early-season varieties are ready to harvest as soon as the plants start to flower, about 60 days after planting. If you aren't sure, try lifting a test plant. If the tubers are too small, leave the plant for another week before digging up any more. Those first "new" potatoes are such a treat, it's worth digging a few plants for a meal.

- An alternative method, which leaves the undersize tubers to continue growing, is to plunge your hand into the hills and feel for egg-size tubers. Remove only one or two tubers from each plant. When you return to the plants for another harvest, the tubers will be larger.

- Mid-season varieties are normally ready to harvest in about 80 days, and you can harvest them fresh—before the skins begin to become tough—or let them mature. When the plant leaves start to die down, the skins on the tubers will harden. Once this happens, you can dig up and store these potatoes until the end of December.

- Late-season varieties are ready for harvesting after about 90 days, usually two weeks after the tops die down, as long as there's no threat of frost. Use a fork to loosen the soil; then remove the tubers with your hands to avoid skewering them with the fork. Choose a dry fall day, and lay out the tubers to dry for a few hours.

- At this point reject any damaged tubers for storing; they're fine to use immediately. Spread out the remainder in a cool, dark place for about a week to cure them. Then store the tubers in paper or burlap sacks in a cool, dark place for use through winter.

After harvesting, let potatoes air dry for a few hours.

FAQ

Q My potatoes are dying from some type of disease. Can you tell me what is it?

A Late blight can attack potatoes in areas that have humid weather with warm days and cool nights. The leaves and stems will develop brown blotches, and this disease can spread rapidly through a crop. The only recourse is to cut off the top growth to prevent the fungus from washing down to the tubers. After the harvest, destroy all soft or rotting tubers regularly. In the future, plant only certified disease-free seed potatoes. You can spray a copper-based fungicide to help prevent an attack.

Q Why have some of the plant's leaves turned yellow and crinkled?

A Potatoes can be afflicted by several viruses, which are spread by aphids or infected seed tubers. Destroy any affected plants. Always buy certified disease-free seed potatoes and cover the crops with floating row covers to keep aphids off.

Q Why are my potatoes suddenly wilting?

A The most likely cause is root nematodes. These destroy the roots so the plant cannot draw up sufficient water in hot weather. If you examine the roots, you'll notice small round lumps. Look for resistant varieties and practice crop rotation to limit the damage. (See "Crop Rotation," pages 22–23.)

Q What is making holes in the leaves?

A The most likely culprit is the Colorado potato beetle and their dark orange grubs. Handpick or crush any you see, or if there are too many, spray with an insecticide containing pyrethrum.

Radish

Colorful roots with a zesty flavor

RADISHES ARE SO QUICK AND EASY TO GROW that you can enjoy several crops through the year. Because they take up little space, radishes are the perfect fill-in crop. (See "Intercropping," pages 40–41.) You can fit them between large or slower-growing vegetables, or use them to fill space that won't be occupied for the four weeks or so that it takes them to grow. It's not just the roots that add a hot crunch to salads—the pods are edible, too.

 ## SOW

Sow small amounts every 10 to 14 days from early spring, as soon as the soil can be cultivated, until fall. In hot-summer areas, stop sowing during the summer, but continue sowing right through winter.

- Loosen the soil to make a seedbed and sow into furrows ½ inch (1cm) deep and 6 inches apart. As a fill-in crop, sow midway between adjacent longer-term crops.

- Sow the seeds thinly and when the seedlings appear, usually in less than a week, thin them to about 1 inch (2.5cm) apart.

Varieties

- **LONG-ROOT** cultivars include 'French Breakfast', which is a red type with a white tip (25 days), and 'White Icicle', which is an all-white cultivar (30 days).

- **ROUND, RED** varieties include 'Cherry Belle' (23 days) and 'Sparkler' (25 days).

- **'EASTER EGG'** is a round mixture of different colors, including violet and pink (28 days).

- **'MUNCHEN BIER'** is the cultivar to grow if you want to try radish pods.

 ### GROWING IN CONTAINERS

Summer radishes are also quick container crops. Sow thinly, aiming for a seed every 1 inch (2.5cm) or so—they'll push apart as they grow. Because they are light feeders, use them to occupy containers before tender crops or after greedier crops have finished.

 ## grow

Summer radishes should grow quickly and without interruption, so make sure you keep the soil moist at all times. Radishes do not require much attention and will not need feeding.

- Apply a thin mulch to help retain moisture; it will also help to suppress weeds.

grow: radish pods

If left too long, radishes will bolt, producing huge sprays of flowers followed by shiny, pointed green pods. If this happens to your plants, collect the young pods and eat them—they are crunchy and slightly hot.

 Grow radishes with cabbage crops to lure flea beetles away from the leafy vegetables.

③ harvest

Start pulling individual roots when they reach 1 inch (2.5cm) in diameter, leaving the remainder to continue growing. Alternatively, pull up as bunches and discard the undersize roots.

- Once they reach 2 inches (5cm), they may start to become tough and pithy—move on to the next batch.

- Use right away or refrigerate for a day or two.

FAQ

Q Why are my radish leaves full of holes?

A Radishes are members of the cabbage family, so they are attacked by the flea beetle, especially during the hotter months. This is not a big problem because you can simply discard the leaves.

Winter radish

large roots, either hot or mild

ALSO KNOWN AS DAIKON OR MOOLI, the winter radish produces large roots.

① sow

Sow thinly in midsummer so the harvest coincides with the first fall frost. Thin to 6 inches (15cm) apart in rows 10 inches (25cm) apart.

② grow

Apart from the occasional weeding and watering, they require little attention.

Varieties

- **'APRIL CROSS'** is a long, pointed, all-white cultivar with a mild flavor (65 days).

- **'BLACK SPANISH ROUND'** is a hot-flavored cultivar with black skin and white flesh (60 days).

- **'SUMMER CROSS'** is another long, pointed type with a mild flavor (45 days).

③ harvest

You can pull the roots anytime and use them fresh as summer radishes. They will store better if you leave them to develop to their full size and color. Leave in the garden until needed, but dig before the soil freezes.

- Hot types have a better flavor when cooked. Milder types are best raw or grated into salads and can be bland when cooked. You can dice larger roots and use inplace of turnips.

The winter radish is also known as daikon radish.

Sweet potato

a hot-weather producer of sweet roots

UNLIKE POTATOES, SWEET POTATOES THRIVE IN HOT WEATHER. They are normally a crop for the southern states, where they should get the minimum of 100 warm days and nights that they need. Because the slightest frost will kill the vines, it is risky to attempt to grow them in colder areas. However, if you pick a quick-yielding variety, they are still well worth a try. Nutrient-packed sweet potatoes are often confused with yams, but yams are from Africa and Asia, while sweet potatoes are an American native.

 SOW

Sweet potatoes are grown from rooted cuttings known as slips. Buy certified disease-free slips from a nursery or mail-order supplier, or raise your own slips from saved tubers. Slips from a mail-order supplier may be wilted or seem dead, but they will recover when planted.

- Plant the slips deeply, so the first leaves are level with the ground.

- For the best results, make sure you plant the slips in loose, stone-free soil with little or no fertilizer.

SWEET POTATOES WERE AN IMPORTANT SOURCE OF NUTRITIOUS FOOD FOR THE FIRST AMERICAN COLONISTS, AS WELL AS FOR SOLDIERS DURING THE REVOLUTIONARY WAR.

SOW: growing your own slips

Use your own tubers or those from a friend only if you know they are free of disease. Do not use store-bought sweet potatoes—these are treated to prevent growth.

- Take a medium-size, healthy tuber and put it in a container so the bottom third is immersed in water. Put it in a warm, sunny place to sprout. When the sprouts are 6 inches (15cm) long, pull them off and place in water or damp sand until roots grow.

- Harden off these slips before planting them outside. In colder parts, first repot them into small pots containing seed-starting mix; then harden off before planting them outdoors.

Varieties

- **'BEAUREGARD'** is a high-yielding cultivar with red skin and light orange flesh; it is suitable for most areas with long growing seasons (105 days).

- **'GEORGIA JET'** also has red skin and orange flesh; this cultivar is also suitable for cooler areas (90 days).

- **'VARDAMAN'** has a golden skin, orange flesh, and shorter vines; it is a good choice for smaller gardens or containers (110 days).

Use garden wire or twine to help keep vines off the ground.

2 grow

Mound up the soil until about 8 inches (20cm) high, with 3 feet (90cm) between rows, and plant the slips about 18 inches (45cm) apart.

- In cooler regions, grow sweet potatoes in raised beds. Warm the soil by covering it with black plastic; then plant the slips through cross-shaped slits. Cover with floating row covers early and late in the season to protect the crop from frost and prolong the season.

- Once established, sweet potatoes do not need to be fed or watered.

- As the temperature increases, the vines will grow rampantly. Lift the vines off the ground to prevent them from rooting as they grow. This concentrates the plants' energy back to the initial roots, where the tubers will form.

3 harvest

Let the plants die down; the first frost will kill the tops. Dig the tubers. Cure them by sitting them in the sun for a day; then in a warm, humid place for 10 to 14 days. Wrap each tuber in newspaper, or place the tubers on racks, and keep in a cool, dry place for up to five months.

When digging up the tubers, avoid piercing the skin with your fork.

FAQ

Q What has been burrowing into my sweet potatoes?

A If you live in the South, sweet potato weevils can burrow into the tubers. Cleaning up crop debris and following a crop rotation plan will help reduce damage. (See "Crop Rotation," pages 22–23.)

Q What is nibbling my sweet potato leaves?

A Flea beetles are the most likely culprits. The best preventive measure is to cover the crop with a floating row cover.

Turnip

white roots and succulent greens

TURNIPS ARE SO QUICK-GROWING THEY MAKE A USEFUL FILL-IN CROP among the more slow-growing members of the cabbage family. Apart from the sweet, slightly hot-flavored roots, they provide valuable greens in spring and fall.

 sow

Turnips are generally hardy, so you can start sowing them a few weeks before the last frost date. They take only eight weeks, or even less, to produce usable roots; make several sowings through the season.

- In warm regions, stop sowing before the hottest part of the year, but for a fall crop start sowing again from late summer through fall.

- Turnips benefit from a moist, fertile soil, so work in an inch (2.5cm) of well-rotted organic matter or a generous amount of a plant-starter fertilizer before sowing.

- Make seed furrows ¾ inch (1.5cm) deep and 6 inches (15cm) apart. Sow thinly and water well.

- Thin the seedlings to 4 inches (10cm) for roots or 1½ inches (3cm) for turnip leaves.

2 grow

Turnips should grow rapidly. However, lack of water will make the turnips hot and woody. Water them regularly during dry spells. Give a thorough soaking once a week instead of just wetting the surface.

- Keep weeds down by applying a mulch, which will also help retain moisture. Otherwise, regularly hoe between the rows, but avoid damaging the roots with the blade.

- Like their leafy relative the cabbage, turnips are susceptible to insect pests—flea beetle, cabbage root maggots, and cabbage caterpillars. Covering with floating row covers before the seedlings appear should keep all these pests away.

Varieties

- **'HAKUREI'** is very fast, has flattened white roots, and is a good choice for greens (38 days).

- **'PURPLE TOP WHITE'** is a standard bicolored cultivar (55 days).

- **'TOKYO CROSS'** is a fast-growing all-white globe, good for baby roots (40 days).

3 harvest

Lift turnips when they reach 2 inches (5cm) as baby roots or let them grow to 4 inches (10cm) across. Trim off the leaves. The roots will stay fresh in the refrigerator for up to two weeks but are tastier when just picked.

- Turnip has a hot flavor raw, but is milder when cooked.

- Cut greens for cooking when plants are 6 inches (15cm) high. Leave a stump 1 inch (2.5cm) high, and more leaves will grow. Keep cutting until the plants begin to seed.

FAQ

Q Why are there tunnels in my turnips?

A These tunnels were probably made by cabbage root maggots, which appear early in the season. Protect your plants with a floating row cover, or plant in late spring or midsummer.

Rutabaga

a cool-weather crop

A WINTER STAPLE, rutabaga is good as a hearty roasted vegetable or in stews.

 **SOW**

Sow in midsummer for a fall harvest. Rutabaga takes as long as four months to grow, so it will be in the garden for a long time. Sow thinly into furrows 1 inch (2cm) deep and 15 inches (38cm) apart. Thin the seedlings in stages to 9 inches (23cm) apart.

Varieties

- 'AMERICAN PURPLE TOP' is a standard cultivar with a purple top and yellow flesh (100 days).

2 grow

Rutabaga needs little attention, apart from occasional weeding and watering to prevent the soil from drying out completely deep down.

3 harvest

You can leave rutabaga in the garden until needed. In areas with hard freezes, cover rows with deep mulch or lift the roots and store them in a root cellar or in boxes of barely damp sand.

Florence fennel

a bulb with a mild licorice flavor

THOUGH NOT A ROOT, FLORENCE FENNEL forms a swollen stem base that is eaten as a vegetable.

 **SOW**

Florence fennel needs a cool but frost-free period of about 100 days. Very hot or cold weather or lack of water will make it bolt or produce tough stringy bulbs.

- In areas with a short summer, start seeds in small pots in a warm place. Harden off, and plant out when there's no chance of a late frost. In warmer areas, you can sow seeds directly in spring or summer. In the hottest areas, sow in midsummer for a fall harvest. Space plants about 12 inches (30cm) apart.

 **grow**

Keep seeds and seedlings moist. Water regularly to keep the soil moist and ensure uninterrupted growth. Feed occasionally in summer with fish emulsion.

3 harvest

You can harvest the bulbs when they are 3–5 inches (7.5–12.5cm) across. Cut the aboveground bulb from its roots; trim off the leaf stalks; and use immediately.

10

Heat-Loving Vegetables

TOMATOES BELONG TO A LARGE, DIVERSE FAMILY that provides several of our favorite edible plants, including potatoes. Tomatoes are deservedly the number-one garden crop. There are tomato cultivars available that will bear successfully even in the coldest areas, but other members of the family, such as eggplant and peppers, need heat to flourish. Regardless, all the vegetables in this chapter are prime candidates for containers and will reward you with tasty crops all summer—though some of them will need a long, hot summer to grow.

If you like Mexican cuisine, try the tomato's less well-known relative, the tomatillo, and its sweeter version, the ground cherry (or cape gooseberry). We've also included okra, which hails from Africa. It appreciates the same growing conditions as peppers and eggplant, so if you can grow these vegetables, okra is worth a try.

If you are a beginner, you can simply purchase transplants from a garden center. However, all of the plants in this chapter are easy to grow from seeds. For the enthusiast, saving seeds for next year is easy. (See "Sow: Saving Seeds," page 162.)

Eggplant

beautiful in the garden, delicious on the plate

ALTHOUGH THE NAME "EGGPLANT" DERIVES FROM TYPES that bear white, egg-shaped fruit, the most familiar varieties are dark purple and the size of ostrich eggs. You can grow eggplant varieties similar to those commonly available in the supermarket, but why confine yourself to purple when there are so many interesting colors from which to choose? Unlike many other vegetable plants, eggplant is attractive enough for a flower border or prominent container planting. Eggplant will grow in most hardiness zones, but these are heat-loving plants that can be temperamental in the North. Choose short-season varieties to grow in these areas.

SOW

Unless you want a lot of plants of the same variety, buy young plants from your garden center in late spring. They are not difficult to start from seeds, but they need plenty of heat to start them off.

- To raise eggplant from seeds, start them in divided seed-starting trays eight weeks before the last frost date. Keep them as warm as possible (80°F/27°C is ideal), using a warming mat to provide bottom heat if necessary.

- Wait until the soil reaches 70°F (21°C) before planting transplants outside. Try not to disturb the root ball and space them 24 inches (60cm) apart each way. In areas with a longer growing season, plant a second crop about four months before the first frost.

Eggplant is available in a variety of shapes and colors.

Varieties

Standard cultivars have the familiar large, slightly bulbous, shiny black fruit found in the supermarket. Choose from 'Black Beauty', a classic large, dark purple eggplant (80 days); 'Dusky', a good choice for the North (63 days); and 'Purple Rain', which has light purple fruit, flecked with cream.

- **'FAIRY TALE'**, a modern, less spiny variety, produces bunches of small elongated fruit up to 4 inches (10cm) in length, beautifully striped white and purple; good for containers (65 days).

- **'ICHIBAN'** is an Asian type with elongated, dark purple fruit (70 days).

- **'KERMIT'** has small, mottled, round green-and-white fruit, about 2 inches (5cm) across—a real conversation piece in a container (60 days).

- **'ROSA BIANCA'** is an Italian heirloom with white-and-mauve striped fruit, best for warm areas (75 days).

- **'SNOWY'** has medium-size, elongated, pure white fruit (60 days).

GROWING IN CONTAINERS

The eggplant is a great container plant, attractive enough to hold its own with ornamental plants—but with the bonus of tasty fruit, too. In a small container about 12 inches (30cm) in diameter, they make neat bushes that are covered in soft leaves and bright yellow flowers. Choose a modern, less spiny variety with plenty of small fruit—'Fairy Tale' is one of the best. Feed eggplant regularly with a tomato fertilizer.

 2 grow

Eggplant prefers plenty of heat, so give it a sheltered position, away from wind, in full sun in cooler areas. It also likes a rich but well-drained soil that warms up quickly in spring.

- In cooler areas, use raised beds, floating row covers, or plastic sheets to increase the soil temperature. Covering the plants with floating row covers will also keep pests away.

- Farther south, they will thrive in the heat and grow into large bushy plants. Staking or other methods may be necessary to keep the fruit off the soil.

- Water regularly, trying to keep the leaves dry—a drip irrigation system is a good investment here. Mulch around the plants with organic matter when the soil is warm to retain moisture and keep weeds down.

- Apply a high-potassium fertilizer to keep the plants growing strongly and encourage the crop to grow rather than the leaves.

 3 harvest

Cut an eggplant when it reaches about half its full size. It will be sweet and tender and this will encourage the plant to keep producing. Don't let the fruit reach full size, or it will become tough and seedy.

- Choose an eggplant with shiny skin; if the skin is dull, the fruit may be bitter.

Use upturned pots to keep the fruit raised off the ground.

FAQ

Q Why are the leaves on my eggplant turning yellow?

A Examine the undersides with a magnifying lens—the tiny creatures you'll likely see are spider mites, which suck sap. Spray the plants with a strong stream of water from a hose.

Q What's eating the leaves?

A Colorado potato beetle can be as much of a nuisance on eggplant as on potatoes. Handpick the beetles and grubs and squash the eggs; or spray with an organic insecticide if severe. Floating row covers should keep them off the plants.

Pepper & Chili

from sweet and mild to fiery hot

WHETHER YOU LIKE SWEET, CRUNCHY BELL PEPPERS or super hot chilies from the Mexican border, there are peppers to suit all tastes. These are easy plants to grow from seeds; they are even easier to grow if you buy named plants from your garden center in late spring. Peppers are not only well worth space in the garden, but they make great container plants. The plants need little care—just a regular supply of water. Most do best with plenty of heat and a long growing season, but there are also varieties that can succeed in the coldest areas.

 SOW

Buy young pepper plants in late spring, especially if you want to try a variety of shapes, colors, and levels of heat. (See "Measuring the Heat," page 158.) They are easy to grow from seeds, but need plenty of warmth to germinate and are slow to grow to transplanting size.

- Start the seeds off in individual pots or divided seed-starting trays about eight weeks before the last frost date. The ideal germination temperature is around 80°F (27°C). You may need a warming mat to provide adequate bottom heat and grow lights to provide sufficient light.

- Wait until the soil reaches around 70°F (21°C) before planting home-raised or store-bought transplants into the garden. Space them 15 inches (37cm) apart.

▲ Bell peppers are the familiar squat, square-shape sweet variety, available in a range of colors, including green, red, yellow, orange, and even purple.

CHRISTOPHER COLUMBUS INTRODUCED THIS AMERICAN VEGETABLE TO EUROPE WHEN HE RETURNED TO SPAIN AFTER HIS FAMOUS VOYAGE.

▲A type of chili, poblano peppers have a hint of heat at a rating of 1,000 to 1,500 heat units on the Scoville scale. At 4 to 6 inches (10–15cm) long, these peppers are good for stuffing, or let them ripen and dry as 'Ancho' chiles.

Varieties

There are two main types of sweet peppers: bell peppers and banana peppers. There are many types of chilies with varying degrees of heat, from mild to very hot. Harvest days are from planting out to green fruit; the higher number is for fully ripe fruit. Peppers grow slowly in cold soil, so choose cultivars to suit your climate.

- **'ACE'** is an early bell pepper, reliable in short-season areas; it ripens to bright red (60–80 days).

- **'ANAHEIM'** is a mild chili pepper, with long tapered green fruit ripening to red (77 days).

- **'BLUSHING BEAUTY'** is a big, sweet bell pepper that starts yellow and develops a pink-red blush when mature (72 days).

- **'CALIFORNIA WONDER'** is the standard bell pepper with large, blocky fruit that turns from green to red; ideal for stuffing (75 days).

- **'CARMEN'** is a modern hybrid of Italian-style banana peppers; light green to bright red and pointed (60–80 days).

- **'EARLY JALAPENO'** is a mild chili with blunt, dark green fruit 3 inches (7.5cm) long (60–80 days).

- **'GYPSY'** is a banana pepper with beautiful elongated tapered fruit that turns from yellow to orange to red; good for short-season areas (65–85 days).

- **'HOLY MOLE'** is a very mild chili with dark green fruit 7–9 inches long (18–23cm) that ripens to dark brown; good in Mexican cuisine (85 days).

- **'HUNGARIAN HOT WAX'** is a large, fairly mild, pointed pepper that ripens through yellow to red (70-95 days).

- **'MARIACHI'** is a hybrid chili culitvar with mild but very attractive carrot-shaped, yellow and red fruit 4 inches (10cm) long (65 days).

- **'SWEET BANANA'** another banana pepper, has pointed yellow fruit 6–7 inches (15–18cm) long that ripens to red (72 days).

- **'SWEET CHOCOLATE'** is an unusual reddish-brown bell pepper, good for short-season areas (65–90 days).

- **'THAI HOT'** is a very hot chile with, bright red fruit 3½ inches (9cm) long (75–95 days).

▲ Habanero peppers need a long hot season to produce 2-inch-long (5-cm), extremely hot fruit—their Scoville scale rating can be 200,000 heat units or greater! They ripen from green to gold before they mature to orange.

▲ Banana peppers, another type of sweet pepper, have long pointed fruit that grows up to 6 inches (15cm) long; the fruit can be yellow, orange, or red when ripe.

Measuring the Heat

The heat found in chili peppers comes from a chemical called capsaicin. Heat is measured in Scoville units. Bell peppers have none, while the hottest habanero peppers have 200,000 units or more. As a general rule, larger chilies are milder than tiny ones, but check the seed packet. In hot chilies, the seeds and their membrane have the most heat; remove these before adding chilies to your recipe to reduce the burn. When handling chilies make sure you wear rubber gloves to protect your hands—and never rub your eyes.

Green peppers will eventually ripen to red if left on the plant.

 GROWING IN CONTAINERS

Sweet peppers and chilies in particular make neat, bushy container plants. Choose varieties that are naturally compact, such as 'Baby Belle', or cut back 8-inch (20cm) or longer branches by one-third to encourage bushiness. Using a small container, about 8 inches (20cm) in diameter, will also keep the plant compact, but it will need more frequent watering. Keep the plants well watered—a drip irrigation system will cut down on your work—and feed regularly with a high-potassium tomato fertilizer.

 grow

Peppers need a lot of warmth, so choose a spot sheltered from wind in full sun; in short-season areas, a raised bed is ideal because the soil will warm up more quickly. Cover the soil with a black plastic sheet to help warm it, retain moisture, and prevent weeds.

- Peppers need a moderately rich soil, so work a little organic matter into the bed before planting. The soil should be free-draining, too.

- Cover new transplants with floating row covers to keep them warm and keep pests away.

- Some varieties may need staking to stop them from falling over; however, most varieties will form compact bushes. If necessary, prune any long shoots to keep the plants neat and encourage branching.

- Water the plants regularly to keep the soil just moist, but not too wet, about 1 inch (2.5cm) a week. Too little water can stress the plant and affect the fruit. Avoid watering from overhead, which can wash away pollen and decrease the number of peppers you grow. A drip irrigation system is ideal, and it will also save on work.

- If you haven't covered the bed with plastic, mulch around the plants with organic matter when the soil is warm to retain moisture and keep weeds down.

- Apply a balanced fertilizer, such as compost, to produce a strong plant, but switch to a high-potassium fertilizer once the fruit begins to form.

You can use a sharp knife to harvest any type of pepper.

③ harvest

Cut both sweet bell peppers and chiles at any stage. Green bell peppers will be less sweet and green chilies less hot than fully ripe red ones. However, if you pick the fruit while under-ripe, it will prolong the harvest and you'll have more peppers to pick. Fully ripe peppers usually turn red, but if you let them mature and develop seeds, the plant will stop producing fruit.

- To remove a pepper, use a sharp knife or pruners to cut through the stem of the plant.

- Store peppers in the refrigerator for up to two weeks. Or cut them up into chunks and store them in plastic bags in the freezer.

FAQ

Q Why do some of my peppers have black patches on the fruit?

A This is blossom end rot, which is caused by a lack of moisture when the fruit was first developing. Make sure you keep the soil moist but not wet at all times. You can eat undamaged parts of the fruit.

Q What causes the dry, white patches on the fruit?

A This is known as sunscald. If you garden in a hot area, provide some shade when the sun is at its brightest. By spacing the plants close together in a block, the leaves will shade the fruit.

Q Why are the leaves deformed and mottled?

A The plants have been attacked by a virus. Although there is no cure, the plants can outgrow the problem. In the future, look for virus-restistant varieties.

Okra

A mild-flavored vegetable with an unusual texture

OKRA ORIGINATED IN AFRICA and needs all the heat it can get. It is a crop that thrives in the warmest parts of the South, where the tasty, gelatinous pods are part of the cuisine. However, thanks to plant breeders, there are hybrids that will succeed as a summer crop in the colder North and anyone can try growing okra.

 sow

Okra will not germinate and grow well when the soil temperature is below 70°F (21°C). Wait until the soil is warm enough in milder climates, and sow the seeds directly into the ground about 3 inches (7.5cm) apart in rows 1½–3 feet (45–90cm) apart.

- When the seedlings are large enough, thin to 12 inches (30cm) apart. Most varieties need 50–70 warm days, so sow the seeds at several intervals until about 16 weeks before the the first fall frost is expected.

- In the North and cooler areas, start okra in pots or seed-starting trays indoors about three to four weeks before the last frost date. When the soil temperature reaches 70°F (21°C), plant carefully—okra resents root disturbance—12 inches (30cm) apart. Cover with floating row covers to protect against wind until well established.

Varieties

- **'ANNIE OAKLEY'** is a quick-growing green cultivar, good for all areas (45 days).

- **'BURGUNDY'** has bright red stems and pods up to 8 inches (20cm) long (60 days).

- **'CAJUN DELIGHT'** is a quick-growing, high-yielding cultivar that, despite the name, is good in the North (70 days).

- **'CLEMSONS SPINELESS'** is the standard green cultivar; "spineless" refers to the lack of spines on the leaves (56–60 days).

2 grow

Okra needs a deeply dug, fertile soil, but don't add manure—the nitrogen will encourage excessive leaf growth. Once established, okra needs little attention and has few problems.

- It is reasonably drought tolerant, but in very dry spells, a weekly watering will boost yields. Once the soil is nice and warm, mulch to preserve moisture.

3 harvest

Pick the pods regularly, every other day, when they reach about 3 inches (7.5cm) long. Some varieties are still tender up to 5 inches (12cm) long. Larger pods may be fibrous—add them to the compost pile. Picking regularly will ensure that more pods are produced.

- Pods should snap off cleanly; if not, cut the stalk.

- Wear gloves if the spiny leaves give you a rash.

FAQ

Q Why are the plants stunted and yellow?

A Okra can suffer from soil-living nematodes. Destroy the plants and as much of the root as possible. Grow okra in a different part of the vegetable garden, and include them in a crop rotation in future years. (See "Crop Rotation," pages 24–25.)

Tomatillo

A tart tomato-like fruit with firm flesh

THIS VEGETABLE IS HARDIER THAN ITS RELATIVE, THE TOMATO, and is less likely to suffer from pests and diseases. The fruit itself grows inside a brown, papery husk. Tomatillos are an essential ingredient in salsa verde and other Mexican dishes. The similar ground cherry, also known as the cape gooseberry or physalis, is sweeter than the tomatillo and is used in desserts, salsas, and jams.

1 sow

Tomatillos and ground cherries are as easy to grow from seeds as tomatoes, and they also self-seed readily.

- Sow the seeds in individual pots or seed-starting trays about four weeks before the last frost.

- Sow directly or plant outdoors when the soil has started to warm up, about 3 feet (90cm) apart.

Varieties

- **'DA MILPA'** has green fruit flushed with purple (70 days).

- **'PURPLE'** has dark purple fruit in green husks (65 days).

- **'TOMA VERDE'** is an early green variety (60 days).

2 grow

These are mostly trouble-free crops that grow into large, sprawling plants. Grow them in full sun in soil that is not too rich; they require no additional fertilizer.

- Water only in very dry spells.

- You can prune long branches to keep the plants compact and bushy. Alternatively, grow them inside cages, like tomatoes, to keep them neat.

- Treat them as a member of the tomato family when planning a crop-rotation plan to prevent soil diseases.

3 harvest

The fruit is ready to pick when it is completely full and starts to split its husk. It will often start to drop when ready. Any fruit not gathered will produce seedlings next season, so harvest as many fruit as you can.

- Tomatillos are ripe when they turn yellowish green or purple, depending on variety. Ground cherries will turn golden yellow.

- Both can be stored—leave them in the husks—for a month or two if spread out and kept in a cool place.

- To make removing the husks and the fruit's sticky coating easier, first let the fruit soak in warm water for a minute.

- Tomatillos are best cooked, whereas ground cherries can be eaten raw or added to fruit salads, sweet sauces, and condiments.

Tomatillos have green, papery husks that change color as they ripen.

Tomato

refreshing, juicy fruit in a variety of shapes and sizes

TOMATOES NEED NO INTRODUCTION. Even if you only have space for a modest container, you can grow a plant without much effort in any hardiness zone. With more garden space you can easily grow enough to supply fresh tomatoes all summer, with enough to preserve, dry, or freeze for the winter. (See "Plant Growth Habits," page 165.)

 SOW

If you need only a few plants, or you want several varieties, buy plants—but wait until the soil is warm enough to plant right away. Look for stocky plants with dark green foliage that is free of any obvious pests or diseases. To start from seeds using your own disease-free plants, just throw a couple of over-ripe fruit on the ground and look forward to seedlings.

- In warm areas, wait until the soil temperature reaches at least 70°F (21°C). In the coldest areas, start seeds indoors, about eight weeks before the last expected frost, where you can maintain a steady 70°F (21°C).

- Plant transplants deeply—extra roots are formed along buried stems, which gives the plant a boost. Bury so the lowest set of leaves is on the soil surface.

- Space bush plants 4 feet (1.2m) apart and vine types 2 feet (60cm) apart in rows, with 4 feet (1.2m) between rows. Make sure they don't shade adjacent plants.

SOW: saving seeds

Tomatoes are the easiest vegetables from which to collect your own seeds. The flowers are self-fertile, which means the seeds will produce identical offspring, even if other varieties are growing nearby. Simply pick a ripe fruit of a disease-free heirloom or open-pollinated variety. (Hybrids will not come true from seed.)

- Squeeze the pulp with the seeds into a glass with a little water. Let stand in a warm place for a week. A crust of fungus will form on top of the liquid. Scoop it off. Strain out the seeds resting at the bottom. Let dry on a paper towel, then store in an airtight jar, ready for next season.

▲ Beefsteaks produce huge meaty fruit, weighing up to 1 pound (450g) each, especially if thinned to one fruit per bunch.

▲ Cherry tomatoes produce long strings or bunches of small, sweet fruit.

Varieties

There's a huge choice of tomato varieties. These include giant beefsteaks, slicing tomatoes—which produce medium-size fruit 2 inches (5cm) across and are usually eaten fresh—tiny cherry tomatoes, paste tomatoes, and pear tomatoes. Choose several varieties, considering a combination of plant growth habit, fruit size and color, and how you intend to eat them.

- **'BETTER BOY'**, a beefsteak type, bears red, 1-pound (450g) fruit on indeterminate plants (72 days).

- **'BIG BEEF'** is a modern indeterminate beefsteak hybrid with an old-fashioned flavor. The red fruit weigh up to 1 pound (450g) each. Disease resistant and suitable for all areas (73 days).

- **'CELEBRITY'**, a hybrid slicing-tomato cultivar, bears heavy yields of 7-ounce (200g) red fruit on determinate plants; good disease resistance (70 days).

- **'EARLY GIRL'** is a very early tomato with red slicing fruit, weighing around 6 ounces (170g) each, on indeterminate plants (52 days).

- **'HUSKY GOLD'** is a midsize slicing tomato, with 6-ounce (170g) golden fruit on dwarf indeterminate vines; good disease resistance (70 days).

- **'JULIET'** is a cherry-tomato cultivar with red fruit on indeterminate plants (70 days).

- **'MICRO TOM'** is a determinate type with plants just 6–8 inches (15–20cm) high; it is good in containers or hanging baskets (88 days).

- **'OREGON SPRING'** is a slicing tomato with early and heavy crops of 6-ounce (170g) red fruit, even in the North (60 days).

- **'SUGARY'**, a cherry-tomato plant, produces small, bright red, grape-shaped fruit that hang in bunches on semideterminate plants (60 days).

- **'SUNGOLD'**, a hybrid with orange fruit, is one of the sweetest cherry tomatoes; early (57 days).

- **'SUPERSWEET 100'** is a prolific, indeterminate cherry variety with good disease resistance (65 days).

- **PASTE TOMATOES** bear elongated, fleshy fruit with strong flavors; grow them for canning, sauces, and paste. 'Roma VF', 'San Marzano', and 'Viva Italia' produce plum-shaped fruit, weighing 3 ounces (85g) each, on determinate plants (76–80 days).

▲ Pear-, plum-, and grape-shape tomatoes have a sweet flavor but meaty texture. The fruits may be red, yellow, or orange and are produced on indeterminate plants.

▲ Heirloom tomatoes come in a variety of shapes, flavors, and colors. These grow on either semideterminate or indeterminate plants.

grow

Tomatoes need a rich, well-drained soil, so work in compost or well-rotted organic matter before planting.

- To help warm up the soil, cover the rows with black plastic sheets. You can plant through cross-shaped slits.

- In cold areas, cover newly planted transplants with floating row covers until they are well established.

- Water the plants regularly to keep the soil uniformly moist at the roots; otherwise fruit problems can develop later on. A drip irrigation system is a good investment.

- Feed regularly with a balanced or high-potassium fertilizer—too much nitrogen will produce excess foliage.

Make a small ditch near the plant to hold the water.

 GROWING IN CONTAINERS

Tomatoes grow really well in containers, as long as you water frequently and feed them regularly with a high-potassium fertilizer. Start with a 3-gallon (11L) or larger container and fill it with a rich potting mix. Choose a dwarf determinate or bush variety to save work, but expect to harvest over a relatively short season. A vine or indeterminate variety can be trained up a tepee or trellis support and will produce fruit for a longer period. Cherry varieties and others with small fruit are the best choice for containers, but you can grow any variety if you are prepared to prune the vines and support larger fruit.

grow: training and supporting

Bush or determinate varieties don't need any pruning or training, but they do benefit from support. The easiest way to support them is to cage them. Buy sturdy, funnel-shaped cages from a garden center or make them from 6-inch (15cm) mesh wire. They should be 4 feet (1.2m) high and 3 feet (90cm) in diameter.

- An alternative for keeping the fruit off the ground is to nail a square of wire mesh onto four 1-foot (30cm) posts. Train the plant through the mesh so it sprawls over the top.

Indeterminate varieties will need supporting. A tomato cage is the easiest option. Alternatively, for fewer but slightly larger fruit, train the plants as a single stem by regularly removing any sideshoots or suckers that emerge from where the leaves join the main stem. Be careful not to remove the flower shoots that grow from the stem. As the main stem grows, tie it to a support using plant ties or strips of cloth. There are many methods of support:

- A single wooden stake is the simplest

- A tepee of poles with one plant trained to each pole

- A trellis using wire, plastic, or nylon mesh stretched between posts

Remove sideshoots or suckers.

Staking and training indeterminate plants will produce larger tomatoes.

Plant Growth Habits

Tomato plants are classified based on their growth habits. *Determinate* types are fairly compact and bushy and require no training. The vines are short and stop extending when the fruit is forming. They produce their crop over a relatively short period of about six weeks. Some are so compact that they are ideal for containers or even hanging baskets.

Indeterminate types just keep growing until they are killed by frost. But best of all, they keep producing fruit all season. Left to their own devices they make unruly plants, but can be trained to remain neat. The most efficient way to grow indeterminate varieties is to limit them to a single stem by careful pruning. A bunch of fruit will form at every leaf joint.

A third type is called *semideterminate*. This plant produces short vines, but it bears fruit over a longer period than determinate types.

③ harvest

Once the skin reaches its mature color, the fruit is ready to harvest.

- Pick ripe fruit every other day when they are in full flow.

- If you can't eat them all right away, they'll keep for at least a week in the refrigerator. Let them warm to room temperature to appreciate the full flavor.

- Pick unripe fruit left on the plants when the first fall frosts are due; then bring indoors and put them on a sunny windowsill to continue ripening.

FAQ

Q Why are the tomatoes on my plants splitting?

A Periods of uneven watering, such as drought followed by heavy rain, can cause the skin to crack on the fruit. Water the plants regularly, and use a mulch to retain soil moisture. Harvest heirloom varieties that are prone to cracking two days before they are mature.

Q Why does the fruit have brown patches?

A A sunken brown patch at the end opposite from the stalk is blossom end rot. It is caused by a lack of moisture when the fruit was first forming. To prevent it in the future, keep the soil uniformly moist at all times.

Q Why are some tomatoes misshapen?

A Anything that stresses the plant can result in deformed or scarred fruit, especially high or low temperatures or lack of water. Try to keep the plants growing evenly and protected from wind.

Q What is eating my tomato leaves?

A The usual suspects are tomato hornworm caterpillars, which are large enough to handpick, or Colorado potato beetles—handpick them or spray with an organic insecticide.

Vine Crops

THE CUCUMBER FAMILY IS A LARGE AND DIVERSE ONE and includes a lot of popular vegetables—which are all actually fruit because the edible parts of the plants contain the seeds—including melons, pumpkins, and squash. The only ones treated as dessert are the pumpkins and melons, and who can resist the prospect of harvesting succulent melons from their own garden? As for the rest of the family, the produce is treated as a vegetable, either cooked, such as zucchini and summer squash, or raw in salads, such as cucumbers. When planning which vegetables to grow, remember that no garden should be without at least one pumpkin for the kids to carve at Halloween and another for pumpkin pie on Thanksgiving. And don't forget the versatile winter squash to store from fall to the following spring for roasting and for warming winter soups.

Most of the members of this huge family, especially melons, need plenty of sun and long growing seasons. They can all be large, sprawling plants that require plenty of room. However, in most cases, there are compact bushy versions available—so you have no excuse for not making space for them if you can provide them with the right growing conditions.

Cucumber

refreshing, crisp salad staple

APART FROM A LITTLE VITAMIN C, cucumbers don't have much nutritional value. However, summer salads just wouldn't be the same without their cool crunch. If you grow pickling types, you can enjoy the pickled version all through winter, too. Cucumbers can be rampant vining plants, so grow them on trellises, or try modern bush varieties that are small enough for a container and will still produce plenty of normal-size fruit.

 SOW

In warmer areas, you can sow seeds directly into the soil. In cooler areas with a short growing season, start seeds in individual pots indoors, where you can maintain a temperature of 70°F (21°C).

- Whether you sow directly or plant transplants, wait until the soil reaches a steady 65°F (19°C).

- Harden off the plants before planting them outdoors.

- Sow thinly in rows, especially if you are using trellis supports, and thin seedlings or space transplants 12–18 inches (30–45cm) apart.

- Cucumbers can also be grown on mounded-up soil, which will improve drainage. Add plenty of compost when you make hills about 6 inches (15cm) high and 4 feet (1.2m) apart. (See "Hill Sowing," page 32.) Sow six seeds per hill and thin later to the best three plants.

The fruit forms beneath the plant's large, attractive blossoms.

Varieties

Choose a bush variety for growing in containers. For pickling, look for a variety with small fruit. For people who have trouble digesting cucumbers, burpless cultivars are available.

- **'ALIBI'**, with fruit up to 4 inches (10cm) long on compact vines, is suitable for pickling (55 days).

- **'BURPEE PICKLER'**, a pickling variety, produces a prolific crop over a long season (53 days).

- **'BUSH CHAMPION'** is a compact bushy plant that bears a heavy crop (55 days).

- **'DIVA'**, an all-female slicing variety, provides a big yield of sweet, thin-skinned fruit (58 days).

- **'FANFARE'** is a compact slicing vine with fruit 8–9-inches (20–23cm) long (63 days).

- **'SALAD BUSH'** bears normal-size (8 inches/ 20cm) fruit on compact bush plants (57 days).

- **'STRAIGHT EIGHT'**, a slicing variety, has fruit 8 inches (20cm) long with good flavor (58 days).

- **UNUSUAL CULTIVARS** include 'Armenian', which has pale green, ribbed fruit with a mild, sweet flavor (70 days), and 'Lemon', with sweet round, yellow fruit, 3–4 inches (7.5–10cm) across, that are good for salads or pickled (65 days).

 To prevent powdery mildew, grow plants on a trellis for better air circulation and

GROWING IN CONTAINERS

You can grow just about any cucumber in a largish container—one with at least a 4-gallon (15L) capacity is ideal. If you opt for a vining type, provide a strong tepee for it to scramble up, or place it next to a trellis. Alternatively, try one of the compact bush varieties. A drip irrigation system will take the work out of regular watering, but don't forget to use a liquid fertilizer regularly.

 grow

Cucumbers need full sun and rich, well-drained soil. Work an inch (2.5cm) or so of well-rotted manure into the soil before planting or sowing.

- In cooler areas, cover the soil with a black plastic sheet a few weeks before transplanting to help warm it up. In all areas, water the soil thoroughly, and cover with black plastic or mulch to retain moisture and suppress weeds.

- Water regularly—a drip irrigation system is ideal—and feed regularly, too, with a balanced or high-potassium fertilizer. Too much nitrogen will produce leaves, not fruit.

Pinch off the vines at the top of a trellis to encourage sideshoots.

grow: trellis varieties

Trellised vine varieties take up less room; the increased air circulation reduces disease problems; and the fruit is easier to pick. Put the trellis in place before you sow or plant transplants.

 harvest

Pick cucumbers young and keep picking. Check the plants every other day and cut pickle varieties when 3–4 inches (7.5–10cm) long and slicing types when 6–8 inches (15–20cm) long. Don't let them reach full size and start producing seeds or the crop will tail off.

- Pickling varieties crop over a short period, but slicers hould keep going for weeks.

FAQ

Q Why don't my cucumbers set fruit?

A Pollination can be poor early in the season, especially in wet weather or if pollinating insects are scarce. Hand pollinate by gently pushing a brush into male flowers, then female ones. (These have a bulge beneath the petals.)

Q Why are my plants covered in white powder?

A This is a disease known as powdery mildew. It is usually worse in warm, moist weather. Destroy severely affected leaves and spray with a solution of baking soda. In the future, look for resistant varieties.

Q What's caused my plants to suddenly wilt?

A Bacterial wilt is spread by cucumber beetles. Destroy any affected plants. In future years, prevent cucumber beetles by covering the young plants with floating covers until they flower.

to help prevent the disease from developing.

Melon

juicy, refreshing summertime treat

WHERE MOST OF THE CUCUMBER FAMILY are barely sweet, melons are deliciously, sugary sweet. Once you've experienced the flavor of homegrown melons and learn to gauge when they are at their peak of perfection, you won't want to be without at least one plant in the plot. At one time melons were crops for the South. However, thanks to early-ripening, more compact varieties, melon can now be grown in all hardiness zones as long as you choose the right cultivars. Watermelons are only for long-season areas but are grown in the same way as other melons.

 SOW

Don't rush sowing seeds or planting transplants outdoors.

- In northern and colder areas, start seeds indoors in individual pots. Maintain a temperature of at least 70°F (21°C). Harden the plants off and delay planting outdoors until the soil temperature is at least 65°F (19°C).

- In warmer areas, as long as the soil is 65°F (19°C) and it is within two weeks of the last expected frost date, you can sow the seeds directly in the ground.

HIEROGLYPHICS SHOW THAT THE EGYPTIANS ENJOYED MELONS IN 2400 BC.

Varieties

- **CHARANTAIS** are small French melons with orange flesh and green or gray skin. 'Edonis' (70 days) and 'Honey Girl' (75 days) have typical 2-pound (900g) fruit.

- **CRENSHAW** types bear large oval melons with yellow skin and pale green or salmon-colored flesh. 'Burpee Early Sweet' has 15-pound (6.8kg) fruit with pink flesh and is early enough for all zones (85–90 days).

- **GALIA** has green netted skin and pale green flesh with a subtle flavor. 'Passport' bears 5-pound (2.3kg) fruit and is suited to all areas (73 days).

- **HONEYDEWS** are winter melons that have smooth, round fruit with white skin and flesh that is green, white, pink, or orange. 'Early Dew' has 3-pound (1.4kg) fruit with pale green flesh (75 days); 'Orange

Sorbet' has 7–8-pound (3.2–3.6kg) fruit with pale orange flesh (82 days).

- **MUSKMELON,** also called cantaloupe, has orange flesh with a musky, sweet flavor and a netted skin. 'Ambrosia' has small 5-pound (2.3kg) fruit with firm pale orange flesh (90 days).

- **SPANISH** melons bear 4-pound (1.8kg) fruit with smooth yellow skin and pale green flesh. 'Amy' has smaller fruit with white flesh (70 days).

- **WATERMELONS** are available as bush varieties with small melons at 5 pounds (2.3kg), icebox types with manageable vines, or the classic huge melons weighing 20 pounds (9kg) or more. 'Crimson Sweet' has large red-flesh fruit on disease-resistant plants (85 days). 'Moon and Stars' is an heirloom with large green fruit splashed with yellow (100 days). 'Sugar Baby' is a good cultivar with medium-size, red-flesh fruit (80 days).

② grow

Melons are large plants that need plenty of room to grow and a rich, well-drained soil. Work in a layer of compost before planting.

- In warmer areas, plant in "hills" of mounded-up soil, 6 feet (1.8m) apart for trailing watermelons, 5 feet (1.5m) apart for trailing melons, and 3–4 feet (90–120cm) apart for bush varieties. (See "Hill Sowing," page 32.) Sow six seeds per position; thin to the best three seedlings later.

- An alternative for all areas, but especially cooler ones, is to cover the bed with black plastic. This helps warm the soil as well as retains moisture and suppress weeds. It also helps keep the fruit clean. Make cross-shaped slits to plant through, 4 feet (1.2m) apart each way for trailing varieties and 3 feet apart (90cm) for bush types.

- In cooler areas, cover the young plants with floating row covers to keep them warm and prevent insect pests.

- Melons need plenty of water, at least an inch (2.5cm) per week. However, withholding water for about a week before harvesting should increase the sweetness of the fruit.

- You can grow varieties with small fruit in rows, trained on trellises. Sow or plant them 3 feet (90cm) apart and make sure they won't shade adjacent crops.

- Support fruit on trellised plants with slings made of plastic mesh, such as an old onion bag, attached to the trellis. Place a board, tile, or upturned pot under the fruit of trailing plants to keep them off the soil.

③ harvest

Judging the precise moment to cut fully ripe melons can be tricky. Key indicators are when the blossom end feels slightly soft, when the skin color changes, and when the last leaf before the fruit turns pale. Ripe melons also give off a sweet fragrance when ripe.

- Muskmelons will detach from the vine, but they are best if cut off just before this happens.

- Watermelons give off a dull sound when thumped and the base, where it rests on the soil, should be fully colored.

- Melons will keep for a week or two uncut in a cool place.

Some melons have smooth skin, while others have textured skin.

FAQ

Q What's nibbling my melon leaves?

A The striped cucumber beetle is the most likely culprit. Handpick or spray with an organic insecticide because the beetle's grubs can also attack the roots and spread bacterial wilt disease. Floating row covers should keep them off.

Q Why aren't my melons as sweet as they should be?

A There are several possible causes: cold soil, insufficient nutrients in the soil, or a cultivar not suited to your climate. Another reason might be that there's too little foliage for the number of fruit. In this case, thinning the developing fruit in the future might help.

Pumpkin & Winter Squash

The giants of the garden

THESE ARE THE BIG BOYS OF THE CUCUMBER FAMILY, and they are heat-loving vegetables that need a long growing season. Pumpkins can reach 25 pounds (11.4kg)—and that's not including the really huge ones. Pumpkins are at their best in late fall, but unfortunately, they don't store well. Winter squash are equally demanding of space, but more compact varieties are available for smaller gardens. They are much easier to store than their pumpkin cousins—in some cases, all the way through winter until the following spring. They taste great, too.

 1 **SOW**

Don't rush sowing seeds or planting transplants outdoors.

- In warmer areas, sow the seeds directly into the soil, 1–2 inches (2.5–5cm) deep. Wait until a couple of weeks after the last expected spring frost or until the soil temperature is above 60°F (15.5°C). Sow up to four seeds per planting position, and thin later to the strongest two seedlings.

- In colder areas, start the seeds indoors, where you can maintain a temperature of 70°F (21°C). Sow the seeds individually in pots.

- Space bush and semitrailing types 3–4 feet (90–120cm) apart each way and vining types 5–6 feet (1.5–1.8m) apart.

Both pumpkins and winter squash have hard, inedible rinds.

Acorn (left) and delicata squash are two types of winter squash.

 Using black plastic sheets instead of organic mulch will help prevent squash bugs

Varieties

PUMPKIN

Pumpkins are a type of winter squash, but they don't develop a hard rind like other winter squash do. Small pumpkins are a good size for eating, with sweet, rich orange flesh. Choose pumpkins for their size, for eating, or for decorating for Halloween.

- **'BABY BEAR'** has small, 1½–2½ pound (0.7–1.1kg), sweet fruit just right for a pie and "naked" seeds that can be roasted (105 days).

- **'CONNECTICUT FIELD'** is a classic, large jack-o'-lantern type, up to 20 pounds (9kg), ideal for Halloween (110 days).

- **'DILL'S ATLANTIC GIANT'** is the one to grow if size matters; it currently holds the world record for the heaviest pumpkin (120 days).

- **'HOWDEN'** is large, up to 25 pounds (11.3kg), with orange fruit that is ideal for jack-o'-lanterns (115 days).

- **'LUMINA'** has white fruit, weighing 8–10 pounds (3.6–4.5kg), with orange flesh; it is ideal for carving or painting (80–90 days).

- **'ORANGE SMOOTHY'** bears 6–9 pound (2.7–4kg) fruit suitable for eating, carving, or painting.

- **'SMALL SUGAR'** bears small, sweet fruit up to 5 pounds (2.3kg) that is ideal for eating; the seeds can be roasted, too (115 days).

- **'SORCERER'** produces orange, 15–25 pound (6.8–11.4kg) fruit with a good handle for jack-o'-lanterns (95 days).

- **TINY PUMPKINS** are borne on plants that produce a lot of fruit no bigger than 3 inches (7.5cm) across, making them ideal for drying and using as seasonal decorations. 'Baby Boo' has white fruit; 'Jack Be Little' and 'Wee Be Little' both have orange fruit (all 95 days).

WINTER SQUASH

All winter squash types have dense, sweet, nutty flesh and store well until the following spring. There are many types to choose from.

- **ACORN** types bear medium-size, ridged fruit ideal for baking or microwaving. These are bush plants, which are useful where space is limited. 'Cream of Crop' has 3-pound (1.7kg) fruit with white skin and orange flesh (75 days). 'Table Ace' fruit weighs 2 pounds (900g) and has dark green skin and sweet orange flesh (75 days).

- **BUTTERNUT** types have buff-colored, club-shaped fruit with the seed cavity in the bulbous end; the neck is solid, with pale orange flesh. 'Butterboy' produces 2½-pound (1.1kg) fruit (80 days). 'Waltham' has uniform 3–4 pound (1.4–1.8kg) fruit with solid flesh (85 days).

- **DELICATA**, also known as sweet potato squash, has a bush habit and produces long cream-and-green striped fruit with sweet potato-like flesh. 'Cornell's Bush Delicata' bears fruit 8 inches (20cm) long (80 days).

- **HUBBARD** types grow fruit pointed at both ends, with blue-gray warty skin and dense orange flesh. 'Blue Hubbard' is large, up to 10 pounds (4.5kg), and stores well (110 days). 'Baby Blue Hubbard' is a new smaller version with fruit weighing just 4–5 pounds (1.8–2.3kg).

- **KABOCHA** types produce medium-size, round, flattened fruit that has a rich flavor and stores well. 'Bon Bon' has dark green fruit and dense, rich orange flesh (95 days). 'Sunshine' bears 4-pound (1.8-kg) fruit with bright orange skin and sweet flesh (95 days).

- **SPAGHETTI** is baked or boiled whole (but first prick the skin). When split open, the flesh is forked out and resembles spaghetti. Most are trailing plants, but modern hybrids are bushes. 'Hasta la Pasta' produces orange fruit 6–8 inches (15–20cm) long (75 days).

Pumpkin & Winter Squash

Kabocha squash (center) stores well.

2 grow

Pumpkins and squash need rich, well-drained soil. Traditionally, they are grown on hills. (See "Hill Sowing," page 32.) Before mounding the soil, mix in a generous amount of well-rotted manure.

- Covering the bed with a black plastic sheet will help warm the soil and suppress weeds, which can be difficult to control once the vines are growing rapidly.

- Cut circles in the plastic for the mounds.

- Although squash will often produce fruit without additional watering, keeping the soil moist during the summer will increase the crop. Give the area a really good soaking every week to wet the soil deeply.

- Vining types will take over the entire garden if you let them. If space is limited, provide trellis supports for the varieties with smaller fruit and train them upward. Be careful that they do not shade your other crops.

- When four to six healthy pumpkins or squash have formed on a plant, prune the shoot tips and remove any other surplus fruit. This will allow the plant to concentrate its energy on producing fewer, but better tasting, fruit.

3 harvest

Leave the pumpkins or winter squash outside as long as possible to ripen fully. If necessary, prune the leaves to expose the mature fruit to the sun.

- In cooler areas, move ripe pumpkins or squash to a sunny, sheltered spot to complete their ripening. Then move them to a warm place indoors (85°F/29°C) to cure for a week. Finally, store them in a warm, dry place. Acorn squash and delicata squash don't need curing and are best stored at about 45°F (7°C).

- Always cut the vine on either side of the fruit stalk, leaving the fruit stalk intact. This will prevent rot from getting into the fruit in storage. Don't be tempted to use the stalk as a handle, and use any fruit with damaged stalks first.

- Generally, pumpkins will not store long, so they are best used during fall. Winter squash stores better and can be eaten during the late fall and through winter.

FAQ

Q Why are my plants suddenly wilting?

A If this happens on one part of the plant, cucumber beetles are probably spreading bacterial wilt. Destroy the plants and cover future plants with a floating row cover. The row cover will also protect the plants from other pests, such as aphids, squash bugs (which can also cause wilt), and flea beetles.

Use tiles, boards, or other materials to raise the fruit off the ground.

Zucchini & Summer Squash

thin-skinned vegetable with a mild flesh

COMPARED WITH SOME MEMBERS OF THE CUCUMBER FAMILY, these are compact plants. However, they are large vigorous bushes and are very productive. Two or three well-grown plants should be plenty for regular pickings of tender 6-inch (15cm) zucchini. Any more and you can expect a glut at some time during the summer. Don't confine yourself to the plain green type of summer squash. There are plenty of shapes and colors to choose from, including round and the odd-looking yellow crookneck squash.

 SOW

Whether you start your seeds indoors or outside will depend on where you live.

- To grow from seeds in warmer areas, wait until a few weeks after the last frost date and the soil temperature is at least 60°F (16°C). Prepare planting hills, working in plenty of compost and mounding up the soil. (See "Hill Sowing," page 32.) Push three or four seeds into the top; thin them later to the strongest two seedlings.

- In colder areas, start seeds in 3 to 4-inch (7.5–10cm) pots about four weeks before the last frost date. Meanwhile, warm the soil by covering it in black plastic sheets. Plant the seedlings outdoors after hardening off and the soil temperature is at least 60°F (16°C). To reduce weeds, plant through cross-shaped slits in the plastic, 3 feet (90cm) apart.

Types of summer squash include patty pan squash (left) and zucchini.

Varieties

There are several types of summer squash that grow on large bush or semitrailing plants.

- **CROOKNECK SQUASH** look similar to straightnecks but have a kink toward the top of the fruit. Cultivars include 'Early Summer Crookneck' and 'Pic n' Pic' (50 days).

- **PATTY PAN SQUASH** have flattened fruit with scalloped edges; pick when 2–3 inches (5–8cm) across. 'Peter Pan' has pale green fruit; 'Sunburst' has yellow fruit (all 50–55 days).

- **ROUND ZUCCHINI** are treated the same as long ones and best picked up to tennis-ball size. 'Eight Ball' has dark green fruit; 'One Ball' has bright yellow fruit (both 40–50 days).

- **STRAIGHTNECK SQUASH** have club-shaped, warty, yellow fruit. Pick when up to 8 inches (20cm) long and the skin is soft. 'Saffron', 'Early Straightneck', and 'Sunray' are typical cultivars (45 days).

- **ZUCCHINI** are all compact bushy plants. Apart from the familiar long green fruit, there are alternative colors and shapes. 'Black Beauty' and 'Raven' are dark green varieties (50 days); 'Spineless Beauty' grows similar fruit but lacks the small spines on the leaf stalks (45 days). 'Burpees Golden' and 'Gold Rush' have yellow fruit (45 days). 'Magda' has cream fruit (50 days).

GROWING IN CONTAINERS

Zucchini and summer squash are good subjects for a container. Remember that when fully grown, although they are bush rather than vining types, they will still make large bulky plants. They can also be greedy, thirsty plants in a container, so the larger the container the better. Drip irrigation will cut down on work. Feed regularly with a high-potassium fertilizer. And don't forget to keep picking fruit every other day.

Crookneck squash grow from the end of a blossom.

 ## grow

Covering plants with floating row covers should help prevent most insect pests from attacking the plants, but take precautions against slugs, which can destroy young plants. Covers will also protect plants from cold and wind until they are well established.

- Don't let summer squash run out of water; they need the equivalent of an inch (2.5cm) of rain each week. Installing a drip irrigation system will save a lot of work.

- Feed regularly with a high-potassium fertilizer—too much nitrogen will encourage excessive leaf growth.

- Remove the covers when flowers appear so the pollinators can do their job (or you won't have fruit).

③ harvest

The only rule for zucchini and summer squash is to keep picking and picking and never let any fruit get too big. The ideal size is 6 inches (15cm) for the long ones and 2–3 inches (5–7.5cm) for the round ones. However, if you notice too many fruit growing, pick them smaller. Use a knife to cut the stalk.

Leave an inch (2.5cm) of the stem attached when cutting the fruit.

Gourds

You can grow the inedible hard-shell and ornamental gourds like other vine crops, but they need a long season and plenty of warmth to dry (110–130 days). Ornamental gourds grow like trailing summer squash, but let them ripen and dry on the vine. Sow gourd seeds on mounded-up soil 6 feet (1.8m) apart once the soil has warmed up, or train the varieties with smaller fruit on a trellis. In colder areas, start the seeds in pots and plant outdoors once the soil is warm enough for squash. Pinch out the tip of the vine when it reaches 6 feet (1.8m) to encourage sideshoots that bear the fruit. If cold weather threatens, finish drying them indoors.

Hard-shell gourds include 'Apple', with apple-shaped fruit for painting; 'Bottle' or 'Birdhouse', which can be hollowed out; 'Snake', which has thin, curly fruit; and 'Speckled Swan', swan-shaped gourds, speckled with green and white. Ornamental gourds need less time to mature, so they are better for northern gardens. They include 'Crown of Thorns', with flattened, spiky fruit, and small egg- or pear-shaped fruit in green or yellow, striped, and bicolored, and often sold in interesting mixtures. Asian gourds and bitter gourds are used in Asian cuisine and are picked when immature and eaten like summer squash. They need high temperatures and a long season.

Bitter gourd

FAQ

Q Why is no fruit forming on my plants?

A Squash produce both male and female flowers (females have a slight bulge beneath them), so your plants may only be producing male flowers early in the season. Cold weather or a lack of pollinating insects may mean female flowers are present but just not being fertilized. Hand pollinate to ensure fruit will develop, using a cotton swab to collect pollen from the male flowers and deposit it in the females.

Q What is causing my plants to suddenly wilt?

A The culprit may be the squash vine borer. Slit open infested vines and squash the grubs. Mound soil around the stems to prevent the adult moths from laying eggs. Covering crops with floating row covers should also prevent them. However, if part of the plant is affected, bacterial wilt may be the problem. Destroy the plants; use a row cover until the blossoms develop to prevent cucumber beetles, which spread the disease, in future plantings.

Q How can I stop the white mold on my zucchini?

A This is powdery mildew, which looks like a dusting of white powder to start with, although the leaves rapidly turn yellow and brittle. It is worse in warm, humid weather. Pick off and destroy affected leaves, and prune plants to improve air circulation and limit its spread.

Q Why is the skin on the fruit pitted?

A The fruit was exposed to temperatures below 40°F (4.5°C). If a cold spell is due at the end of the season, cover the plants with a row cover or harvest the fruit.

12

Herbs & Perennial Vegetables

NO GARDEN SHOULD BE WITHOUT AN AREA FOR CULINARY HERBS. They release scents that lift the spirits, and the flavor of freshly picked herbs can really transform salads and cooked dishes. Although some herbs are annuals that can be planted among vegetables, it is a good idea to devote a bed just for herbs of all kinds. The majority are easy to grow and take up little space, so even if you have a small garden, you can still grow a good selection. In fact, many herbs are attractive enough to grow in flower borders, and they all do well in containers.

Most vegetables are treated as annuals and replanted in the vegetable garden each year. However, there are a few that are perennials, such as asparagus, artichokes (in some regions), and rhubarb, and all are a good choice for the garden if you have the space. Give them a patch of ground all to themselves, and they'll reward you with produce year after year.

Basil

a Mediterranean favorite

THE WARM, PUNGENT AROMA of fresh basil (*Ocimum basilicum*) features in many Italian and Greek recipes. As a garden plant, it is pretty, with a neat habit and small flower spikes that attract bees. There are several variations on the typical basil grown for cooking, such as selections with purple foliage and those with a lemon scent or more spicy flavors. A collection growing together in a window box or flowerpots is attractive and productive, even in the tiniest of spaces.

 ## sow

Basil is tender, and its leaves turn black at the slightest frost. Even in cool weather, growth can slow down. The best way to grow basil is to sow a small amount of seeds every few weeks. Don't sow directly into the ground or plant young plants outdoors until all danger of frost has passed.

- Sow indoors four to six weeks before the last expected spring frost. Put a few seeds in a 3-inch (8cm) pot of seed-starting mix. Keep at 75°F (24°C) until they germinate, usually within two weeks. Let them continue to grow; acclimate the young plants to cooler conditions gradually.

- To sow directly in the ground, wait until the soil temperature is at least 60°F (15.5°C).

2 grow

Once there is no danger of frost, plant transplants 12 inches (30cm) apart for larger types; use about half this spacing for dwarf types.

- Choose a warm, sheltered spot with moist but well-drained soil; avoid cold, damp sites, which will encourage fungal disease.

- In the North, plant outdoors in late spring to early summer. In the South, plant outdoors in the spring. Growing in containers or raised beds is also an option.

- Keep the soil moist and protect plants from slugs.

- Liquid feed with a balanced fertilizer to encourage lush leaf growth.

- Plants that drop leaves or suddenly wilt may be infected with Fusarium wilt. Pull and destroy infected plants.

Varieties

There are basil cultivars with extra-large leaves, which are useful if you need large quantities for making your own pesto. There are also cultivars with really tiny leaves that can be snipped off whole and put into sandwiches or salads.

- **LEMON BASIL** has a lemon flavor.

- **'MAGICAL MICHAEL'** is the most ornamental cultivar, with purple leaves and flowers, and has the classic basil flavor.

- **'NUFAR'** is resistant to Fusarium wilt.

- **'SIAM QUEEN'** has an anise flavor.

3 harvest

Once plants are 5–6 inches (12–15cm) high, pick the young leaves from the top of the stems. This encourages more leaves to grow and results in neat, bushy plants. Remove no more than one-third of the leaves at a time.

 Good soil drainage and air circulation will help prevent Fusarium wilt.

Bay

an evergreen herb with strongly aromatic leaves

BAY (*LAURUS NOBILIS*) CAN BE EITHER a treelike shrub or evergreen houseplant, depending on whether it survives the winter in the garden or stays indoors in a pot.

1 sow

You can buy bay plants as either rooted cuttings, small or large pot plants, or clipped and trained topiary specimens. Prices can vary greatly, with topiary types being the most expensive.

2 grow

In warmer areas, where temperatures don't drop below 10°F (-12°C), grow as an evergreen hedge or a large shrub. The ideal is a warm, sheltered spot in well-drained soil. Where frost is a factor, grow in a container so the plant can be outdoors in summer and indoors in winter.

3 harvest

Simply pick off the leaves as required for soups or sauces. Bay is evergreen so the leaves are available year round. There is no need to dry them unless you have surplus from clipping trained plants in summer.

Chervil

an unusual annual with an anise flavor

FRESH CHERVIL CAN PERK UP a bland salad. It has finely divided leaves that resemble parsley. When dried, it can be used as an ingredient for a bouquet garni.

1 sow

Buy fresh seeds each spring and sow where it is to grow—chervil doesn't transplant well.

- Sow small amounts regularly, every three weeks or so. Early sowings will bolt rapidly and the later sowings will continue until killed by frost. [In mild winter areas, late sowings may survive over the winter.]

- Sow thinly and thin out the seedlings to 6–8 inches (15–20cm) apart.

2 grow

Chervil prefers a shady position in moist soil. Keep this herb well watered or it will bolt even more quickly, especially when grown in a container.

3 harvest

Pick the leaves anytime before the flowers start to open. Start picking leaves early to help delay flowering.

Chives

perennial member of the onion family

ONE OF THE EASIEST HERBS TO GROW, chives have edible hollow leaves and pretty mauve flowers, which can also be eaten.

1 sow

Sow seeds indoors in pots or outside. These will be slow to grow, so allow a year before harvesting. A faster option is to buy plants or get a friend to donate clumps. Thin seedlings or plant clumps 6–8 inches (15–20cm) apart.

2 grow

Chives grow in sun or partial shade in dry or moist soil. The leaves die back in winter in cold climates; in warmer areas, they are evergreen. Fork in some organic matter before planting; water until the plants are growing well.

3 harvest

If you snip off the tips of the leaves, unsightly brown marks will appear at the top of the plant. Instead, use scissors to cut the leaves further down, leaving a 2-inch (5cm) stump to regrow. Stop harvesting three weeks before the first frost date.

Dill

a smaller version of fennel

USE THE LEAVES AND SEEDS OF DILL, which grows to 3 feet (90cm), in fish and potato dishes.

1 sow

Sow seeds directly into the ground in spring, but cover lightly with soil because light improves germination. Keep the bed moist and thin seedlings to 6–8 inches (15–20cm) apart. Sow every three weeks for a continuous supply.

2 grow

A warm, sunny site with poor, well-drained soil is ideal. It can be grown in a flower border. In a small bed, the cultivar 'Fernleaf', at only 18 inches (45cm) high is useful. Make sure you keep it away from fennel to avoid cross-pollination.

3 harvest

The leaves are ready to pick two months after sowing. To harvest the feathery leaves over a long period, choose a cultivar described as being slow to bolt, such as 'Dukat' (also known as 'Tetra') or 'Fernleaf'.

Cilantro & Coriander

flavorful seeds and refreshing leaves

BOTH THE LEAVES AND SEEDS of *Coriandrum sativum* can be used in cooking. The fresh young leaves, known as cilantro, are widely used in Asian and Mexican dishes, while the seeds, called coriander, are used as a spice.

 sow

Cilantro is an annual that does not transplant well. Sow the seeds directly into their final position. This can be either into the ground in rows or scattered into a large container. Sow the seeds every two weeks to ensure that you have a continuous supply, but stop sowing during hot weather.

- Sow seeds 1 inch (2.5cm) deep and 2 inches (5cm) apart, and thin the seedlings to 6–8 inches (15–20cm).

Varieties

- **'DELFINO'** has finely divided leaves that make it an attractive garnish.

- **'LEISURE'**, often described as slow to bolt, is one of the varieties bred for leaf production.

 grow

Cilantro will grow in sun or partial shade in normal soil that has been enriched with some organic matter to keep the soil moist.

- Once the hot weather and long days of summer arrive, the plant will quickly form flower stalks. The white flowers are a magnet for beneficial insects. Although the plants will slow down their leaf production, the flowers will set seed and dry out, and you'll be able to use these plants to harvest the seeds.

 harvest

Start cutting leaves when the plants are about 6 inches (15cm) high. The leaves are usually chopped and scattered onto dishes such as salads or curries. Fine-leaved varieties can be used without chopping. The leaves are best used fresh, but you can also freeze them in ice-cube trays.

- Seed heads will ripen in late summer and fall to the ground; cut them before this happens once they turn brown. Place in a paper bag and dry in a warm, airy place. When completely dry, store the seeds in airtight jars.

Cilantro leaves can be used chopped or whole as a garnish.

Fennel

a tall, elegant plant

FENNEL FOR THE HERB GARDEN HAS THE SAME ANISE FLAVOR and feathery foliage as the vegetable variety of fennel, but not its bulblike base.

1 sow

Sow seeds directly into the ground in spring in cold areas or in fall in southern gardens, when temperatures are 60–65°F (15.5–18°C). Or purchase a young plant in spring or get self-sown seedlings from a friend.

2 grow

Fennel prefers a moist, deep soil so its taproot has plenty of room, but it copes well in free-draining soils, too. Pick a 2 × 2-foot (60 × 60cm) sunny spot. In mild climates where seeds can survive the winter, remove the flowers before they shed their seeds to prevent it from spreading.

3 harvest

Cut leaves when they are large enough to use. Seeds can be gathered once they have dried. Do not grow dill and fennel near each other because they will cross-pollinate and produce inferior seedlings.

Lemon balm

a member of the mint family

PICK SOME LEMON BALM (*Melissa officinalis*) leaves to make a refreshing tea with a hint of citrus.

1 sow

You can buy a plant from a garden center, but lemon balm is easy to grow from seeds. Sow in spring, either indoors in a pot or directly into the garden soil. Germination can take three weeks.

2 grow

Lemon balm will grow in most situations and soils. In hot areas, provide some shade from midday sun, particularly for the yellow and variegated forms. Cut down old foliage and lift and divide the plant in the fall. In warm areas, this herb is a perennial and will self-seed.

3 harvest

Simply cut or pinch off leaves as needed. The flavor of the leaves is best before the plant flowers. If the quality of the leaves is poor, cut back to 2 inches (5cm) above soil level; water; and wait for a fresh flush of young foliage to appear.

 Later in summer, lemon balm's small flowers will attract bees.

Lemongrass

a grasslike herb

A POPULAR INGREDIENT IN ASIAN COOKING, *Cymbopogon citratus*, or lemongrass, has aromatic leaves and lemon-flavored leaf bases. Is is used in a variety of dishes, from soups to spice mixes.

 **sow**

Lemongrass is difficult to grow from seeds and is usually bought from a garden center as a young plant.

- Grow lemongrass in a container because it can be invasive in mild areas. It needs moving indoors during winter in all but the warmest areas because it is hardy in only Zones 9 to 11. Choose a container 12 inches wide (30cm) and fill with a potting mix.

- Alternatively, divide an established clump and replant the divisions.

2 grow

Grow in a warm spot, sheltered from wind, in full sun. Keep well watered in summer and give it a balanced liquid fertilizer. Move indoors in winter; keep just moist.

3 harvest

Detach young stems from the plant and remove the leaves to reveal a stalk with a thick base. Gently crush the base and add to stews or curries; remove before serving.

Marjoram

a relative of oregano

ALTHOUGH A PERENNIAL, sweet marjoram (*Origanum marjorana*) is sometimes treated as an annual herb. Marjoram has a sweeter, more subtle flavor than the more heady oregano.

 **sow**

You can raise marjoram each year from seeds, but it is slow to get going. It is easier to buy a plant from a garden center. Marjoram can also be propagated easily from cuttings.

- Marjoram is hardy up to Zone 6, where it can be treated as a perennial; in cooler areas, treat it as an annual.

- Space plants about 8 inches (20cm) apart).

2 grow

Marjoram requires poor, well-drained soil, so it is a good candidate for a container. Before flowering starts, trim the plant back to encourage fresh growth.

3 harvest

Pick young shoots regularly to keep the plant neat. Dry marjoram for winter use. Strip off the leaves as needed.

Mint

WHILE REFRESHING AS A TEA OR FLAVORING, mint is also an attractive plant and has a lot to offer the cook and gardener. It is a herbaceous perennial, so plants will last for years. In fact, keeping them in their allotted space can be a challenge because they are invasive plants. Spearmint (*Mentha spicata*) and peppermint (*M. × piperita*) are the most useful in the kitchen, but there are many other types, such as the milder apple mint, with its attractive woolly leaves, and the eye-catching variegated ginger mint. A small collection of potted mints is a worthwhile addition to any yard.

 sow

Buy a small plant or get a few pieces of underground stem, or rhizome, from a friend. Plant in a large container in a rich potting mix—simply inserting cuttings just below the soil surface will be sufficient.

- Mint can be invasive, so it is best grown in a raised bed where the roots can be confined or in containers sunk into the soil with 2 inches (5cm) of the rim above ground.

grow

Keep plants well watered and feed with a balanced liquid fertilizer. If grown in a container, you can keep it in partial shade or full sun.

- Mint is fairly tolerant. If it starts to wilt because watering has been neglected, cut the top growth back severely, water well, and the plant will grow back.

- These plants can "run out of steam" in a container because they are so vigorous. Repot them every one to two years, replanting some of the newer rhizomes into fresh potting mix.

- Remove flowers as soon as they form to prevent them from seeding.Plants raised by seeds do not come true so your distinct collection could become a motley crew.

 harvest

Mint is a vigorous plant so start harvesting as soon as new growth emerges. Pinch out the growing tips so you get fresh young leaves, and at the same time, help to create a bushy plant. Later, cut the top half of the young stems and strip off the leaves.

- For fresh mint over winter, tip the plant out of its pot and select some runners to cut from the parent plant. Plant in a fresh pot and cover with 1 inch (2.5cm) of potting mix. Water and keep in a cool, well-ventilated place.

Mint's lush green leaves make it an attractive container plant.

Oregano

THE LEAVES OF OREGANO (*Origanum vulgare*), which is a perennial, add flavor to Mediterranean dishes. There is also a Greek species (*O. v.* subsp. *hirtum*) and an Italian species (*O. majoricum*).

 sow

Raising plants from seeds can provide variable results, so buy potted plants from a garden center or take divisions in the fall or stem cuttings in the spring or fall. Oregano varies in flavor, so before choosing a plant, rub a leaf and then taste it.

 grow

Oregano thrives in full sun and in a well-drained soil, and dwarf types are suitable for containers. Oregano may not survive really cold winters; digging up small plants and keeping them in pots on a sunny windowsill over winter is an option.

 harvest

Pick leaves as soon as the young plants are established. Once the plant starts flowering, the flavor will diminish. For larger quantities, cut back plants when 6 inches (15cm) tall, again before they flower, and finally in late summer. After each cutting, there will be fresh growth.

Rosemary

AS WELL AS NEEDLELIKE LEAVES AND PALE BLUE FLOWERS, rosemary has a strong flavor and a distinctive aroma. It is hardy in only Zones 8 to 10; elsewhere, treat it as an annual.

 sow

Buy a plant or ask a friend for some cuttings (taken in mid- to late summer). Plant outdoors in spring in light, well-drained soil—fork in some gravel or sand to improve the drainage if the soil needs it.

- Keep moist until the roots are established.
- Alternatively, choose a dwarf cultivar and grow in a container of free-draining potting soil; in winter, bring it indoors and keep well lit (with 4 hours each day of direct sunlight or 12 hours of artificial light).

 grow

In mild areas and well-drained soil, rosemary is care-free. In containers, water when the soil is moderately dry.

 harvest

Pinch out the stem tips for some fresh leaves—this will also keep the plant bushy. On mature plants, remove a few branches—this will provide a supply of leaves that you can freeze or dry and will also improve the shape.

Parsley

a great standby in the kitchen

PARSLEY IS NOT ONLY A YEAR-ROUND GARNISH, but the tasty, nutritious chopped leaves are also delicious in soups, sauces, and salads. There are two types: the strong-flavored, tight, curly parsley (*Petroselinum crispum* var. *crispum*) and the sweeter, flat-leaf variety known as Italian parsley (*P. crispum* var. *neapolitanum*). Parsley is a biennial, so it produces a crop of leaves in the first year; in the second year, it sends up tougher flower stalks before flowering, setting seed, and dying. Gardeners often treat it as a hardy annual because the best leaves are produced in the first year.

 sow

You can buy parsley plants from a garden center, but parsley is easy to grow from seeds. Start with a fresh packet of seeds and be patient. Parsley seeds need two to four weeks to germinate, during which time the soil needs to be constantly moist.

- Sow seeds in small pots in a warm place (82°F/18°C); then repot into larger outdoor containers. Or sow seeds directly into the ground when the soil temperature is at least 50°F (10°C). Sow seeds indoors in early summer for a fall crop in the North.

- Plant transplants when they are four to six weeks old, being careful to avoid damaging the roots.

- Grow in rows 10 inches (25cm) apart and thin plants to 8 inches (20cm) apart.

 grow

Parsley does better in cool, partial shade and in fertile, moist soil. Consider growing some plants in rows in the vegetable garden or in ornamental borders.

- Cover with a floating row cover to keep insect pests away.

- Mud splashes can spoil parsley, particularly the curly types. Look for cultivars with long stems, or mulch around the plants. Keep the mulch an inch (2.5cm) away from the stems to avoid crown rot, and water the plants carefully to avoid splashing.

 harvest

Start to cut leaves when the plants are 6 inches (15cm) tall. Cut the stems 1–2 inches (2.5–5cm) above the crown so the plants can produce more leaves. If you need a lot of parsley, cut the whole plant.

- The stalks have a lot of flavor but can be tough, so use them in stock and soups.

- Parsley is best fresh, but you can store it in a plastic bag in the refrigerator; it also freezes well.

Look for long stems on curly-leaf parsley to avoid mud splashes.

Sage

an herb full of aroma even when dried

THE SAGE USED FOR COOKING is a perennial that is hardy in Zones 4 to 8, and many of its cultivars are attractive foliage plants with variegated purple, green, or cream leaves.

 sow

It is easier to start with a small plant in spring. Seed-raised plants need two years before harvesting, and the cultivars with the most attractive foliage are grown from cuttings. Plant in a well-drained soil in a sunny position.

 grow

As perennials, sage plants fit in better in perennial borders than a vegetable patch.

● In warmer zones, sage grows as an evergreen shrub—

the main limiting factor is waterlogged soil over winter, so containers or raised beds are a useful alternative.

● Cut back young specimens by one-third each spring to stimulate fresh growth.

 harvest

Sage has a strong flavor so use only a few leaves at a time—simply pluck them off the plant. Sage leaves will dry well.

Savory

a substitute for ground pepper

CHOOSE BETWEEN SUMMER OR WINTER SAVORY, or grow both for year-round use. Savory adds a peppery flavor to bean, cheese, and egg dishes.

 sow

Sow the annual summer savory (*Satureja hortensis*) or the perennial winter savory (*S. montana*) where they will grow in spring. Thin them to 8 inches (20cm) apart for summer savory, 12 inches (30cm) for winter savory.

 grow

Savory will tolerate hot dry conditions and poor soil. Summer savory can be grown in the vegetable garden;

winter savory is best in an herb bed but is attactive enough for an ornamental border.

● Cut established winter savory plants back to stop them from sprawling and to encourage fresh growth.

 harvest

Pick leaves as needed once the plants reach 6 inches (15cm) tall. When summer savory has flowered, cut the whole plant and dry it for winter use. Continue picking winter savory in winter—it is better fresh.

Tarragon

a perennial with a subtle licorice flavor

FRENCH TARRAGON GOES WELL WITH FISH AND CHICKEN dishes and is also used to make tarragon vinegar. It will do best in areas with cool summers and a distinct dormant period.

sow

French tarragon (*Aretemisia dracunculus*) does not produce seeds, so you'll need to buy a plant. Don't confuse it with Russian tarragon (*A. dracunculus var. dracunculoides*). Give the plant 12 inches (30cm) to itself.

2 grow

French tarragon requires a well-drained soil and full sun, which makes it a good container plant. Or grow it in a raised bed with other drought-tolerant herbs, such as thyme. Each summer, as it starts to flower, cut back the top growth to encourage fresh leaves. In colder areas, cover with straw to protect it over winter.

- After a few years the clump may become too congested. Dig it up; remove some pieces of younger roots with shoots attached; and replant them.

3 harvest

Cut or pinch out the top third of the stems for use in the kitchen. Use the leaves fresh or to flavor vinegar.

Thyme

a shrubby perennial with tiny leaves

THERE ARE HUNDREDS OF THYMES but most cooks opt for common thyme (*Thymus vulgaris*), which imparts a warm spicy flavor to meat, cheese, egg, and pasta dishes.

sow

You can raise some types from seeds, but it is easier to start with small plants in spring. Plant in a well-drained soil or potting mix in sun or partial shade.

2 grow

Thyme is neat in habit but can get swamped by more vigorous herbs. A rock garden or on top of a wall are locations worth considering. Some low-growing, matlike varieties can be tricky to harvest, but growing them in raised beds, hanging baskets, or window boxes makes harvesting easier—and the leaves should be less muddy. Plant 6–12 inches (15–30cm) apart, and shear back after flowering to keep them bushy.

harvest

Cut off some stems, and remove the leaves in the kitchen. Thyme dries well.

Globe Artichoke

a distinctive gourmet vegetable

IF YOU HAVE A TASTE FOR ARTICHOKE HEARTS, it is worth growing your own, and once established they should keep on producing flower buds for years to come. Globe artichokes need plenty of space, but they are one of the most architectural of vegetables and worthy of a place in the flower border. They are hardy to Zone 7; in the coldest regions, grown them as annuals.

 sow

For a perennial crop in the warmest areas, buy young plants of a good strain. Globe artichokes are easy to grow from seeds and this is the best option in cooler areas, where it is grown as an annual crop.

- Sow seeds ½ inch (1cm) deep in 3-inch (7.5cm) pots about 8 to 12 weeks before the last spring frost. They germinate best at around 75°F (23°C). If necessary, transfer them into 4-inch (10cm) pots.

- After carefully hardening them off, plant in their final positions outdoors after the last frost date. In colder regions, the temperature should remain below 50°F (10°C) for ten days—this tricks the plant into flowering in its first year, instead of producing only leaves. It behaves as an annual does and you don't need to worry about protecting it over the winter.

Varieties

- **'GREEN GLOBE IMPROVED'** is a good choice for perennial plantings.

- **'IMPERIAL STAR'** is a cultivar bred for growing as an annual in northern areas (95 days).

- **'VIOLETTA'** is a perennial cultivar with attractive purple buds.

 grow

Dig or rototill the area deeply, adding plenty of organic material and removing any weeds at the same time. Allow 3–4 feet (90–120cm) between plants and 5–6 feet (1.5–1.8m) between rows as a perennial crop, and 2–3 feet (60–90cm) apart as an annual crop.

- Control weeds and water regularly. A mulch of organic matter will help preserve soil moisture and suppress weeds.

- Feed monthly with a balanced fertilizer during the growing season.

- Cut perennial plants to ground level after harvesting the buds. They will resprout soon after.

- If the plants become dense clumps, divide them so each division has at least two buds. Replace the original plant and any others that are growing poorly.

- In late fall, cut plants to ground level; cover with mulch.

 harvest

Perennial plantings will bear in spring with a smaller crop in the fall each year. Those grown as annuals will crop once in the fall.

- Cut the flower buds when full size and still firm, when the lowest scales just start to open.

- After cooking, discard the "choke," which is the immature flower. The fleshy base beneath and the bases of the scales are what you eat.

Asparagus

PERHAPS THE ULTIMATE GOURMET VEGETABLE, asparagus spears are at their best when freshly harvested. However, asparagus is not a crop for the impatient—you'll have to wait two years for the first taste, and you'll need three years before you have a decent crop. You'll need plenty of plants and a lot of space to grow enough for a feast, and even then the season lasts only six to eight weeks. However, if you can wait that long and have the space, asparagus is certainly worth the initial effort—and once it starts cropping, it should continue year after year with little work on your part.

 SOW

You can grow asparagus from seeds, but because it takes three years until you get your first crop, most people start with one-year-old crowns—the underground stem base and roots. You can buy these from a garden center or a mail-order supplier as dormant crowns.

- Plant asparagus in fall or spring—spring is best for cooler areas, fall for warmer areas.

- As a rough guide, ten well-established plants should yield about 7 pounds (3kg) of spears each season.

Varieties

Older varieties need more space than modern types and have both male and female plants. The females bear red berries that self-seed. Modern hybrids are more compact and produce only the more productive male plants. Look for:

- **'JERSEY' SERIES,** such as **'JERSEY KNIGHT'** and **'JERSEY SUPREME',** which are rust-resistant varieties.

- **'PURPLE PASSION'** is a hybrid, but not all-male; the purple spears are sweeter than green types.

Spread out the roots of the asparagus crowns when planting.

 grow

Because asparagus is such a long-term crop, spend some time getting the soil right.

- Asparagus prefers a light, free-draining soil with a neutral pH (6.5–7.5); add lime if your soil is more acidic.

- Cultivate the soil as deeply as you can, working in at least an inch (2.5cm) of compost the previous fall. Be careful to remove every scrap of perennial weed and hoe off annual weeds a couple of times. Add a generous amount of potassium and phosphate fertilizer, too.

- Dig a trench 6–8 inches (15–23cm) deep and 12 inches (30cm) wide. Make a ridge of compost down the center of the trench. Space the crowns 18 inches (45cm) apart, straddling the ridge of compost so their roots spread down either side.

- Cover the crowns with soil and gradually fill the trench once the shoots start to appear.

- If you want more than one row, space them at least 3 feet (90cm) apart.

- The major work involved in growing asparagus is keeping the weeds under control. Mulch with a weed-free compost of other organic material around the plants. Or hoe between rows but not too close to the base of the plants.

- Water newly established beds regularly—setting up a drip irrigation system is most efficient. After two years, the plants will take care of themselves.

- Feed the plants in late spring or early summer when you stop cutting. Apply a balanced fertilizer or dress with compost. This will feed the fronds that, in turn, will supply next year's spears.

- Leave the ferns until they die back completely after a couple of hard frosts. Then cut them to about 12 inches (30cm) from soil level and mulch the rows. You can pull out the dry stems in spring.

3 harvest

In the first year, don't be tempted to pick any spears. Let them all grow into ferny fronds to help build up the crowns.

- In the second year, you can cut spears for a limited period. After a month, let the fronds grow.

- In the third year, you can start to harvest for a full six to eight weeks.

- Wait until the spears are 6–8 inches (15–23cm) tall and the tips are still tight. Snap them cleanly at soil level or cut them with a knife just below soil level.

- Because the spears grow so quickly, harvest every other day. If you do not pick a sufficient amount, keep them in a refrigerator until you have enough for a meal.

- In the unlikely event that you have a surplus, asparagus freezes well.

FAQ

Q Small striped beetles are attacking my asparagus. What should I do?

A Asparagus beetles and their unattractive grubs can be a real nuisance. Severe infestations can defoliate crops and reduce future yields. Spray regularly with an organic insecticide, such as pyrethrum.

Q My asparagus foliage is turning yellow and dying. What is the cure?

A Asparagus suffers from rust disease, which is worse in warm, humid weather. Destroy affected fronds. In warmer areas, plant asparagus wider apart to allow air circulation and choose a rust-resistant variety.

Tender young asparagus spears fresh from the garden are a real treat.

Horseradish

useful as a spicy condiment

THIS PERENNIAL IS NOT RELATED TO THE SIMILARLY NAMED ANNUAL RADISHES, but it does have roots that are spicy hot. Like Jerusalem artichokes, any piece of root is capable of producing a new plant—this is useful for propagating, but the plant can be invasive. For this reason, and because it is a perennial, horseradish is best confined to an unused corner of the vegetable garden, where it will provide roots without becoming a nuisance.

 sow

Horseradish is grown from pieces of root rather than seeds. Buy and plant a root in the spring and by fall you should have a large plant.

 grow

Because it is a perennial and can be invasive, it is usually confined to a poor or shaded part of the vegetable garden. If you will need more than one plant, space the root cuttings at least 12 inches (30cm) apart.

- Except for watering early on if the soil dries out, horseradish is carefree. Giving it a mulch will help suppress weeds and retain moisture.

 GROWING IN CONTAINERS

Horseradish is not a particularly attractive plant, but confining it to a container will stop it from spreading around the garden. Choose a pot at least 12 inches (30cm) across and half sink it into the ground to save watering as often. Harvesting is simple: tip the plant out of the container; select a healthy piece of root; and replant it for next year.

3 **harvest**

For the best flavor, wait until after the first few frosts before harvesting.

- Dig up the plant and replant a sideshoot; trim off the top; and store the rest of the roots in a box of moist sand.

- If the ground doesn't freeze in your area, leave the plant in the ground and mulch it; dig roots as you need them until spring. Don't harvest while the plant is actively growing because the flavor will be poor.

- Grate horseradish for use as a garnish or in horseradish sauce carefully—it can irritate the eyes and skin.

The leaves and other parts of the plant are rarely attacked by pests.

Jerusalem Artichoke

an American "sunflower"

THIS PLANT'S NAME IS ACTUALLY A CORRUPTION OF THE ITALIAN FOR "SUNFLOWER."
These tall plants with their yellow flowers make an effective barrier or screen during summer. The roots are so prolific that, unless you gather every single one, it can become a real menace. Nevertheless, it couldn't be much easier to grow and behaves as a perennial crop. The tubers have a texture like water chestnuts and a nutty taste.

1 SOW

Instead of seeds, Jerusalem artichokes are normally grown from tubers. Most gardeners who grow this crop will be happy to give you some spare tubers.

- Plant in spring after the last expected frost date, or in fall four weeks before the first expected frost date.

- Give them room to grow by spacing the tubers 12 inches (30cm) apart and bury them 4–6 inches (10–15cm) deep.

Varieties

- There are few named cultivars, but the one to look out for is **'FUSEAU'**, with large, less-knobbly tubers, which makes preparation a lot easier.

2 grow

This is an easy-to-grow crop that can be mostly ignored. Although Jerusalem artichokes will grow in any soil and even in partial shade, they will do best in rich, well-drained soil.

- Water the plants until established and mulch to conserve soil moisture. Once established, they need no help.

- The plants will normally reappear the following year because it is difficult to remove all the tubers. In fact, it can become invasive if you aren't careful—don't inadvertently add pieces of root to the compost pile.

GROWING IN CONTAINERS

Jerusalem artichokes are an unusual subject for a large container, one that has at least a 2–gallon (7.5L) capacity. Put a medium-size tuber halfway down the container as you fill it. The plants will get tall but need little attention apart from watering. When the tops have completely died down, empty the container and collect the tubers. Put one back for next year. This is a good way to grow a few Jerusalem artichokes if you find them too invasive in the garden.

3 harvest

When the tops die back in the fall, mulch the area. This will help to keep the ground from freezing so you can leave the tubers in the garden until you need them.

- Because the flesh discolors quickly, keep them whole until the last minute before using them; then peel and cook them right away.

Remove all the tubers when you harvest the Jerusalem artichoke.

Rhubarb

tender red stalks used in desserts

JUST BECAUSE PEOPLE USE RHUBARB TO MAKE SWEET DISHES doesn't make it a fruit. Botanically, rhubarb is really a vegetable, and a perennial one. It will require plenty of room in a vegetable garden; however, rhubarb is one of the most low-maintenance crops you can grow. Apart from an annual mulch of manure, you can completely ignore it. Confine it to a sunny corner of the vegetable garden, and it will reward you year after year with a crop of red stalks.

 sow

In colder areas, grow rhubarb as a long-term perennial. It is easier to buy a plant or a division from a garden center than it is to grow rhubarb from seeds. Most gardeners will be happy to give you a division, too.

- Plant where rhubarb has space to grow into a large plant. Give it at least 3 feet (90cm) each way all to itself.

- In mild-winter areas, the cold spell may not be long enough to break the plant's dormancy and produce stalks.

Applying an organic mulch will help keep rhubarb growing.

 grow

Rhubarb will be productive year after year for 20 years or more. It does, however, prefer a rich, well-drained soil—too heavy or wet and the crown may rot. If flower shoots are produced, cut them off early or they will weaken the crown.

- Once established, rhubarb needs little maintenance, but it likes moist soil. If you harvest it heavily each year, mulch it each fall with well-rotted organic matter to keep it growing strongly—this will also prevent weeds.

- After several years, the clump may become congested and the center might start to die back. Dig out the whole clump in early spring and split healthy sections off the outside of the clump. These divisions should contain at least three or four plump buds and plenty of roots. Discard the old center of the clump. If you replant a young division in the same spot, dig the area over to break up the soil, and work in plenty of organic matter.

Varieties

- **'CANADA RED'** has sweet, bright red stalks and is a good choice for cooler areas.

- **'STRAWBERRY'** has greenish pink stalks.

- **'VALENTINE'** has tender, pink-red stalks and is one of the cultivars with the best flavor.

The stalks of the leaves are used for cooking.

grow: forced rhubarb

You can have rhubarb earlier in the year by forcing it into growth. If you have divided an old clump and have too many plants, this is a good way to use them. Dig them up, and leave them outside in fall to expose them to a couple of frosts. Then plant them in pots and bring them into a cool but frost-free basement or garage. Cover with black plastic to exclude light and check them every couple of weeks. After a few weeks, the stalks should be ready for cutting. You can replant forced rhubarb crowns, but wait a year before cutting again.

3 harvest

Don't harvest the first year, but you can take a few stalks the second year. In the third year, start harvesting the young stems as they begin to appear in spring.

- When a stem reaches 12–15 inches (30–40cm) high, twist it as you pull it to snap it off the crown; or cut it with a sharp knife. Continue harvesting for up to two months; then let the plant recover. Never remove more than one-half of the leaves at any given time.

- You may get a smaller harvest during the fall.

- To prepare rhubarb for eating, cut off the leaves; these contain high levels of oxalic acid, which is poisonous if eaten. However, they can be safely composted. The leaf stalks—the part you eat—contain very low levels of this chemical but are safe to eat when cooked.

FAQ

Q What are the insects infesting my rhubarb plants?

A Rhubarb is generally trouble free, but can be attacked by curculios—yellow-gray beetles about ½ inch (1.25cm) long. Handpick them or spray with an organic insecticide, and destroy any nearby dock plants, their alternate host plant.

Q Why has my rhubarb started to die?

A The most likely cause is phytophthora crown rot. This is most common on waterlogged soil. Destroy the existing plant, and replant a fresh crown on a new site with good drainage.

13

Garden Fruit

IF YOU ARE PLANNING TO START A VEGETABLE GARDEN, consider planting some fruit, too. Strawberries are a summer essential and fit in well with vegetables. Brambles—fruit-bearing bushes with thorns, such as raspberries, blackberries, and their relatives—are easy to establish and will reward you with pounds of fruit each year. Blueberries can be more of a challenge because they are fussy about soil, but the fresh berries will be worth the effort. Fully ripe grapes picked fresh off a vine are another late-summer treat. And in some states, you can also add currants and gooseberries to the list of fruit to grow in your garden.

Unlike the majority of vegetables, most garden fruit will need a permanent home. Because they will provide a plentiful crop of fruit every year, dedicating a part of the garden solely to them won't be a waste—as long as you take time first to prepare the soil. The only exception is strawberries, which produce the best fruit for only a few years. However, this isn't a big problem because strawberry plants easily multiply from runners. Even the brambles are remarkably simple to propagate; once you have established a couple of plants, you can multiply them to fill up the garden with fruit-bearing plants.

Strawberry

NO GARDEN SHOULD BE WITHOUT STRAWBERRIES. There's nothing to compare with a warm, fully ripe berry right from the plant, and they couldn't be much easier to grow. Simply plant a few and after a few years you'll have more plants than you'll know what to do with—and as many berries as you can eat. Even if you don't have space in the garden, strawberries make attractive container plants. The only downside is that they fruit over a short period. You can overcome this by planting several varieties to spread the harvest from early summer to fall.

SOW

For a plant that propagates itself by runners so enthusiastically, it is tempting to take a few spares from a friend or neighbor. However, because strawberries are attacked by viruses and other diseases, it is always safer to purchase guaranteed virus-free started plants from a reputable garden center or mail-order supplier. You'll then be able to easily multiply your stock in the following years. (See "Maintaining the Bed," page 202.)

- Spring is the best time to plant; it will allow the plants time to become established before winter.

- Plant in rows 18 inches (45cm) apart with 3 feet (90cm) between rows. Plant them at the correct depth—the top of the crown should be just above soil level.

If propagating stawberries from runners, make sure they are free of disease.

Varieties

June-bearers produce a heavy crop over a short period in summer. This is good news if you want to process the fruit, but not if you prefer to eat them fresh. Within this group, early and late croppers help extend the season.

- **'EARLIGLOW'** is an early maturing and disease-resistant cultivar.

- **'HONEOYE'** is resistant to diseases and has large fruit; although it is reliable, it doesn't have the best flavor.

- **'SPARKLE'**, a late variety, has good flavor and is hardy, so it is a popular choice in the North.

Everbearers and day-neutral strawberries produce smaller quantities of berries but over a longer season, often with a peak in June and August.

- **'FORT LARAMIE'** produces large, bright red fruit; they are the most cold-tolerant cultivar, so they are a good choice for the North.

- **'OGALLALA'** is a hardy cultivar that tolerates dry conditions well.

- **'OZARK BEAUTY'** provides heavy yields of large, tasty, dark red berries; this cultivar has good disease resistance.

② grow

You'll need to keep weeds under control. You can hoe between rows, but mulching with straw is the best option. Alternatively, you can plant through cross-shaped slits made in black plastic sheets. Cover the plastic with wood chips or a similar type of material to create a more attractive appearance.

- During cold weather, protect the plants by covering the rows with loose straw. Because the blossoms are sensitive to frost, cover the rows with a row cover.

- As soon as the first flowers appear, cover the beds with bird netting to stop birds, squirrels, and other animals from taking the fruit. Slugs and snails can damage the fruit, too, and damp straw provides cover for them. Use traps to reduce numbers.

 GROWING IN CONTAINERS

Strawberries are easy plants to grow in containers. You can use any decent-size container, or buy a special strawberry pot that has holes around the sides. One trick is to use two containers: one with new plants and one with second-year plants, which will have a better crop and deserve the more prominent position. Use a good, but not too rich potting mix; water regularly, especially after the first flowers form; and feed with a high-potassium fertilizer—one with too much nitrogen will encourage too much leaf growth.

Alpine Strawberries

These plants produce fruit similar to wild strawberries, with diminutive but intensely flavored berries. However, unlike the regular strawberries with large fruit—which are hybrids and won't grow true from seeds—alpine strawberries are usually grown from small seeds, and they are less likely to be affected by pests and diseases. You can plant alpines to create an attractive edible edging for a flower border; they are also suitable for growing in containers.

Start the seeds in seed-starting trays that contain a seed-starting mix; cover with water-retaining granules, such as perlite; and keep them in a cool, light place to germinate. When the seedlings have a couple of leaves, transplant them into individual pots. Plant them outside after the last spring frost. They will behave like everbearers and should continue cropping for several years before you need to replace them. 'Alexandria' and 'Mignonette' are the cultivars you are most likely to find.

grow: maintaining the bed

The yield of your plants will drop in the third or fourth year, so you'll need to start new plants. Strawberries are susceptible to many insects and diseases, including some insects that thrive in the lawn, so it is better to grow them on soil that has not been previously covered by grass.

- After five or six weeks, new plants will begin to grow runners, and these will produce new, rooted plants. For the best berries, let each parent plant produce only five runners, and allow each runner to produce only one new plant. Wait four or five weeks before cutting the runner between the parent plant and the newly rooted plant. Meanwhile, prune off any additional runners where you don't want new plants.

- In the first and second year, remove old leaves, mulch, and any unwanted runners in fall. Cultivate the soil between rows to help the plants in the following year.

- In year two or three, start a fresh bed elsewhere with store-bought plants. Or use rooted runners from your existing bed if you are sure they are not diseased.

- Once the yield has diminished in the original bed, dig up the plants and dispose of them.

Strawberries have the most flavor when freshly picked.

③ harvest

You need to pick strawberries on the day they ripen because overripe fruit deteriorates quickly once picked. However, under-ripe fruit can be too tart.

- Ideally, pick every day in peak season in morning, when the fruit is cool and the dew has dried.

- Store the berries in shallow layers in the refrigerator. Don't wash them until just before serving, which will help retain their vitamins and keep them fresh.

- Whole strawberries don't freeze well, but freeze any surplus to make puree or jam later on.

FAQ

Q Why are my strawberry plants stunted?

A White grubs that live in the soil, and later turn into June bugs, love the roots. They are most common on beds that were recently lawn grass. If you grow strawberries where vegetables have grown for several years, you may avoid these grubs. Another possible cause is a type of root weevil, a small black or brown beetle. Destroy the plants and start a new bed elsewhere (weevils don't travel far).

Q What can I do about my unhealthy-looking plants?

A Unfortunately, strawberry plants suffer from a lot of diseases. Leaf spots, wilt, and powdery mildew affect the leaves, while red stele, root rot, and root knot nematodes affect the crown and roots. Viruses can cause mottled and distorted leaves. Choose a disease-resistant cultivar and clear old strawberry plants every few years to prevent diseases from becoming a problem.

Q Why are my strawberry leaves curled?

A The most likely cause is cyclamen mites, which are tiny creatures invisible to the naked eye. They prefer humid conditions and multiply rapidly, causing severe damage. Chemical control is difficult, but biological control using predatory mites is possible.

Blueberry

a native American shrub

ONCE ESTABLISHED, BLUEBERRY PLANTS YIELD A REASONABLE CROP of tasty, nutritious berries every year. Maintenance is easy after the initial planting, but they are particular about where they will grow. If you can grow azaleas or camellias in your garden, you'll have no problem with blueberries. Otherwise, you can amend your soil or grow them in containers to provide them with acidic soil. However, just think of the pleasure of harvesting fresh berries from your backyard.

 SOW

You should be able to find potted blueberry bushes in any good garden center or from a mail-order supplier. It is best to start with small plants. While they take longer to crop, they should become better established.

- Buy potted plants and plant anytime in the fall or spring, provided the ground isn't frozen. In most areas, early spring is best.

- Unless you have a self-pollinating type, the flowers must be cross-pollinated to produce fruit. To guarantee a good crop, plant at least two different varieties with a similar bloom period. Plant them close together so that pollinating insects cross-pollinate them.

- Space high-bush and rabbiteye types 5–6 feet (1.5–1.8m) apart in rows 8 feet (2.4m) apart; space low-bush types 2 feet (60cm) apart in rows 3–4 feet (90–120cm) apart—they will form a low hedge.

Blueberry's blooms and foliage make this an attractive plant.

Varieties

- **LOW-BUSH** blueberries are the hardiest type. The plants reach 1–3 feet (30–90cm) high and spread up to 8 feet (2.4m). Good cultivars include 'Butte' and 'Top Hat'.

- **HIGH-BUSH** types are slightly less hardy but they should grow in most areas. In the South and some other regions, these can make big plants up to 6 feet (1.8m) high and wide. Good cultivars include 'Bluecrop' (mid-season), 'Bluejay' (mid-season), 'Blueray' (mid), 'Chandler' (mid-late), 'Earliblue' (early), 'Herbert' (mid), 'Ivanhoe' (early), 'Jersey' (late), all good for most areas. In warm areas, choose 'O'Neal' or 'Sharpblue'.

- **HALF-HIGH** types are crosses between the low-bush and high-bush types, and produce bushes reaching 2–4 feet (60–120cm) high and wide with big berries. Good cultivars include 'Early Bluejay' (early), 'Northblue' (mid-season), 'Northcountry' (mid), 'Northland' (mid-season), and 'Patriot' (early).

- **RABBITEYE** blueberries are the least hardy, but they will tolerate drier soils and are a good choice for warmer regions. However, they need a winter chilling period so are not suitable for areas with mild winters. They make the biggest plants, up to 15 feet (4.5m) high and 6 feet (1.8m) wide. Good cultivars include 'Beckyblue', 'Bonita', 'Climax', and 'Tifblue' (all mid-season).

Blueberry

② grow

Blueberries need a very acidic soil. Before you think about growing blueberries in the garden, check the soil pH. (See "Finding Out About Your Soil," pages 16–17.) If it is 4.5–5.0, which is very acidic, you'll be able to grow blueberries—they may even be growing wild in your neighborhood. Unfortunately, garden soil is rarely this acidic, but the situation can be rectified. (See "Get the Soil Right," opposite.)

- In the first year after planting, remove all flowers so the plant puts all its energy into establishing its roots and forming a good framework of branches.

- Blueberries fruit on shoots that are one to four years old; after that, the crop starts to decline. Prune lightly during the next three years to keep the bush neat and open.

- After the fourth year, cut the oldest branches down to ground level in the dormant season. At the same time, remove any weak or damaged shoots and try to keep the center of the bush open and uncongested. In the South, prune out shoots of high-bush varieties taller than 5–6 feet (1.5–1.8m). In the North, they won't get this tall.

- Because blueberries root close to the surface, ensure that they are never short of water, especially after flowering and when the berries are swelling.

- Apply a balanced fertilizer in the spring. Fertilizers that are based on aluminum sulfate are a good choice for blueberries.

- Do not hoe around blueberries; control weeds by regular mulching or hand-weeding.

- You'll need to keep birds from stealing the ripe fruit. Erect a framework to hang bird netting when the first fruit starts to ripen.

 ## GROWING IN CONTAINERS

If your soil is above pH 6.0 and contains lime, preparing a bed for blueberries can be difficult work. Fortunately, they'll grow well in a container. Fill it with an acidic soil or potting mix. Choose a half-tall or a compact high-bush variety. Water regularly to keep the compost just moist, and feed with an aluminum sulfate fertilizer once or twice during the growing season.

Make a small ditch near the plant to hold the water and keep the soil moist.

Blueberries are attractive plants to keep in a container on the patio.

grow: get the soil right

If your soil pH is in the range of 5.0–6.0, you can still grow blueberries successfully. You'll need to add plenty of sphagnum peat or other acidic organic matter. You can also add granular sulfur to further acidify the top few inches. These plants like plenty of organic matter such as compost, leaves, and manure. If your soil is above 6.0, consider growing blueberries in containers or prepare a special bed for them, replacing the existing soil with a something more suitable. (See "Growing in Containers," opposite.)

- Blueberries are shallow rooting plants and need a well-drained soil. If it's likely your soil will be waterlogged in winter, grow blueberries in a raised bed. Remove the existing soil down to at least 2 feet (60cm), and refill with an acidic soil mix. Some gardeners line the hole with boards to prevent the natural soil from mixing with the added soil. Mulch the bed with organic matter, and check the pH before planting.

- Each year, add a mulch and check the soil pH. If necessary, adjust the pH with granular sulfur.

THE EARLY AMERICAN COLONISTS USED BLUEBERRIES BOILED IN MILK TO MAKE GRAY PAINT.

3 harvest

The berries are ready when they develop a bloom, but taste a few before picking in earnest. Once ripe, they will keep in good condition on the plant, so you don't have to pick more than once a week.

- The berries will keep for several days when picked and freeze well for winter use.

FAQ

Q I've got grubs in my blueberries. How do I prevent them in the future?

A Blueberry maggots and cherry fruit worms are the most likely culprits. Both feed inside developing berries, causing them to become soft. Clear up any fallen berries to help prevent the grubs from surviving on them over the winter.

Q Why are some of my berries turning black and shriveling up?

A Sounds like mummy berry, a fungal disease that attacks the shoot tips and flowers. The affected berries will be rubbery and ridged and have a white growth inside. Later, they shrivel up and drop. Pick off affected berries, and clear up any fallen mummies to prevent the disease from surviving over the winter.

Q Why do my blueberries have unhealthy-looking yellow leaves?

A If the soil pH is too high, the plants will start to show symptoms of nutrient deficiency. Check and, if necessary, correct the soil pH. Give them a boost with a foliar feed containing iron and magnesium.

Q Why are the stems covered in spots?

A This could be due to stem canker, where small, swollen spots or lesions appear and, in severe cases, shoots may die off. Prune out and destroy affected canes. There are no suitable fungicides, but look for resistant varieties.

Blackberry & Hybrids

sweet, plump, deep-colored berries

BLACKBERRIES AND RASPBERRIES ARE BOTH BRAMBLES, usually with thorns, but they differ in two respects. Unlike raspberries, blackberries don't sucker. However, they have an even more effective way of taking over your garden if you let them. Each shoot roots when the tip touches the ground and produces a new plant. Leave them untrained and you'll soon have a blackberry thicket! The berries won't let you know when they are ready to pick either—unlike raspberries, the central plug comes away with the berries. Otherwise, blackberries and raspberries are grown in the same way. There are several blackberry relatives that are also worth considering if you have the space. Blackberries are suitable for all but the coldest and warmest zones.

 SOW

Buy plants in the dormant season to plant in the spring in colder areas and fall or spring in warmer areas, any time the ground is not frozen. Follow the advice for raspberries. (See "Raspberry," pages 212–213.)

- Blackberries are more vigorous than raspberries, so space them 5 feet (1.5m) apart in rows 6 feet (1.8m) apart.

Varieties

- **'CHESTER'** is a hardy cultivar with thornless canes that bear large, firm, but not tart, berries.

- **'EBONY KING'** is another hardy cultivar with thornless semi-upright canes; the plant produces large sweet berries.

- **'TRIPLE CROWN'** has vigorous thornless canes with large juicy berries; this is a good heat-tolerant cultivar.

 grow

Prepare the soil deeply with plenty of organic matter and remove perennial weeds.

- Growing blackberries against a fence is an easy way to support them. Or provide a post-and-wire trellis, and tie in the new shoots regularly. (See "Supporting Brambles," page 212.)

- Prevent the shoots from reaching the soil and rooting to keep them under control.

Training a blackberry up a trellis is one way to make picking the berries easier.

grow: training blackberries

Blackberries fruit on one-year-old canes, so you won't get a crop the year after planting.

- In subsequent years, tie the new canes to a fence or trellis.

- Cut old canes to the ground after they have finished fruiting. Also remove weaker canes if the plant starts to become crowded (wear gloves unless it's a thornless cultivar).

- Tie the new canes securely in a fan shape to make picking easier and allow air to circulate freely.

The berries will turn a deep black color as they ripen.

3 harvest

The fruit is ready to be picked when it reaches full size and is black and lustrous. Picking the fruit will encourage the plant to produce larger fruit later on.

- If you are worried about insects lurking inside the fruit, soak the berries in salted water to expel them.

- Blackberries freeze as easily as raspberries do. Both make great jam, too, if you have a surplus.

Blackberry Relatives

The boysenberry is a trailing relative of the blackberry, with long thornless canes bearing tart, black berries 2 inches (5-cm) long; it is cold tolerant. The loganberry has a similar habit to the boysenberry; 'Thornless' has long, dark red berries that are tart and full of flavor.

FAQ

Q The tips of my blackberry canes are wilting. Why?

A The raspberry cane borer is the most likely culprit. Prune the cane below the damaged area and cut it open. You'll find a fat grub, which, left to its own devices, will continue burrowing down the cane.

Q Why are my leaves yellow and mottled?

A Virus is a serious problem on bramble fruit. Buying virus-free plants helps, but the plants can be infected by aphids. Dig up and destroy affected plants because they will just get weaker and the crop will tail off. Unfortunately, there's no cure.

Q Why are some of the canes dying?

A This is caused by a disease called spur blight. It affects older canes, so although you'll lose part of this year's crop, new shoots should not be affected. Spraying with a fungicide in spring and again in fall should control it.

Q What are the orange spots on my bushes?

A Orange rust affects blackberries in particular. Unfortunately, it is difficult to control, but keeping the bushes uncrowded and avoiding excess nitrogen fertilizer should help.

Currant & Gooseberry

great berries for pies, purees, and preserves

CURRANTS AND THE CLOSELY RELATED GOOSEBERRY ARE EXCELLENT plants and are both grown in the same way. They make neat bushes, needing no support and only a little pruning each year to keep them productive. Once established, they should keep going for years. The berries are sweet when fully ripe, with more than a hint of acid. If you live in certain states, there are restrictions on growing them because of white pine blister rust. As long as you don't live in one of these areas, there's no reason not to have a few bushes in your garden, even if among ornamental plants.

 ## sow

Currants and gooseberries are sold in containers or as bare-root plants in spring—look for plants that are fresh out of the ground with a good ratio of root to top growth. Buy one-year-old plants. Although they will take a couple of years before you can harvest large quantities of fruit, they are easy to establish.

- Plant bare-root types immediately, or if the ground is not ready, bury the roots in a pot of moist potting mix to keep them from drying out. Better still, look for plants in large pots ready to put straight into the garden.

- Give the plants an area 4–5 feet (1.2–1.5m) in diameter each or plant 4–5 feet (1.2–1.5m) apart in rows.

sow: growing restrictions

The *Ribes* species, which includes the gooseberry and the European black currant, are affected by a disease known as white pine blister rust. It hardly affects the *Ribes* species, but it is a devastating disease on its alternate host, the native white pine. Thus, currants have a bad reputation and although federal restrictions have been lifted, there are still laws in many states on planting currants and gooseberries if there are stands of white pine nearby. Catalogs usually list restricted states because it is illegal to ship the plants to them. Check with your local Cooperative Extension Service to see what the restrictions are before you start planting any of these fruit.

 ## grow

Both currants and gooseberries are easygoing plants. If you can, dig or till the soil deeply and work in some compost or organic matter before planting.

- In subsequent years, apart from keeping the area around the plants free of weeds and providing a little general-purpose fertilizer, they require little attention.

- Water the plants if the soil starts to get too dry, especially when they have finished flowering and the fruit is starting to swell.

- As with all fruit that grows on bushes, cover the ground around the plants with mulch, such as compost or another organic material. It will help take care of the weeds, retain moisture, and provide sufficient nutrients. Alternatively, use a plastic sheet combined with an annual fertilizer.

- The bushes don't need pruning for the first three years. Thereafter, you should treat them as typical garden shrubs: first cut out old, damaged, or congested shoots; then thin the center of the plant to allow air movement. The aim should be a neat, open bush with a good balance of one-, two-, and three-year-old shoots.

Varieties

- **BLACK CURRANT** types have "strigs" of fairly large rich, black fruit and are sweet when fully ripe. 'Ben Sarek' is a modern Scottish cultivar that makes a compact bush, ideal for smaller gardens, but with large berries; 'Consort' is a classic blister rust-resistant cultivar.

- **RED CURRANT** types bear long "strigs" of small, bright red, sharp fruit, ideal for making jelly. 'Red Lake' is popular but susceptible to powdery mildew. 'Redstart' is a high-yielding cultivar.

- **WHITE CURRANT** types are similar to red currant types but the fruit is semitransparent, yellowish white in color, and fairly tart. 'White Imperial' is a widely grown cultivar.

- **GOOSEBERRY** types have been bred with few spines. The fruit ripen to gold or red. 'Captivator' is a mildew-resistant, nearly thornless cultivar with tasty pink berries. 'Invicta', a mildew-resistant cultivar, has tart, pale green fruit good for cooking. 'Pixwell' is a variety with medium-size berries that ripen to pink. 'Poorman' has large red fruit that can be eaten fresh.

- **JOSTABERRY** is a cross that combines the larger fruit of a gooseberry with the rich color of a black currant and a taste somewhere between the two; it is resistant to blister rust and mildew.

Gooseberries (center) and currants appear different but are closely related.

3 harvest

The trick with all members of the currant family is to leave the fruit on the plant as long as possible. Pick too soon and they will be too tart, and you'll have to add pounds of sugar to make them palatable. However, let them ripen fully on the plant and they'll become sweet. When you can eat a black currant or gooseberry straight off the bush without wincing, the berries are about ready to be picked.

- You will, of course, need to keep the local bird and squirrel population off them. Temporary netting should do the job.

- Some older gooseberry varieties can be spiny, so wear gloves to protect your hands.

- Currant and jostaberry varieties are spineless. The fruit is best picked in bunches or "strigs;" remove the stems once you get the fruit indoors.

FAQ

Q What is causing my gooseberry plants to be covered in white mold?

A Unfortunately, both currants and gooseberries are susceptible to American mildew (the white powdery mold later turns brown) and powdery mildew. Both are hard to control and worse in warm, humid summers. If this is a regular problem, replace bushes with resistant cultivars. Keep the bushes open and uncrowded to improve air circulation. Use a recommended fungicide or try a solution of baking soda.

Q What's caused the discolored leaves on my currants?

A Anthracnose is another disease that affects these plants. Keeping your bushes open and free of weeds should help. However, if the discoloration becomes severe, spray with a suitable fungicide.

Grape

THERE ARE TWO APPROACHES TO GROWING GRAPE VINES. Train them as climbers on an arbor and leave them more or less to their own devices, appreciating their shade and the bunches of grapes as a bonus. Or train them as a productive crop to maximize your harvest of sweet, juicy grapes. Whether you grow them for eating fresh or making your own wine, you'll appreciate the superior flavor.

 SOW

Buy strong one-year-old plants from a garden center. These will become better established than two-year-old plants, but you'll have to wait longer for a crop.

- Choose a variety suited to your location, particularly if you live in cooler areas.

- Plant in the spring in rows with about 8 feet (2.4m) between plants. If you plant more than one row, space them 8 feet (2.4m) apart, too.

 grow

Grapes prefer a deep, sandy soil that warms up quickly in spring and drains quickly. It should be reasonably fertile but not too rich. Too many nutrients will just encourage leaf growth, not fruit.

- The vines will need supporting. Put these in place when you plant the row. For a post-and-wire system, hammer a stout post at each end of the row and halfway between each plant. Remember that these will be standing for many years because this is a long-term crop. Run two wires (at least 9-gauge) between the posts 2–4 feet (60–120cm) high and secure them well.

- In the first year, water the plants to help them become established and let them build up strong roots.

- Mulch around the plants to warm the soil, retain moisture, and suppress weeds.

- Water vines regularly during spring and summer, but stop when the fruit starts to swell.

- Apply a little fertilizer in early spring, if the plants need it, or a small quantity of compost. Do not overfeed.

- Mulch the rows with straw or a similar material for winter protection, but remove this in the spring. Clear debris from under the rows before mulching the next fall to deter pests.

grow: training and pruning

Training grape vines can sound daunting, but follow the advice below and after a few years it will become a routine job. This system of training will work well for American and European grapes and their hybrids. For muscadines, use a T-shaped post structure supporting two top wires.

- In early spring in the second year, before the buds break, cut the plant back to a single stem with no sideshoots. Allow four buds to develop into sideshoots, two in each direction, and as they grow tie them to the wires if they don't cling naturally—two on the top wire and two on the bottom wire. Remove all buds that start to grow in other directions along these shoots.

- In the third year, fruit will be produced along the sideshoots. Allow four buds to grow from the main stem. These will replace the fruiting branches next year.

- In early winter, cut the branches that bore fruit back to the main stem; tie the four replacement shoots to the wires. Remove all other growth. Repeat this step each year.

 Homegrown grapes lack the pesticides often associated with commercial crops.

Varieties

- **AMERICAN GRAPES** have skin that slips free from the flesh of the grape. Good cultivars include 'Canadice' and 'Reliance', which are both red-skinned and seedless; 'Concord Seedless', a seedless version of a favorite blue-skinned grape; 'Glenora', a hardy cultivar with black, seedless grapes; and 'Marquis', a white, seedless cultivar that is early and hardy.

- **EUROPEAN** cultivars are best in warm areas; the skin on the fruit adheres to the flesh.

- **HYBRIDS** between American and European types will grow in cooler areas. Good cultivars include 'Himrod Seedless' and 'Lakeland Seedless', which are productive, seedless, white dessert grapes.

- **MUSCADINE GRAPES** are native to the southern states and grow well in warm areas. They have tougher skins than other grapes and ripen bronze to dark purple. Cultivars include 'Carlos' and 'Ison'.

A tepee can support grapes if a fence or wall space is not available.

3 harvest

Leave the bunches on the vine as long as possible because grapes do not continue to ripen after being picked. When ripe they will have reached their full color and have a "bloom," and the bunches will detach easily from the vine.

- Grapes will keep for weeks in a refrigerator and can be turned into jelly, juice, or even homemade wine. You can also use the larger leaves in early summer for stuffing.

FAQ

Q What's eating my vine leaves?

A The Japanese beetle is the most likely culprit. If damage becomes severe, spray with an organic insecticide, such as neem, or apply beneficial nematodes.

Q What's eating my grapes?

A The grubs of the grape berry moth damage the flower bunches and young fruit and later hollow out ripening fruit. If this is a serious problem, watch for early signs and spray with a suitable insecticide. Tidy up dead leaves and debris each fall, too.

Q I've noticed spots on the leaves. Will they affect the crop?

A Grape vines are attacked by several diseases. Circular reddish spots with a black margin indicate black rot, while yellow spots with a downy mold on the undersides indicate downy mildew. Both diseases also attack the flowers, resulting in either shriveled or moldy fruit later on. Both can be controlled by modern fungicides, but removing leaf debris in fall will help prevent the diseases from surviving over the winter.

Raspberry

Brightly colored, plump delicious berries

ONCE RASPBERRIES START PRODUCING FRUIT, it can be hard to keep up with them. Summer raspberries fruit on one-year-old stems, referred to as "canes." At the end of each summer, the canes produced in that year should be tied to a frame to support next year's berries. If this sounds like too much work, everbearing raspberries fruit on the current season's canes in midsummer and again in fall, and they don't need any permanent support. Grow both kinds and choose an early and a late summer variety, and you'll have fresh raspberries until fall.

 SOW

If you know someone who grows raspberries, there's a good chance they'll be happy to give you some spare canes to get you started. One thing you need to know about raspberries is that once they are established, they start to spread out and take over the whole fruit patch. If you acquire canes in this way, check that they are cropping well and free of disease and that they are a good cultivar. If you cannot be sure, play it safe and buy guaranteed disease-free canes from a reputable supplier in the dormant season. Raspberry canes are often sold as bare-root plants. Check that they are not dry and that they have at least one stem about ½ inch (1.25cm) or a little less in diameter and plenty of root. You may also find plants for sale in pots. Keep these in their pots until you are ready to plant.

- When you get bare-root plants home, plant them immediately if possible. If not, dig a hole and bury the roots to keep them cool and moist.

- Plant raspberries 2 feet (60cm) apart in rows 6 feet (1.8m) apart. It is always best to put in the supports before planting. Plant them just slightly deeper than they were originally growing.

- Water the canes in well and keep them moist until the plants are well established and growing strongly.

- Cut the original shoots back to about 2 inches (5cm) from the soil surface.

SOW: supporting brambles

You can train raspberries and blackberries up a fence or leave them unsupported, but it is better to grow them in a row, supported on wires. The canes will have plenty of air and you can pick the berries from either side.

- Set a post at each end of the row and at 6- to 8-foot (1.8–2.4m) intervals. Brace the end posts with diagonals to support the weight of mature plants. Run a strong wire on the sides of each post at about 6 feet (1.8m) above the ground and attach it securely. Attach one or two wires at 2- to 3-foot (60–90cm) intervals from the ground. Having two wires will let you tuck stray canes between them without tying them to the wires.

There's nothing like the first ripe raspberries of the summer.

Varieties

Reliable summer-fruiting cultivars include:

- **'BRISTOL'** produces vigorous upright canes with large, dark berries.

- **'JEWEL'** has vigorous upright canes and is early ripening; it is disease resistant and winter hardy.

- **'KILARNEY'**, a midseason cultivar, has sweet, bright red berries; hardy.

- **'LATHAM'**, an easy-to-pick midseason cultivar.

- **'ROYALTY'** bears large, sweet purple berries on vigorous canes.

- **'TULAMEEN'**, a late cultivar, has heavy yields of tasty, dark pink fruit; very hardy.

Good cultivars of everbearers to choose include:

- **'CAROLINE'**, a newer cultivar with tasty fruit.

- **'FALLGOLD'** has unusual golden fruit; hardy.

- **'FALL RED'** is another popular established cultivar with bright red, tasty fruit.

- **'HERITAGE'**, a popular cultivar, bears sweet red berries.

2 grow

Prepare the bed well, by digging it deeply and working in plenty of compost or well-rotted manure, and there will be only a little work each spring.

- Simply add a generous mulch of organic matter to feed the canes, retain moisture, and suppress weeds. You can use black plastic or landscape fabric for the paths between rows.

- Water the plants regularly if the weather is hot and dry—a drip irrigation system or soaker hose is a good idea.

- Once the canes are well established, you may need to dig out suckers that stray too far from the original row.

grow: training summer berries

Don't expect any fruit in the first season. As the canes grow, tuck them between the wires or tie them to the wires to keep them upright. If they grow beyond the top wire, arch them down and tie them. The canes grow in the first season. In the second, they produce fruit, so you'll always have a mixture of fruiting and new canes.

- At the end of the summer, cut all the old canes that have borne fruit to the ground and remove them. Then select six of the strongest new canes, and tie them in a fan shape to the wires. If you opt for two wires, you can tie any new canes onto one wire and the older fruiting canes to the other to keep them apart.

- During the season cut out any weak canes and remove any canes that appear between the rows.

grow: pruning everbearers

These produce fruit in the late summer and fall on the new growth. Once they've finished fruiting, simply cut all the canes to the ground. Next year you will get new canes and another crop. You don't need to provide any support unless the clumps become too unruly.

- Fall-bearing raspberries will produce a summer crop on canes left unpruned, but you'll get a bigger crop if you do prune and let them fruit only in the fall.

3 harvest

Raspberries are ready to pick as soon as they reach full size and are bright red (or bright yellow in yellow-fruit varieties or black in black-fruit varieties). Ripe fruit should fall off the plant easily when touched, leaving the green plug attached to the cane.

- Be careful when handling ripe fruit because raspberries are easily damaged; use shallow containers to avoid piling them too deeply, which can crush them.

- Raspberries will keep a few days in the refrigerator, but they are better eaten immediately. If you can't, freeze any surplus. Spread them in a single layer on cookie sheets to freeze before transferring to bags or containers.

Glossary

ACIDIC Soil with a low pH, below 7.0 and unsuitable for plants that prefer alkaline soil.

ALKALINE Soil with a high pH, above 7.0, also called lime soil, and unsuitable for plants that prefer a neutral or acidic soil.

ANNUAL A plant that grows from a seed and flowers in the same year; most vegetables are annuals.

BARE ROOT Plants that have been grown in the soil, then lifted out of it and sold to gardeners without being planted in pots.

***BACILLUS THURINGIENSIS* (BT)** A naturally occurring bacteria that is lethal to caterpillars but harmless to other animals and most insects. It is sold as a soluble powder to kill caterpillar pests.

BALANCED FERTILIZER A fertilizer with equal parts of the three main nutrients needed by plants: nitrogen, phosphorus, and potassium.

BENEFICIAL NEMATODES Minute worms that can be bought and spread on the ground to kill soil pests.

BIENNIAL A plant that produces a storage root in its first year and flowers in the second year; most root crops are biennials.

BLANCH To cover plants to exclude light and make the leaves or hearts pale and milder in taste.

BOLTING When a plant sends up a flower stalk early due to unfavorable growing conditions. *See also* "interruption to growth."

BORDEAUX MIXTURE A mixture of simple chemicals originally used to control diseases on vines but useful on other fruit, too. However, it is does not wash away from foliage easily and can eventually build up to toxic levels, so if you use it, do so sparingly.

BRASSICA The family of plants that includes cabbage and its many edible relatives, from turnips to cauliflowers.

BROADCAST To scatter seeds in patches rather than along single rows to produce a mass of leaves, a technique useful for salad greens.

CANKER A dead spot on a plant stem resulting from a disease caused by a fungus or bacterium.

CLOCHE *See* "hot cap."

COLD FRAME An outdoor, boxlike structure with a plastic or glass top similar to a window that is used for starting seeds and protecting young plants in cold weather.

COMPOST Dead plant matter collected into a pile that rots down; it produces a useful material that can be used as a mulch or as a soil additive.

COVER CROP A crop grown not to eat but to cover bare soil to keep it in good shape; *see also* "green manure."

CROP ROTATION A method of preventing pests and diseases by moving crops to a different part of the vegetable garden year to year in a set sequence.

CULTIVAR A named form of a fruit or vegetable that is guaranteed to be distinct from other varieties and conforms to a description; the name is usually enclosed in single quotes.

CUT-AND-COME-AGAIN A technique of cutting salad greens so that the plants resprout to provide a second and third crop of leaves.

DETERMINATE Plants, such as tomatoes, that grow to a set height and produce most of their fruit at the same time; *see also* "indeterminate."

DIBBLE A tool with a pointed end that increases in diameter, used for making planting holes in the soil.

DIVISION A section of a perennial plant that has been pulled or cut away from a mature plant; this technique can be used to increase several perennial herbs.

DORMANT The state of a plant when it is alive but not actively growing. Plants may be dormant when conditions are not suitable—for example, during winter when the temperature is cold.

DRAW HOE A hoe with the blade at right angles to the handle, which is pulled toward you to remove weeds.

EARLY Varieties of fruit or vegetables that crop faster than other varieties; *see also* "main crop."

F1 HYBRID Seeds produced by crossing two specific parent types; hybrid varieties produce plants that are vigorous and almost identical to each other.

FERTILIZER Any product containing a concentrated form of nutrients that plants need to grow. Fertilizers can contain man-made chemicals or products of natural origin—the latter is an organic fertilizer.

FLOATING ROW COVER A translucent material made from spun plastic that can be used to cover crops, keeping them warm while letting air and rain through; it also keeps insect pests out.

FORCE To cover crops before they start into normal growth to produce pale tender leaves or hearts.

FUNGICIDE A chemical or natural product used to kill or prevent diseases caused by fungi.

FURROW A narrow, shallow trench made in the soil so that seeds are buried at the correct depth and in straight lines.

GREEN MANURE A cover crop grown especially to dig into the soil to help add organic matter.

HANDPICK To remove insects or other small garden pests from plants by picking them off manually. You can use tweezers or other implements to help remove them.

HAND PULL Removing weed seedlings by hand from among rows of crops, where a hoe cannot be used.

HARDEN OFF To get plants that were started off indoors used to being outdoors by leaving them outside for longer each day over a period of a week or so.

HARDPAN A layer of hard soil beneath the surface often caused by repeatedly cultivating to the same depth. It can lead to poor drainage and poor root growth.

HARDY Describing a plant that is more tolerant of cold weather; some can survive frosts. (See "Heat & Hardiness," pages 24–25.)

HEIRLOOM VARIETY An open-pollinated plant that has been around for a long time, usually from before 1940, sometimes kept going by gardening enthusiasts.

Glossary

HERBICIDE A chemical for killing weeds.

HILLING A technique in which seeds are planted in a small hill, or mound, of soil, usually about 12 inches (30cm) high or the technique of pulling soil up around the plant as it grows. This hill protects the neck of these plants, which are susceptible to rotting.

HORTICULTURAL OIL A solution of natural oils used to kill insect pests and acceptable to organic gardeners.

HOT CAP A temporary transparent cover for individual plants to protect them from cold weather, also known as a "cloche."

INDETERMINATE Plants, especially tomatoes, that continue to grow from the top and produce fruit right through the summer; *see also* "determinate."

INSECTICIDAL SOAP A natural product used to kill insect pests and that is acceptable to organic gardeners.

INSECTICIDE A chemical for killing insect pests. Most are developed from man-made chemicals, but some are produced from naturally occurring chemicals, suitable for organic gardening.

INTERRUPTION TO GROWTH A setback to a plant due to drought, cold, or heat, which stops it from growing or makes it flower early; *see also* "bolting."

LEAF MOLD A compost made from leaves collected in the fall; these rot slowly, so they are often kept separate from other garden waste in the compost pile.

LEGUME A family of plants that includes peas and beans; all have the ability to turn nitrogen in the air into nitrogen salts they can use as food.

LOAM A soil that contains a fertile mixture of sand, clay, and silt.

MAIN CROP Varieties of fruit or vegetables that are ready for harvesting within the main bearing period; early or late varieties bear outside this period.

MILKY SPORE DISEASE A solution of a natural bacteria that kills the grubs of Japanese beetles.

MULCH A layer of material laid over the surface of the soil to retain moisture, prevent weeds, or protect it from cold, heat, and wind. It may be organic, such as compost, or inorganic, such as a plastic sheet.

NEMATODES Minute worms that are abundant in the soil. Although they are mostly harmless, there are a few that can harm garden plants.

NO-DIG A method of managing a vegetable garden that relies on adding organic mulch each year to improve the soil, instead of digging.

NPK The ratio of the main plant nutrients in a fertilizer—nitrogen, potash, and phosphate—and given on the package in percentages, such as 7:7:7.

OPEN-POLLINATED Seeds collected from plants that have been pollinated naturally; seeds of open-pollinated varieties produce plants that are all slightly different from their parents.

ORGANIC Anything that is of plant or animal origin; also used to describe a way of gardening that uses only organic materials.

ORGANIC MATTER Bulky material, such as manure or garden compost, that is used to improve soil and help feed plants.

OVERWINTER To keep plants growing through the winter to crop in the following spring; also refers to when insects and other creatures survive outdoors during the winter.

PERENNIAL A plant that keeps growing for years, flowering each year, such as most fruit and some herbs and vegetables.

PESTICIDE Any chemical used to kill pests, sometimes used as a general term to include fungicides and herbicides, too.

PH The measure of whether a soil is acidic or alkaline. A pH of 7.0 is neutral, higher than this is alkaline and lower is acidic.

PRICK OUT To separate seedlings started in the same container and plant each in its own pot.

PUSH HOE A hoe with a flat blade that extends from the end of the handle. It is pushed away from you to remove weeds.

REPOT To move a seedling or a started plant into a larger pot.

ROOT NODULE Lumps on the roots of peas and beans that convert nitrogen in the air into food.

SEED STARTER TRAY A plastic tray divided into several square divisions; a seed sown in each will produce an easily separated seedling to plant outdoors.

SET Started onion bulbs ready to grow into mature plants as an alternative to growing from seeds.

SIDE-DRESS To scatter fertilizer along a row of half-grown vegetables to boost its yield.

SLOW RELEASE A fertilizer that is made to release its nutrients over a period of weeks or months instead of all at once.

STARTED PLANT Plants grown from seeds in divided trays and available from garden centers when ready to plant outdoors.

SUCCESSIONAL SOWING Sowing small amounts of seeds of a particular vegetable several times during the season instead of just sowing once. This helps to spread out the harvesting period.

TENDER A plant that does not survive cold conditions or frosts.

THINNING The act of removing extra seedlings from a row to provide sufficient growing space for the remaining plants.

TILTH The condition of the soil after it has been broken down and raked to create a fine, crumbly texture suitable for planting seeds.

TOP-DRESS Scattering fertilizer over the soil before sowing a crop; it does not need to be mixed in.

TRANSPLANT A young plant grown from a seed in a pot to be planted outside when conditions are suitable; also the act of planting out started plants.

VARIETY *See* cultivar.

Resources & Suppliers

useful addresses and other contact details

On the following pages, you'll find organizations and other resources that can provide supplemental information about gardening to use alongside this book, as well as just a few of the numerous vegetable garden suppliers. It is not intended as a listing of the products and manufacturers represented by the photographs in this book.

ORGANIZATIONS AND OTHER RESOURCES

American Horitcultural Society
7931 Boulevard Dr.
Alexandria, VA 22308
(800) 777-7931
www.ahs.org
A network of experts that provides horticultural help for home gardeners.

Cornell University Department of Agriculture
134A Plant Science Building
Cornell University
Ithaca, NY 14853
(607) 255-4568 or 255-1789
www.gardening.cornell.edu/
Provides information on soil and vegetable gardening.

Extoxnet
Ace.orst.edu/ino/extoxnet
A cooperative involving the University of California-Davis, Cornell University, the University of Idaho, Michigan State University, and Oregon State University, providing information on pesticides.

Herb Society of America
9019 Kirtland Chardon Rd.
Kirtland, OH 44049
(440) 256-0514
www.herbsociety.org
Provides information to promote the use of herbs.

The Massachusetts Department of Agricultural Resources
1251 Causeway St., Ste. 500
Boston, MA 02144
(617) 626-1700
www.mass.gov/agr/gardening/vegetables/
Provides links to sites on homegrown vegetables.

Native Seeds/Search
526 N. 4th Ave.
Tucson, AZ 85705-8450
(520) 662-5561
www.nativeseeds.org
Established to preserve native American seeds.

The Ohio State University
16 Howlett Hall
2001 Fyffe Ct.
Columbus, OH 43210
(614) 292-3866
plantfacts.ohio-state.edu
Provides information for gardening throughout the United States and has more than 60,000 pages of Extension fact sheets and bulletins.

Seed Savers Exchange
3094 North Winn Rd.
Decorah, IA 52101
(563) 382-5990
www.seedsavers.org
Dedicated to saving and sharing heirloom seeds.

United States Department of Agriculture
1400 Independence Ave.
S.W. Washington, D.C. 20250
www.usda.gov
Provides a plant database that includes weather information and advice on food preservation.

SOIL TESTING

(Many state universities and local Extension services will also provide soil testing.)

Peaceful Valley Farm Supply
P.O. Box 2209
Grass Valley, CA 95945
www.groworganic.com
Supplies organic seeds and related products.

Soilperfect
1511 East Main St.
Belleville, IL 62222
www.soilperfect.com

SUPPLIERS

VEGETABLE SEEDS AND PLANTS

W. Atlee Burpee & Co.
300 Park Ave.
Warminster PA 18974
(800) 333-5808
www.burpee.com

The Cooks Garden
P.O. Box C5030
Warminster, PA 18974
(800) 457-9703
www.cooksgarden.com

Evergreen Y. H. Enterprises
P.O. Box 17538
Anaheim, CA 92817
(714) 637-5769
www.evergreenseeds.com
(Asian vegetables)

Gurneys Seeds and Nursery
P.O. Box 4178
Greendale, IN 47025-1491
(513) 354-1492
www.gurneys.com

Henry Fields Seeds and Nursery
P.O. Box 397
Aurora, IN 47001-1496
(513) 354-1498
www.henryfields.com

Heirloom Seeds
P.O. Box 245
W. Elizabeth, PA 15088-0245
(412) 384-0852
www.heirloomseeds.com

Ed Hume Seeds
P.O. Box 73160
Payallup, Washington 98373
(253) 435-4414
www.humeseeds.com

Johnnys Selected Seeds
955 Benton Ave.
Winslow, ME 04901
(877) 564-6697
www.johnnyseeds.com

Park Seed Company
1 Parktown Ave.
Greenwood, SC 29647
(800) 213-0076
www.parkseed.com

Pinetree Garden Seeds
P.O. Box 300
New Gloucester, ME 04260
(207) 926-3400
www.superseeds.com

Seeds of Change
(888) 782-7333
www.seedsofchange.com
(organic seeds)

Seeds from Italy
P.O. Box 149
Winchester, MA 01890
(781) 721-5904
www.growitalian.com

Southern Exposure
P.O. Box 460
Mineral, VA 23117
(540) 894-9480
www.southernexposure.com

Stokes Seeds
P.O. Box 548
Buffalo, NY 14240-0548
(716) 695-6980
www.stokeseeds.com

Territorial Seed Company
20 Palmer Ave.
Cottage Grove, OR 97424
(541) 942-0510
www.territorialseed.com

Thompson & Morgan
220 Faraday Ave.
Jackson, NJ 08527-5073
(800) 274-7333
www.tmseeds.com

Totally Tomatoes
334W Stroud St.
Randolph, WI 53956
(800) 345-5977
www.totallytomatoes.com

Veseys Seeds Ltd.
P.O. Box 9000
Calais, ME 04619-6102
(800) 363-7333
www.veseys.com

POTATOES

Ronniger Potato Farm
12101 2135 Rd.
Austin, CO 81410
(877) 204-8704
www.ronnigers.com

Wood Prairie Farm
49 Kinney Rd.
Bridgewater, ME 04735
(800) 829-9765
www.woodprairie.com

FRUIT SUPPLIERS

Millers Nurseries
5060 West Lake Road
Canandaigua, NY 14424-8904
(800) 836-9630
www.millernurseries.com

Stark Bros. Nurseries and Orchards
P.O. Box 1800
Louisiana, MO 63353
(800) 325-4180
www.starkbros.com

GARDENING SUPPLIES

Down to Earth Distributors
P.O. Box 1419
Eugene, OR 97440
(800) 234-5932
www.down-to-earth.com

Gardens Alive
5100 Shenley Pl.
Lawrenceburg, IN 47025
(513) 354-1482
www.gardensalive.com

Garden Harvest Supply Co.
2952W 500S
Berne, IN 46711
(260) 589-3384
www.gardenharvestsupply.com

Gardeners Supply Co.
128 Intervale Rd.
Burlington, VT 65401
(800) 235-6739
www.gardeners.com

Index

Index

Photo Credits

Front cover: Photolibrary/Garden Picture Library/Fredrich Didlillon (background). Ian Armitage (TR); Getty Images/Nordic Photos (MR); Ian Armitage (BR).

Back cover: Shutterstock/Lori Froeb (Background); Shutterstock/Christine Van Reeuwyk (BL); Shutterstock/Anne Kitzman (BM); Shutterstock/Arturo Limon (BR).

Ian Armitage: 9; 72; 83 (BR); 88 (BL); 94 (TL); 180 (TR); 186 (BR); 187 (BR); 189 (TR); 191 (TR); 211 (BL).

T. C. Bird: 49 (TR); 113 (BL).

Jane Courtier: 108 (BR); 109 (TR).

Dr. Michael Denner: 149 (L).

DK Images: Pia Tryde 18 (BL); Emma Firth 23 (ML, MR); Peter Anderson 45 (TL).

GAP Photos Ltd.: Graham Strong 14 (BL); Mark Bolton 23 (B); Paul Debois 67 (TR); Visions 204 (BR); Friedrich Strauss 206 (BL).

Harper Garden Images: Jerry Harper 11 (TR).

Harris Seeds: 176 (L).

Neil Hepworth: 4 (TL, BL); 5 (BR, BL); 76 (T); 102 (BR); 110 (BR); 111 (BR); 118 (BL); 122 (TR); 131 (BR); 134 (TR); 136 (TR); 146 (TR); 148 (TR); 156 (TR, CR); 170 (TR); 182 (TR); 202 (BL).

Johnny's Selected Seeds: 94 (BL); 128 (BL); 129 (BR); 141 (BL); 160 (TR); 181 (B); 187 (TR); 189 (BR).

Mariquita Farm Photos: 151 (BR); 154 (BL).

Thomas Morgan: 76 (C); 77 (BL, BC).

Photolibrary.com: Jennifer Cheung 3; Garden Picture Library/Jaqui Hurst 6; Oxford Scientific/Geoff Kidd 15; Guy Moberly 23 (BR); Botanica 26; Index Stock Imagery/Bill Gillingham 33 (BL); Garden Picture Library/Michael Howes 37 (R); Garden Picture Library/Chris Burrows 37 (TL); Garden Picture Library/Francois De Heel 42, 73 (TR); Garden Picture Library/Dennis Davis 53 (TR); Botanica/Ragan Romy 56 (BR); Garden Picture Library/Howard Rice 70, 85 (R); Garden Picture Library/Stephen Hamilton 81 (TR); Garden Picture Library/Mark Turner 96 (BR); Nordic Photos/Svenne Nordlov 103 (BL); Schnare & Stief 103 (TL); Garden Picture Library 104; Garden Picture Library/James Guilliam 115 (BR); Nordic Photos/Olle Akerstrom 116; Botanica/Rob Casey 132; Image Source 143 (BR); Garden Picture Library/David Cavagnaro 149 (R); Tim Hill 157 (BL); Botanica/Sandra Ivany 161 (BL); Botanica/James Baigrie 163 (BR); Garden Picture Library/Juliet Greene 165 (TL); Garden Picture Library/Chris Burrows 168 (BL); Garden Picture Library/Linda Burgess 178; Botanica/Bob Stefko 182 (BR); Imagestate/Foodfolio Foodfolio 183 (BR); Botanica/Linda Lewis 184 (BR); Garden Picture Library/MarkBolton 185 (BR); Botanica/Rachel Weil 190 (TR); Garden Picture Library/Susan McCafferey 190 (BR); Garden Picture Library/Stephen Hamilton 195 (BR); Tracey Kusiewicz/Foodie Photography 198; Garden Picture Library/David Cavagnaro 203 (BL).

Photos Horticultural: 107 (BR).

Photoshot: Tim Harris 161 (TR).

Denis Ryan: 8; 22; 32 (BR); 35 (TR); 36 (BL); 54 (BL); 55; 90 (BR); 93 (C); 145 (BL); 155 (R); 169 (BL); 174 (BR).

Shutterstock: Norman Chan 5 (MR); Arturo Limon 69 (TR); Arnaud Weisser 74 (BL); Slowfish 75 (TR); Olga Shelego 76 (BR); Lori Froeb 77 (TR); Anne Kitzman 78 (BL); Laurent Renault 80 (BR); Travis Klien 82 (TR); Isakov Eduard Olegovich 84 (TR); Sally Scott 86; 95 (TR); Nigel Paul Monckton 89 (BL); Iain Frazier 91 (BL); Margita 92 (BL); Peter Doomen 98 (TR); Robyn Mackenzie 98 (BR); Harris Shiffman 99 (TL); Wilee Cole 100 (BL); Candace Schwadron 101 (TL); Christopher Elwell 102 (TL); LockStockBob 106 (TR); ale1969, 107 (TR); Joseph Galea 111 (BL); David Andrew Gilder 119 (L); Vishal Shah 125 (BL); Ye 126 (TR); South 12th Photography 127 (TR); Norman Chan 129 (TL); Rafa Fabrykiewicz 142 (BR); Nicola Keegan 144 (TR); Craig Hansen 147 (BR); JackK 150 (TR); Colin and Linda McKie 156 (BR); Beth Whitcomb 157 (BR); Dwight Smith 166; Stacey Lynn Brown 171 (BL); Andrew Cribb 172 (BL); Tony Strong 174 (BL); Blanche Branton 175 (BL); Joanna Wnuk 181 (TR); Kuehdi 185 (TR); Elena Schweitzer 194 (TR); Winthrop Brookhouse 194 (BR); Christine Van Reeuwyk 204 (BL); P. Kruger 209 (BL).

Jason Smally: 144 (BR).

Roy Williams: 17 (TL, TR).

Mark Winwood: 1; 5 (TL, TM, TR); 9 (BR); 13 (TL); 16; 19; 20; 21; 28 (BL); 30; 31 (BL, BR); 32 (TR); 34 (BL, BR); 38 (BL); 39 (BL); 40 (BR); 44 (BL); 46 (TR); 47 (BL); 48 (BL); 50 (BL); 51 (TL); 52 (BL); 59 (BR); 61; 62 (BL); 63 (TL); 64 (TL); 66 (BL); 68 (BL); 77 (BR); 79 (B); 92 (TR); 97 (BL), (R); 112 (L); 113 (R); 115 (L); 119 (BR); 121 (TR); 123 (TL), (BR); 130 (BR); 135 (BL); 139 (BL); 138 (TR); 139 (BL); 140 (BL); 141 (TR); 151 (TR); 152; 159 (L); 162 (BL, BR); 163 (BL); 164 (BL, BR); 172 (R); 176 (R); 184 (TR); 188 (BR); 192 (TR); 193 (BL); 196 (BL); 197 (L); 200 (BL); 201 (BL).

ART WORK: 24, 25.

Have a home gardening, decorating, or improvement project?
Look for these and other fine Creative Homeowner books wherever books are sold

COMPLETE HOME GARDENING
Expert advice for creating flower, herb, and vegetable gardens.

Over 1,000 photographs and illustrations.
400 pp.
9" x 10"
$24.95 (US)
$27.95 (CAN)
BOOK #: 274021

COMPLETE HOUSEPLANTS
Secrets to growing the most popular types of houseplants.

Over 480 photographs and illustrations.
224 pp.
9" x 10"
$19.95 (US)
$21.95 (CAN)
BOOK #: 274820

COMPLETE ROSES
Information on planting and growing popular rose varieties, including heirloom types.

Over 280 photographs and illustrations.
176 pp.
9" x 10"
$16.95 (US)
$18.95 (CAN)
BOOK #: 274061

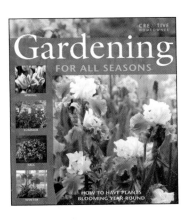

GARDENING FOR ALL SEASONS
Strategies for keeping your garden blooming year-round.

Over 780 photographs and illustrations.
320 pp.
9" x 10"
$21.95 (US)
$23.95 (CAN)
BOOK #: 274013

COMPLETE TREES, SHRUBS & HEDGES
Guides to selecting and growing trees, shrubs, and hedges.

Over 700 photographs and illustrations.
240 pp.
9" x 10"
$19.95 (US)
$21.95 (CAN)
BOOK #: 274222

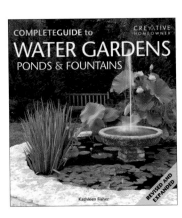

COMPLETE GUIDE TO WATER GARDENS, PONDS & FOUNTAINS
Secrets to creating garden water features.

Over 600 photographs and illustrations.
240 pp.
9" x 10"
$19.95 (US)
$21.95 (CAN)
BOOK #: 274458

For more information and to order direct, go to **www.creativehomeowner.com**